Anonymous

Lynn:

Its representative business men and points of interest

Anonymous

Lynn:
Its representative business men and points of interest

ISBN/EAN: 9783337713133

Printed in Europe, USA, Canada, Australia, Japan

Cover: Foto ©ninafisch / pixelio.de

More available books at **www.hansebooks.com**

ITS

REPRESENTATIVE BUSINESS MEN

AND

POINTS OF INTEREST.

NEW YORK:
MERCANTILE ILLUSTRATING COMPANY
38 TIMES BUILDING.
1893.

LYNN AND ITS POINTS OF INTEREST

Everybody knows Lynn and everybody knows that Lynn is the "Shoe City" and is a very busy, wideawake and prosperous community, but everybody does not know that its population is greater than that of any other city east of Boston, that its growth is so steady and rapid that the population and valuation are increasing at a rate so exceptional as to be almost phenomenal, and that Lynn is as beautiful and desirable as a place of residence as it is prominent and successful as an industrial centre. Yet such is the case, and the city of Lynn must seem a veritable wonder to those whose experience has been such as to make them believe that a prosperous manufacturing town must necessarily be grimy and smoke-laden ; must practically be controlled by a few corporations and must contain many great tenement houses and a few mansions—neat and comfortable homes for the people being chiefly conspicuous by their absence.

In all the republic there is no city the story of whose origin and development is of more interest, for although Lynn is not situated upon what is commonly known as historic ground and has been remarkably free from the strifes, the important occurrences and the momentous events which are intimately associated with the history of other old Massachusetts towns, still it has well borne its part in the great struggle against adverse conditions the outcome of which has made New England in many respects the leading section of the country, and while Lynn has done her full share of the work of maintaining and promoting the interests of the nation she has received very little aid in the utilization of her own resources and may be truthfully called a self-made city that won success by courage, industry, enterprise and perseverance. Most of the important manufacturing towns in New England owe the origin and development of their industries to their being so favored by the existence of valuable water powers or other favorable natural conditions as to attract the attention of outside capitalists, but Lynn has no such natural advantages and is essentially a modern industrial centre, for her factories are not the outgrowth of by-gone conditions but rather the product of the demands of the times. Lynn is not "a city built around a waterfall," and hence she is not a city whose industries had their origin in what is now the bygone supremacy of water power. It is an open secret that steam has so far superseded water power that many a manufacturing town would never be established where it now is were it not established already; and it is obvious that steam and its ally—electricity—are destined to work many wondrous changes in industrial circles in coming years.

Lynn will not suffer from, but on the contrary will be greatly benefitted by, these changes. Her location and her facilities are such as to enable her to compare favorably with any other New England city as regards the cost of steam power, and some idea of the advantages this city offers for the carrying on of modern industries may be gained from the fact that Lynn was chosen as the site of what is now one of the greatest electrical establishments in the world.

Lynn is so essentially modern a city, so free from grass-grown streets, rotting wharves, tumble-down buildings and other ancient belongings, that it is difficult to realize that this is one of the oldest communities in the country, a year older than Boston itself; but nevertheless, it is so old that more than two and a half centuries have passed since its birth, the first settlement having been made in 1629. The pioneer settlers were Edmund and Francis Ingalls, who had previously lived in Salem (or Naumkeag as it was then called), but were not entirely content there and so asked Governor Endicott for definite permission to locate elsewhere. As they had no use for the governor's settlement the governor had no use for them, and so he told them to go where they pleased, and in June, 1629, they decided upon a location and with the aid of Salem friends built a log cabin and thus began the new settlement.

Three more families joined them during the first year and about fifty more families came during the second year, so that at the close of 1630 the future "Shoe City" was fairly under way. But nearly a decade elapsed before the name of Lynn was given to it, the original name of the territory being Saugus, which means great or extended and was chosen by the Indians on account of the spacious beach near the official residence of the Sachem of the region. This residence was on Sagamore Hill, close by the end of Long Beach, at Swampscott, and nearly all the Indians in this vicinity lived either on Sagamore Hill or in Nahant.

The freedom of the early settlers at Salem, Lynn and other points along the coast, from trouble with the Indians was probably chiefly due to their having arrived at a time when tribal warfare and a disastrous plague had almost destroyed the savages and so reduced their power as to discourage them from making any attempt to repel the invaders. Had they tried to establish settlements on these shores during the time when this region was but a part of the great territory ruled by the famous chief Nanapashewlt they would doubtless have met with bitter opposition, but as he had been slain during the long and destructive war with the Tarratives, and as the majority of his followers had perished during that struggle or during the awful scourge that visited them soon after, both the power and the confidence of the Indians were so impaired that they were in no condition to offer resistance to the white men. After the death of Nanapashewlt his sons assumed control of the tribe, but they were merely local chiefs and were by no means feared by the whites, although their names alone were imposing enough to inspire respect, the sachem of Naumkeag being called Winnepoykin, the sachem of Saugus, Montowawpate, and the sachem of Nahant, Poquanam. But such names were altogether too formal for common every day use, so the settlers changed them to Sagamore James, Sagamore George No-nose and Duke William. Although the Indians applied the name Saugus to the beach near their headquarters, it was used by the whites to designate a much more spacious region, for the original Saugus comprised the present towns of Saugus, Lynnfield, Reading, Wakefield, Swampscott and Nahant, besides the city of Lynn. Lynnfield (which then included Reading and Wakefield) was separated from the parent town in 1814, Saugus in 1815, Swampscott in 1852 and Nahant in 1853.

After 1630 the growth of the settlement proceeded steadily and rapidly, and it was during that year that the freemen of Saugus first took their seats in the General Court, this action being accepted as amounting to practically the same thing as the incorporation of the town, for it was never formally incorporated. The change of the town's name to Lynn was almost equally informal, for the only official record of it is "Saugus is called Lin," the General Court so voting on the 15th of November, 1637. There is no positive surety as to why the name Lynn was adopted, but it is supposed to have been chosen in honor of Rev. Samuel Whiting, who came from King's Lynn in England. In its original form the word from which the name is derived means spreading waters and so is particularly adapted to a place situated as is Lynn, "the city by the sea" as some call it in preference to the more prosaic title of "shoe city." At first the Lynn people had to travel to Salem in order to attend divine worship, but they established a church of their own as soon as possible, and in 1632 the first church was organized. It has continued ever since and is said to be the oldest society in the country that still adheres to the original creed, it being indeed the oldest orthodox Congregational church in the world. After the change of name to Lynn, in 1637 the next important event in the history of the town was the establishment of the iron works in 1643. This was not only the first but the only industry of the kind in the colonies, and it seemed as if it could hardly fail to be a profitable undertaking, for there was an ample supply of bog iron to draw from and the works produced charcoal iron of excellent quality. But the enterprise was a failure and although it was continued for many years it was unprofitable from the first. Even the people of Lynn did not encourage it, and some historians think that their action in this matter was prompted by jealousy and distrust of an undertaking founded by outsiders and backed by foreign capital and was but an indication of the spirit which has animated Lynn people from the first, a disposition to " paddle their own canoe," to develop their own town, and to found and

BIRDS-EYE VIEW OF LYNN.

manage their own industries. Not that they have followed a "dog in the manger" policy—on the contrary they have always welcomed new enterprises and conducted the affairs of the community in a broad and progressive manner that has invited wide-awake men and has made Lynn as throughly an " up to date " city as can be found in the entire country—but they have by no means encouraged the establishment of great enterprises whose ownership and management would be outside the city, and that is one reason why Lynn is a most excellent place to live in, and to work in, and why it is not disfigured by numerous great tenement houses, but has a larger percentage of dwelling houses owned by their occupants than any other city but one in the country. The iron works were in charge of Joseph Jenks, who was a thorough mechanic and is credited with being not only the manufacturer but the designer of the first fire engine ever made in this country. The first iron casting ever made on this continent was produced at these works, and is still in the possession of a descendant of the original owner. It is a small covered kettle which will hold a quart and weighs about three pounds, and it is really artistic in design and excellent in workmanship. The farmers should be especially interested in the history of the old Lynn Iron Works, for it was here was manufactured in 1646 the first American scythe, it being invented by Joseph Jenks and being a most pronounced improvement on the short, broad and straight " bushwack " scythe which it superseded. The dies from which were made the famous " pine-tree shillings " and other pine-tree coinage were made here in 1652. The iron works were carried on for nearly half a century in spite of the feeble support they received, the enterprise being discontinued in 1688. For many years the chief industries of the Lynn people were planting and fishing, and more than a century passed before there was even the least approach to the establishment of the business which was destined to make Lynn known throughout the country as the Shoe City. Some believe that one reason for the great success attained by this community is the concentration of effort brought about by lack of natural advantages, for there were no valuable water powers here to attract various industrial enterprises; there was no spacious and easily accessible harbor to lead to the people engaging in commerce; and hence all the settlers had to choose between was farming and fishing. However this may be it is certain that the town increased steadily in population and in wealth, and although its growth was for a time slow in comparison with that of some of its more favored neighbors, it was, on the whole, more assured and more permanent.

The tanning industry was begun here at a very early date, but it never attained large proportions and was soon removed to Salem, Peabody and other places to which it was better adapted.

Shoemaking was begun almost as soon as the town was founded, but none but local needs were supplied and by no means all of those, for the few who made shoes at all made them almost entirely for their own families.

The honor of being the representative pioneer professional shoemaker of Lynn is accorded to John Adam Dagyr, a Welshman who came here in 1750. He was an excellent workman and evidently was possessed by that enterprising and progressive spirit which will assure success in almost any undertaking, for he took apart and carefully examined the best European shoes obtainable, and was not satisfied until he had not only equalled but surpassed them in workmanship. Other workmen learned from him; more skilled shoemakers came to Lynn from England, and the excellence of Lynn shoes soon began to be generally known, as is indicated by the following extract from the *Boston Gazette* of 1764:— "The women's shoes made at Lynn do now exceed those usually imported, both in strength and beauty, but not in price." Of course the demand for such footwear could not fail to rapidly increase, and some idea of the rapidity of that increase may be gained from the fact that 80,000 pairs of shoes were made in Lynn during the year 1767.

CHURCH

Of course the industry was almost ruined by the shaken condition of trade during the Revolutionary times, and in the war of Independence the Lynn people showed the same courage and determination which they had shown when the attempt was made to rob them of Nahant. This attempt was made away back in 1688 by Edward Randolph, who was known as the evil genius of New England and who was as dangerous as he was unscrupulous, for he not only had no regard for the rights of others but as the secretary, counselor and friend of Governor Andros was in a position to do great injury to the colony. He petitioned the Governor for a gift of Nahant, and when the Lynn people received notice of this petition they held a town meeting and forwarded to the Governor and council a strong protest against the granting of the request; their objections being that the peninsula belonged to the town and was of so much service that its loss would be a serious damage to public and private interests. Randolph was not easily discouraged, however, and he renewed his petition and denied that Lynn had any legal right to claim Nahant as the town had never been incorporated. The townspeople answered this by an extended and explicit

A MODEL SCHOOL BUILDING.

declaration signed by seventy-four of the leading inhabitants, but probably the matter would have been decided in favor of Randolph were it not for the successful uprising of the people, the result of which was the placing of Andros and Randolph in Fort Hill prison. Many of the Lynn people hastened to Boston to take a hand in the affair, and, to quote from Randolph himself, when they reached there they were "like so many wild bears," which is pretty good evidence that they had reached the limit of their patience and were determined not to submit to any more tyranny.

From the very beginning the Lynn people showed a disposition to protect themselves by force if necessary, for the first military company was organized in 1630, it being well equipped and provided with two iron cannon. The nearest approach to a fight with the Indians within the limits of the town was made in 1631, when a portion of the company was on guard at night on account of expectation of an attack by the savages. An arrow shot from a bush near by passed through the clothing of the commanding officer and then the guard fired a volley and retreated as it was too dark to engage in open combat. The next morning several cannon shots were fired into the woods and the settlers stood ready to defend their homes but no foes appeared and in the future the settlement remained unmolested.

When the Pequot war broke out, in 1636, one of the companies that saw the most active service, during the first campaign, was commanded by a Lynn man, and when the second expedition was taken, in 1637, the town furnished twenty-one men. Lynn also took a prominent part in the King Philip war, for although too far away from the fields of battle to be exposed to any immedi-

LYNN AFTER THE FIRE, 1889, FROM BROAD STREET.

ate danger the town appreciated the importance of that deadly struggle and knowing that its outcome would decide the question of supremacy between the whites and the Indians, it contributed freely both men and means and thus done much to aid in the advancement of settlements throughout New England. During the French and Indian war many Lynn soldiers saw active service, notably a company which started from Lynn for Canada, May 23, 1758, and of which two were killed on the field of battle.

A resolution passed at a meeting held December 16, 1773, may be taken as a fair expression of the spirit shown by the people in resisting what they considered unfair government exactions; "We highly disapprove of the landing and selling of such teas in America, and will not suffer any teas, subjected to a parliamentary duty, to be landed or sold in this town; and we stand ready to assist our brethren in Boston and elsewhere, whenever our aid shall be required, in repelling all attempts to land or sell any teas poisoned with a parliamentary duty." Some of the Lynn people were present at the famous Boston tea-party, and some of the leading Lynn ladies called upon a storekeeper in town who was known to have some tea on hand and demanded that it be destroyed,— which shows that the townspeople not only said what they ought to say but meant just what they said. Lynn was well represented at the battle of Lexington and four of her sons were killed and several wounded. A few days afterward a Committee of Safety was formed; an alarm company or company of "Minute Men" was organized, and night watches were established. The people were ready for battle at a moment's notice and they not only carried arms when they attended meeting on Sunday but the minister was equally well equipped; he appearing with his powder horn under one arm and his sermon under the other, and resting his musket against the pulpit when he began the service.

Lynn furnished nearly two hundred soldiers during the war, fifty-six of whom were killed;

and among the Lynn contingent were two colonels, three captains, five lieutenants, five sergeants, six corporals and about one hundred and seventy privates. The town was poor and no business whatever was done at this period, but still Lynn contributed very liberally and within two years granted more than seventy thousand pounds, old tenor.

As soon as the Revolution was over the people went earnestly to work to restore the industries which had been so seriously injured by enforced neglect, but recovery was very slow and much of the gain that had been made by long and patient effort was lost during the enforcement

SIDE VIEW OF FLOATING BRIDGE.

of the Embargo Act, in 1808, and during the progress of the second war with England in 1812. Perhaps the most exciting event of the latter struggle, so far as the residents of Lynn were concerned, was the contest between the English frigate Shannon and the American frigate Chesapeake, for it took place where every detail of it could be seen from the heights of Nahant and the housetops of Lynn, and it is safe to say, there was not a person in Lynn who did not see some of it at least, for of course the people were deeply interested in the struggle, and the record of the American tars had been such as to make everyone confident that the result of this fight would be the surrender of the Shannon. But joyous hope was changed into sorrowful despair, for Captain Lawrence of the Chesapeake was killed, the American flag was lowered and the captured vessel was taken to Halifax.

The story of Lynn's action during the Rebellion cannot be fittingly told in a few words and therefore we shall make no attempt to present it to our readers. Suffice it to say that within five hours after the reception of President Lincoln's call for troops, Lynn had two complete companies armed and ready for duty, and the patriotism of her sons was such as to cause the sending of the famous despatch: "We have more men than guns; what shall we do?" And the readiness and courage then shown was but an example of that displayed by Lynn throughout the long and terribly destructive war, not only was every call for troops quickly and fully answered, but every possible encouragement and help was given to the Union cause; and the simple fact that Lynn furnished 3,274 soldiers, or 230 more than her full quota, is of itself conclusive evidence that her sons did not shrink from putting their principles into practice. The soldiers' monument which was erected in City Hall Square, in 1873, is a fitting memorial of those who perished in the cause of freedom, for it is an allegorical and truly classic work of art in bronze, and although not so showy as some of the numerous soldiers' monuments to be found throughout the North, still it is more truly impressive and reflects credit alike upon the artist who designed it and the committee who entrusted him with the work. The sculptor was an American artist, and the casting of the statues composing the monument was done in Munich, Bavaria. The cost of the memorial was $30,000. It is fitting that a city which made so honorable a record during the Rebellion should be the home of the largest G. A. R. post in the country. General Lander, Post 5, has more than 1,100 members; was organized in 1867, and has expended more than $100,000 for charitable purposes, the annual outlay now exceeding $5,000.

SOLDIERS' MONUMENT AND COMMON, LYNN, MASS.

THE LYNN OF TO-DAY.

A steady and rapid increase in population and wealth is the best possible indication that can be given that a city is a good place to live in and to do business in, especially when—as in the case of Lynn—this increase has been going on year after year. In 1870 the census showed that Lynn had a population of 28,233; in 1890 the census showed an increase of nearly 100 per cent., the population being given as 55,727.

The whole of Essex county has been prosperous during the past score of years, and the population has increased 62,595, but as the increase in Lynn alone was 27,494, it will be seen that this city is responsible for more than two-fifths of the favorable showing made by the county. And an almost equally large proportion of the increase in valuation should be credited to the shoe city. The valuation of the county increased $87,659,539; the valuation of Lynn increased $20,379,046.

As Essex county is composed of thirty-five cities and towns, it goes without saying that the growth of Lynn is almost phenomenal.

The population of the city is now estimated to be at least 60,000, and—what is still more gratifying—the increase in dwelling houses corresponds with that in the population, for Lynn is no "tenement city," and her residents are the best housed people in the country. The report of the inspector of buildings shows that during the year ending December 31, 1892, more than 1,000 permits to erect new buildings were issued in this city, or more than three for every working day in the year, including holidays. This was a greater increase in the number of dwellings in proportion to population than was made by any other city in Massachusetts, and it was not brought about by any "boom," or by the establishment of some giant enterprise that brought with it hundreds of people, but was simply the result of the ordinary growth of the city.

There are some very handsome and costly mansions in Lynn, and many tasty and stylish houses of the type one finds in the more select suburbs of Boston, but the greater number of dwelling houses in this busy city are such as are within the means of the average wage earner— that is to say they are neat, spacious and comfortable, devoid of expensive ornamentation, but still pleasant homes, agreeably located and well cared for. Lynn is the "Massachusetts Phila-

OCEAN STREET, LYNN.

delphia" in one respect, for a very large proportion of the dwelling houses are owned by their occupants, and the advantages of the co-operative bank are well appreciated and largely utilized. One reason of this is Lynn is the kind of a city that attracts intelligent and well-informed people. Wages average high here compared with those paid in the same lines of industry elsewhere, and the cost of living is low compared with that of the average manufacturing city. There is a large amount of land eligible to build upon—land that requires no "filling in," no expensive blasting of rocks, and that is by no means remote from the centres of industry and trade.

As a rule the prices of land for residential uses has been maintained at a moderate rate, and although some of the land in the business section is so high in price as to seem almost "out of sight" in comparison with what it was a few years ago, the policy of real estate owners in Lynn is conservative and fair, and no would-be buyers are frightened away by exorbitant prices.

Some very able men have devoted themselves to the development of Lynn's suburbs, and the result is that the work has been skilfully carried on and all unnecessary expense avoided.

Enterprise is shown in the selection and division of large estates; the laying out and grading of spacious streets, the planting of shade trees, and the securing of adequate draining, lighting, and watering service; and good judgment is shown by the choice of sites that are reached by the electric railways and so are easily accessible at all times of year.

From the very beginning Lynn has shown a disposition to encourage individual and discourage corporate effort, but this has not been carried to excess, and so the city has escaped the evils which attend either extreme. No doubt the most important factor in the successful solution of the problem how to steadily hold a leading position among New England's industrial centres has been the possession of a distinct industry in which capital is not combined in huge corporations and syndicates. At one time the shoe industry was in the hands of a comparatively few great firms, but that time is now long gone by, and Lynn shoe manufacturers are as numerous as they are enterprising. A wide distribution of capital is the key to the situation now, and this division gives abundant opportunities to individuals for business and for employment. In the average manufacturing city or town where the corporations have sway, the removal of one of those corporations would mean serious injury to the community and ruin to not a few of its storekeepers. But that is not the case at Lynn. The wage earner is bound to no one factory, and the manu-

LAKESIDE.

facturer is bound by no cast-iron agreement which makes him subject to orders and prevents him from protecting his own interests and profiting by his own ingenuity and enterprise. There is an immense field of employment for the workman, and no manufacturer can drive him out of town simply by discharging him. The more factories there are, the more chance there is for the best men to reach the top, and the more chance there is for reasonably continuous employment. There is also more chance for success in business, as there is "a fair field and no favor" and one does not have to overcome a strong combination in order to gain a foothold.

One needs no stronger proof of the intelligence and the true democracy of the residents of Lynn than that afforded by the character of the public works and institutions. On every hand one can see indications that the citizens spend money freely for public improvements, and yet discriminate keenly and distinguish extravagance from judicious generosity.

Lynn has a most excellent water service, an extensive and efficient fire department, a very comprehensive educational system and many well equipped school-houses; a first-class city hospital, an elaborate and handsome city hall, and the largest and most picturesque public park in New England. The streets are brilliantly lighted; the city is kept in excellent hygienic condition, and there is evidence of wealth, culture and refinement on every side. Lynn is one of the very few cities in the vicinity of Boston that are "self-contained," or, in other words, have such home industries and home stores as to render them almost independent of the metropolis. This is no "Boston bedroom," and the percentage of those who reside in Lynn and work in the "Hub" is very small indeed in comparison with that of most adjacent cities and towns. One result of this is that the local business is very extensive and is increasing in accordance with the population. The time was when many Lynn people bought the most important articles they required at Boston, but they do so no longer, for the simple reason that they know they can now buy them as cheap or cheaper at home. The Lynn merchant is not obliged to pay such phenomenal rent as his Boston competitor is obliged to extract from his customers; he can buy his goods just as cheaply; he offers just as great a variety, and he deals with just the same houses that supply the Boston stores. Visit the business section of Lynn at any time of year and compare the goods and prices with those of Boston, and you will need no further explanation why Lynn people prefer to do their buying at home. The leading stores of the shoe city will not suffer a bit by comparison with those of Boston; they are equally well equipped, well stocked and efficiently managed, and the prices really average lower than those quoted at the Hub. Lynn is the centre of trade for miles around, for the residents of the neighboring municipalities appreciate the advantages of patronizing establishments where desirable goods can be obtained at bottom prices, and they know that no gain in style, quality or variety of the goods open to inspection will be secured by visiting Boston.

NAHANT STREET FROM BALTIMORE STREET.

TRANSPORTATION FACILITIES.

A city whose goods are sent to every part of the country and every part of the world necessarily requires a most extensive transportation service, and that of Lynn is enormous in magnitude as is indicated by the fact that the output of a single Lynn company in one year amounted to 2,000 car loads at 20,000 pounds per car, enough to make up 100 full trains. The steam railway service is furnished by the Boston & Maine and the Boston, Revere Beach and Lynn railway companies, but all the freight is handled by the Boston & Maine as the Boston Revere Beach & Lynn is a narrow gauge road, devoted exclusively to passenger traffic. It is a decided benefit to the city, however, as it provides an excellent service, has done much to reduce passenger rates to points between Boston and Lynn, and has made every point along the coast accessible. The Boston & Maine system has become so extended and plays so prominent a part in the commerce of New England that it has a national reputation, and there is no need of our entering into detail concerning the character of the service afforded. Suffice it to say the Lynn manufacturer can promptly ship his goods to any part of the United States or Canada, or to any seaport in the country, and also can obtain any needed supplies—domestic or imported—without undue delay and at moderate freight rates.

LYNN HARBOR.

Lynn has an extended water front and a safe harbor, but the latter was of but little use to her for many years, as a channel for small draft vessels was the only outlet to the sea.

A comprehensive plan of harbor improvement was drawn up in 1867, but the national government did not begin to carry it out until 1884. An appropriation of $60,000 was secured and the channel has been deepened, widened and straightened, so that to-day large coal steamers come up to the wharves and regular lines ply between this port and the great coal regions of Pennsylvania. The work of improvement is still going on and when completed there will be a basin measuring 500x300 feet, containing ten feet of water at low tide and connected with the sea by a channel 400 feet in width. The indications are that the work will be permanently beneficial, for examinations of the parts first dredged show that there has been very small change in the depth since the dredging was completed. Even in its present unimproved state the harbor of Lynn is quite largely utilized, for the value of the goods brought by vessels considerably exceeds $1,000,000 per annum. A regular steamboat service between Boston and Lynn was established about a year ago and is of much convenience to the business men of the shoe city, as they ship a great deal of freight by this line.

FLOATING BRIDGE IN GLENMERE ROAD.

STREET RAILWAYS.

The street railway service of Lynn is so comprehensive, so frequent, and so ably managed that it is considered superior to that of any other city in the country, with the exception of Boston, and it is far from being a mere local system, as it is the second largest controlled by any one street railway company in the State. Anything even approaching a detailed description of this system would occupy many pages of space, but some idea of its magnitude and completeness may be gained from the statement that it connects with Boston and with each other the cities and towns of Lynn, Chelsea, Revere, Everett, Malden, Saugus, Melrose, Stoneham, Wakefield, Woburn, Swampscott, Marblehead, Salem, Peabody, Danvers, Beverly, Wenham and Hamilton, with a prospect of extension to other important sections of Essex and Middlesex counties and connections with other street railway systems. These municipalities are all related to each other in a business as well as social way, and the passenger traffic between them is very great and is steadily increasing. And the present indications are that the passenger traffic will before a great while be supplemented by the transportation of goods. The shoe and leather industry extends throughout this section and there is considerable traffic between the tanneries of Woburn, Stoneham, Salem, Peabody and Danvers and the shoe factories of Lynn and of the other cities and towns thus connected, and between the various important manufactories of shoe findings in Lynn and the shoe shops in other places. And this traffic will be greatly and quickly increased if the project of establishing a suburban express service over the lines of the Lynn and Boston Railroad Company is carried out—and it probably will be, for it is understood that the management of the company strongly favor the idea, and the charter of the company is such that no legislation will be required to give it authority to carry freight. The steam railways have not been efficient in providing a local freight service, for it does not pay to cart goods to the railway by team, have them carried but a few miles in the cars and then have them loaded on teams again, and so it has been customary to send them by team all the way over the direct highway. But now that these highways are covered by electric railways it will be much cheaper to transport the goods by cars loaded at the door of one factory and unloaded at that of another. The service will, of course, be much more prompt than that afforded by teaming, or by combination of team and railway, and if established on a proper basis it will do much to permanently aid manufacturers throughout this section of the State. And it will also do much to improve roads and to greatly lessen the cost of keeping them in fit condition. The heavy teams which are required for the carriage of express and freight matter are responsible for nearly all the wear and tear on our roadways excepting that due to the weather, and should these teams be

DUNGEON ROCK.

superseded by electric cars the expense of road maintenance would be heavily reduced. The present company will not provide the freight service, the idea being to organize a separate company to run its own cars over the electric railway lines and pay mileage rates for the privilege.

The service will not come into competition with the steam railways to any degree, but will supplement their function in an important direction. Ultimately, however, it seems possible that the steam railways will experience a considerable competition from the electric lines in freight carrying, for the latter bid fair to soon spread a connected network all over the State. Passenger fares by the electric lines are much lower than by the steam lines for corresponding distances, and it is possible that in certain lines of freight transportation they will exert the wholesome influence that they are having in passenger traffic. Lynn will profit greatly by the electric freight service, for it will increase the demand for her products, and will help her manufacturers in the work of securing needed material promptly and cheaply.

The open electric car has been called "the poor man's carriage," and it certainly enables thousands to ride who would otherwise have to walk or stay at home, but it has other merits besides that of affording cheap transportation; it is the fastest vehicle on the road, and the most popular that has yet been placed before the people. The rides from Lynn are many and beautiful. Salem Willows, Marblehead, Lynn Woods—these are visited by many thousand Lynn people every holiday and every evening in summer, and there are various other attractive resorts which are brought so near as to be practically but a step from the shoe city. Truly this is "a most pleasant place in which to live," and it is fitting that this progressive city should have a street car service that leads the van.

ORIGIN AND DEVELOPMENT OF THE SHOE INDUSTRY IN LYNN.

The history of shoemaking in Lynn is identical with the history of shoemaking in the country, for this industry was begun here away back in the sixteen hundreds and has here developed until now the city of Lynn is conceded to be the headquarters of what may be called scientific shoe manufacturing. The first Lynn shoemaker was Philip Kertland, whose name is borne by one of the city streets and who was probably as good a shoemaker as could be found in this country during his time, although he was not exactly an expert at the trade. But the name which is generally associated with the inception of Lynn's shoe industry is that of John Adam Dagyr, a Welshman, who came to what was destined to become the shoe city, in 1750, and laid the foundations of its fame by producing shoes that were equal to the best made in England. The result was that others

RESIDENCE OF E. F. SPINNEY, LYNN.

followed his example; skilled shoe makers emigrating from England and Europe were attracted to Lynn, and Lynn shoes became famous throughout the colonies. Of course they were rough and crude affairs compared with the shoes of to-day but they were fully equal to the best the market afforded, and the demand for them was brisk and constantly growing.

The work of organization proceeded from the first and soon the industry reached a stage where the shoes were cut at the shops of the "bosses" and distributed in the little, square shoe-shops throughout the town to be made; everything, including uppers, soles, linings, thread, wax and nails, being furnished by the bosses. Those were the days when every member of a family " worked for a living," and the women stitched or bound the uppers, while the men prepared the soles and finished the shoes.

Many years passed before labor-saving machinery was introduced and the work was so divided up into specialties that no man could justly claim to be a thorough shoemaker.

What may be called the revolution in shoe manufacturing had its inception in 1862, when the wonderful McKay sewing machine was perfected. Sewing machines had been applied to shoe manufacturing long before then; the first use of them in Lynn occurring in 1852, but it was not until the McKay machine had been made thoroughly practical that pronounced changes took place in the industry. Of this machine it has well been said: "When the great problem of stitching the sole to the upper was solved, the little shoemaker's shops disappeared before the march of the sewing machine, that revolutionizing influence which has made famous the humble pursuit of the cobbler. A resistless combination of cog wheels, so arranged above a heavy framework as to drive an awl like needle through half an inch or more of tough pieces of leather, has built great factories and made thriving cities."

"A swift workman was he who could sew soles to a pair of shoe in fifteen minutes time, yet this wonderful piece of mechanism can sew six hundred pairs within the limits of a working day. The machine which does this work must feed a waxed thread in any direction, so that the shoe rests not on a table but over the end of a horn, from within which the thread, previously waxed, is supplied after being heated by a gas jet within the horn By letters patent, for many years, the company controlling the machine collected a royalty from persons who used it, and one large manufacturer paid in a single year the sum of fifteen thousand dollars for the privilege of using thirteen of them. With several hundred in use, the corporation paid a fancy dividend for many years that was more than the original value of the stock. Rivers have attracted capitalists to build acres of mills on their banks, but this machine has made cities and large towns anywhere."

The expiration of the patents on this machine and the consequent release from the payment of royalty have done much to reduce the cost of footwear, and now some of even the cheapest grades of shoes are sewed on the McKay; but the introduction of other machines has also been an important factor in solving the problem of lessening cost, and notable among them is a "screw driving machine" which makes a screw nail from the end of a coil of brass wire, points it, heads it and drives it in the twinkling of an eye. After the advent of the McKay machine the next notable change in methods of shoe manufacturing was the introduction of steam power. The use of steam in shoe factories did not become general until after the war, so thirty years ago there was not a shoe factory in Lynn run by steam power!

CHURCH, LYNN.

Although shoe manufacturing and the kindred industry, morocco manufacturing, have been the main stays of Lynn for the last half century, their progress has been by no means uninterrupted, and the city owes her leading position as a shoe centre not to exceptional natural advantages or favorable conditions, but to the enterprise, good judgment and determination displayed by Lynn manufacturers in keeping fully up to the times in every respect. There has been a most pronounced change in the general character of Lynn shoes within the past decade, and one need not be very old to be able to remember when the terms Lynn shoes and cheap or inferior shoes were almost synonymous. Another decided change is in the manner of carrying on the business, for while it was once nearly all in the hands of a few great houses it is now distributed among many. The advantages of this change are obvious. Under the old conditions if one of the big concerns should remove it would seriously injure business throughout the city; but now there are so many factories run by so many different houses that the prosperity of the shoe city is subject to that of no one house, however large it may be.

LYNN AND ITS POINTS OF INTEREST.

Not very many years ago the Lynn shoe was looked upon as a cheap article, which was neither stylish nor comfortable. It had a very large sale in some sections, but it was rapidly being driven out of New England because it could not hold its own in competition with the footwear from New York and elsewhere made by manufacturers who catered to the public's demand for footwear that was attractive to the eye, comfortable for the foot, and yet was moderate in price. But things are changed now. The New York shoe can be found in but very few New England stores, and the reason is that the present Lynn shoes are decidedly superior to them in quality and successfully compete with them in price.

WEST LYNN, MASS.

This is the age of specialties, and the leading specialty with Lynn manufacturers is the production of women's footwear, made from special brands of upper stock, stylish in shape, light, durable and comfortable, and sold to the retail trade at from $1.60 to $2.50 per pair. Every manufacturer is producing special lines, to which he gives the most careful attention. Flexibility, durability, comfort and style are thoroughly studied, and constant efforts are made to improve the goods. A few of the larger Lynn concerns produce cheap shoes for the jobbing trade, and there are several manufacturers who produce nothing but the very finest goods, which have a national reputation, but it is on special grades of medium shoes that Lynn is far in the van, and this indicates a most prosperous future, for the demand is certainly for special brands of goods, and no shoe centre compares favorably with the shoe city in catering to this demand.

HOW SHOES ARE MADE.

It would be an unpardonable omission in preparing even the briefest sketch of the city of shoes and her industries not to go into details concerning shoe manufacturing, and yet the subject is so complex and so difficult to make plain to the general public that we can present but the barest outline of it within the limited space at our command. The modern American is so accustomed to taking things as they come and accepting as a simple accommodation things which represent years study and toil, experiment and enterprise that he calmly talks through a telephone to one hundreds of miles distant; hears from a phonograph the voice of one who has long been dead; travels in an "electric" at the rate of twenty miles an hour by means of power transmitted through a wire smaller than his little finger, and profits by these and other marvels in a matter of fact way as if there was nothing remarkable about them. Hence he does not wonder at the remarkable cheapness of shoes now-a-days, and he does not think of inquiring why he can buy for $3.00 a better pair of shoes than he could have bought for $6.00 thirty years ago, even though he knows that those who work at shoe making earn much more now than they did then.

EPISCOPAL CHURCH, LYNN.

The cheapness of modern shoes is a practical exemplification of the truth of that much quoted saying "time is money," for the saving in the cost of footwear has been brought about entirely by the use of machinery and methods which save time. The average cobbler charges you more for the labor he expends in simply soling and heeling your shoes than would be paid for the labor of making three pairs of shoes like them in a factory, and yet his earnings average much less than that of the skilled shoe factory operative, for he has comparatively little help from machinery, hence his productive capacity is but small. But the making of a shoe is no simple thing; a shoe is made up of many different parts, and were all the parts which are combined within it separated from each other and placed side and side, the number and the variety of them would surprise even the least emotional. For instance, in a pair of ladies' button shoes there are 108 distinct pieces, and the material used includes leather, cotton, steel, iron, silk, and many minor articles which are literally " too numerous to mention."

It is indeed a far cry from a Texas steer or a bearded goat to a man's "Blucher" or a woman's "fine button boot," and the processes by which the skin of the animals are made to form the principal part of the foot coverings are, to say the least many, varied and interesting. To begin with, of course, you must "catch your animal;" if he is a steer he will probably come from the west, if he is a goat the chances are that he will come from abroad, for most of our goat skins are imported. Assume him to be one of a drove of cattle slaughtered at Chicago, and after having disposed of his interior department in the shape of "Chicago dressed beef" and under various other names, let us follow his skin or hide to the tanneries and shoe factories. If it is to be converted into sole leather it will probably be sent to central New York; if it is to become upper leather it will receive fitting treatment at Peabody, Mass. No matter where it goes it will be sent in one of two forms, either "dry salted" or "wet salted," for salting is essential in order to prevent it from decomposing. If "dry salted" it will form a part of a large bundle of hides packed flat; if "wet salted" it will be made into a little bundle, bound with rope and thoroughly dampened. Suppose it to have arrived at the tannery in the condition of hairy flabbiness which is the result of "wet salting," how is it treated? Well, it is unloaded more or less tenderly—generally much less than more—then the ropes are removed and the hide is unceremoniously deposited in a "water pit" to soak it and thus prepare it for the scraping, cleansing, pressing, stretching, coloring, and general mauling that it is doomed to undergo before it is fit for admittance to a shoe factory. After remaining in the water pit for several days it is hung over a "horse" (not a real horse but one of the wooden variety) and then the halves of the hide part company forever, as a knife is run along the line where the backbone used to be and the hide is changed into "sides."

OXFORD CLUB HOUSE, LYNN, MASS.

How those sides will be treated next depends upon the methods of the tannery which is preparing them, for some tanners place them in vats and give them a "warm sweat" or a "cold sweat," and others soak them in lime and water, the object of the treatment in both cases being the same—that is to loosen the hair and weaken the grip of the scurf.

The lime method is used in most tanneries and it is certainly the more agreeable (or, perhaps, we should say the least disagreeable) of the two, for even under the most favorable conditions the smells in a tannery do not bring to mind the perfumes of Araby, and hides which are being "sweated" are apt to emit an odor which gives one "that tired feeling," and makes one shiver—whether the "sweat" be hot or cold. The next thing on the programme is the "beaming" or "unhairing" of the hide. It is spread on a rounded wooden form or "beam" which extends from the floor to the height of the workman's waist, and at the end of it he stands and vehemently scrapes the hide with a slightly curved piece of iron which has an upright handle at each end. Then the edges of the skin are trimmed to remove the superfluous parts, and the flesh side is partially smoothed by the operation called "green shaving." If the sides are to be made into upper-leather the shoulders are removed owing to their excessive thickness, and if they ever form part of a shoe it will be in the shape of a sole, heel, counter, or rand, where toughness and stiffness and not softness and pliability are required.

And now the severed and diminished hide is entrusted to the tender mercies of what is called a "pin wheel" and it will be far too well acquainted with the members of that family before it leaves the tannery, for it is destined to be "pin-wheeled" several times and the operation is somewhat agitating to say the least.

The first "pin-wheel" begins the work of removing the lime by repeatedly dousing the hide in warm water, and then it is placed in a vat and "drenched," but the drenching is not simply a "soak," for the hide is turned over and over by a great paddle wheel which is called an "England" wheel but ought to be named after some less peaceable country as it is constantly undergoing revolutions.

Then the hide is again "beamed," and when you are told it is ready to *begin* being tanned you wonder if you will live long enough to see the process completed, as all the treatment which the hide has thus far received is merely preparatory to the work of tanning. It is now placed in a tank of bark liquor and again toyed with by an "England wheel," and then it is removed and allowed to dry for a couple of days so as to season it and make it fit for the reception of the bark. Then it enters the "first layer," or in other words it is spread out in a vat and covered with wet, ground bark. After remaining in this position about a week it is removed to the "second layer," and in about two weeks more to the "third layer" or "splitting layer," to use the technical term, in which it remains about a month. The treatment in each of these "layers" has been substantially the same, the main difference being the difference in the temperature of the various vats. The hide is then hung out to dry for several days so as to lose the superfluous moisture which it has absorbed during its two months' stay in the "layers," and then it is once more cut in halves, but this time the division is one of thickness instead of breadth, for the side

FIRST M. E. CHURCH AND PARSONAGE.

is passed through a "splitting machine" which separates the hair or grain side of the skin from the inner or flesh side, the latter being then known to the trade as a "split." This machine is also intended to make the hide even in thickness by the operation of iron rollers, and its work is supplemented by the hide being next placed upon a "flattening board" and hammered in the thicker parts. Then it is once more caressed by a member of the "pin wheel" family and is soaked in strong bark liquor.

At last the process of tanning has been completed and the hide has become leather, but it is yet far from being "upper" leather, for it has to be "curried" first, and currying is by no means a short or simple operation. To be exact in our description we should state that the process of tanning ends with the removal of the hides from the third or "splitting" layer and that currying then begins, but even in tanneries which have no currying shop attached the splitting and flattening of the hide are almost invariably done before it leaves the premises. When it reaches the currying shop it is placed under a "scourer"—a machine which cleanses, stretches, smooths and compacts the hide—and then it is hung out to dry and is soon brought in again to be dampened for "stuffing" —as the process of filling the pores of the leather with grease is called. In this work the industrious "pin-wheel" lends a hand and the hide is jolted around in a mixture, the main element of which is melted tallow. Then it is allowed to rest for several days so it can peacefully assimilate the tallow, after which it is placed under a "setting out" machine and is again smoothed, stretched and compacted; after which it is "shaped up," or so treated that it will be in the right shape when it gets dry again. Now comes the work of blacking the leather, and the first thing done is the "whitening" of the hide by scraping it with a "whitening slicker." Then it is placed under a "glassing jack," a machine which makes it smoother and more pliable, and then the flesh side of the hide is covered with blacking; the "glassing jack" is again used; the surface is "filled" with paste; the "jack" presses it fervently once more; the hide is dried, then "gummed," then dried again, and now it has become genuine "wax leather" and is ready to be used in the manufacture of the uppers of men's boots. The uppers of women's boots and shoes, in the manufacture of which Lynn leads the country, are almost invariably made of morocco, or in other words, of goat or sheep skins, the tanning of which is done by the use of sumac and gambier instead of hemlock and oak, which are used in the tanning of heavy skins. The process is widely different from that which we saw when watching the manufacture of wax leather, but we have not time to consider it in detail, so let us assume that the work is done and that we have visited a typical Lynn factory to see a kid skin divided and combined with the many other materials essential in the making of a pair of ladies button shoes. It is perfectly safe to assume in advance that the result will be a pair of shoes that combine style, beauty, durability and comfort to a degree surpassed by no machine made shoe in the market, for it is the ability of Lynn's manufacturers to make just such shoes as that, and to sell them at prices which cannot be underbid, that has given the "city of shoes" her present prominence and is increasing her strength every year.

The first thing in shoe manufacturing is the cutting, and this is the only department of the business that is impervious to the action of machinery for so long as machines are destitute of brains and judgment, so long will it be impossible to do the work of cutting profitably by machinery. The only mechanical aid the cutter has is given by the patterns around which he cuts when forming the various pieces which make an upper, and by the knife with which the work is done, for it is "hand work" exclusively. He must economize on material as much as possible; must manage it so that when the pieces are made into a shoe they will be so placed as best to stand the strain without undue stretching; and he must know the qualities of each part of a skin at a glance so as to utilize its virtues and remedy its defects. But he doesn't sit down and study the matter, by a great deal—on the contrary he works as swiftly and as noiselessly as a "pneumatic safety," and the first thing you know he has cut the "vamp," "large quarter," "small quarter" and "button piece" from the skin for each shoe; has cut two pieces of lining from cotton drilling for each shoe and has cut two "top stays," "button stays," "heels stay" and "button-piece linings" from sheep skin—thus providing the twenty pieces which are required in the making of a pair of button shoe uppers.

But of course they have to be united, and when they reach the "stitching room" they are united with a neatness and despatch which would do credit to a minister making one of an eloping couple when the bride's father was rapidly approaching. We will not bewilder our confiding reader with a technical description of the process of making an upper out of a collection of most irregularly shaped scraps, suffice it to say it is done by sewing machines making about a dozen stitches a second, and directed by girls who are evidently keen of sight and sure of hand, for they handle the material with such ease that it seems like carelessness, and yet the sewing is done with the nicest accuracy; the pieces are united, the button-holes cut and finished, the buttons sewed on—and the whole thing has been done in less than a quarter of an hour! If that isn't "hustling" then we have no use for that word in this country. But an upper without a sole is as useless as is a "back number" last to a wide-awake manufacturer and so let us observe the process of making the sole and wedding it to i preordained mate. First, the sole leather is dampened so it will be ready for the severe treatment it is about to undergo. Then it is run between rollers to squeeze or "pack" it; placed in a splitting machine to even it up, and run through a die machine which stamps or rather cuts out the soles. They are operated upon by a channelling machine, which cuts the grooves along which in a machine-made shoe runs the thread which unites the sole and the upper, and then a "feather edging" machine reduces the thickness of the edges of the sole, as the wear comes upon the middle and nothing would be gained by thick edges. The sole is pressed into shape in heavy moulds, and is now ready to meet that long-lost upper. This is the work of the "laster" and perhaps here we have the origin of the expression "last but not least," for although lasting " is almost the final process incidental to shoe manufacturing it is the most important of all, for upon it depends the shapeliness, comfort and a large part of the durability of our footwear. Lasting machines are now used a good deal and they have unquestionably "come to stay" in some departments of the shoe business, but they have thus far proved successful in the production of the coarse grades of footwear only, and it is doubtful if the scope of their usefulness will ever be greatly enlarged, for no machine can remember, think, and reason, and all of these must be done if shoes are to be lasted to the best possible advantage. But how is a shoe lasted by hand? Well, the upper is pulled tightly over a wooden last with an iron bottom; the inner sole is placed in position, the "counter" (or piece which stiffens the heel end of the upper and keeps your shoes from "running down") is placed between the lining and the outside; and the edges of the upper are folded over and fastened to the inner sole by little tacks which are clinched by the iron bottom of the last. This sounds simple enough, and it would be simple enough for anyone to do were it not for the fact that when the pincers of the laster are used in drawing the upper around the sole, if they are not skillfully used the shoe is spoiled in shape and is probably made uncomfortable as well as wrinkled or baggy. But the work is done very quickly and the laster has little chance to go to sleep, for his mouth is filled with tacks; his right hand grasps the pincer which is also

CITY HOSPITAL.

used as a hammer; his left hand grasps the last and holds the edges of the upper in place; and he drives about fifteen tacks and has that shoe lasted before you have satisfied yourself as to "where he is at."

Though the shoe is lasted it is not yet completed, for it must receive a "steel shank," running from the heel to the sole to hold the shank of the shoe in shape and make it "springy;" the outer sole must be placed in position by the "nail tacker," and now the process of union of the upper and soles is to be finished by the McKay sewing machine, which thinks nothing of sewing through half an inch of leather, and which runs at such prodigious speed that it can easily sew a pair a minute. In union is strength but in this case not beauty until the shoe has passed through a "beating out" machine which perfects its shape; "trimming machines" which cut and shape the edges of the sole; which are then covered with blacking and burnished until they shine like the proverbial heel of a gentleman of Ethiopian descent. The bottom of the sole is pressed against a sand-papered wheel which makes some forty revolutions a second and which "buffs" the leather so that it looks as soft and almost as white as new fallen snow and it seems almost a shame to soil so immaculate a sole by contact with things earthy. And that shoe is not fit for wear yet, for we have not seen it receive a heel, and a heel-less shoe is like a worthless check —it looks good enough but nobody wants it. A heel is a collection of "lifts" or pieces of leather which are punched out by the use of dies; piled upon one another until the heel is high enough; temporarily fastened together by tacks and penetrated around the edge by small holes for the reception of the nails which are to be driven in later. A long, narrow piece of leather, thick on one edge and thin on the other and called a "rand" is placed between the heel and the shoe to make the heel level, and then a "heeling machine" drives the nails home, cuts off superfluous leather and thus fastens and forms the heel. A "breasting" machine pares down and smooths the front part of the heel; rapidly revolving wheels grind off the rough parts, after which the heel is blackened and polished until its shine is equal to that of the edges of the sole. If the bottom of the sole is to be made as pretty as possible it is covered with a coat of "finish" and then rubbed by a revolving brush until its "hard finish" is perfected. The next thing to do is to paste a kid lining over the inner sole, then the trade mark will probably be stamped into the outer sole by a "monogram machine," the shoes are buttoned up, placed in a more or less ornamental pasteboard box and are now "ready for business." It will be seen that the making of those shoes has necessitated the use of many machines—some of which are intricate and costly—has required the employment of skilled and reliable labor and has convinced anyone who saw the process that there is nothing lazy about shoe manufacturing. And it takes capital, experience, brains and energy to carry on a shoe factory successfully. Even assuming that a manufacturer made but one style and grade of shoe (and there are but very few such manufacturers in Massachusetts) it would be absolutely necessary for him to have a costly plant of machinery, tools and patterns in order to meet competition; and as a typical Lynn factory produces all the way from twenty-five to one hundred styles, the expense of lasts and patterns alone is a very important item, especially as styles change so rapidly that lasts and patterns which turned out goods that could not be made fast enough a year ago, may this year be so "out of date" and useless as not to be worth the room they occupy. Lynn shoes are made to fit the feet, and that means the variety of sizes and widths in each style requires an enormous number of lasts and patterns. This policy has been perfected to such an extent that it is now not only possible but easy to get a "ready made" pair of shoes that will fit as perfectly as if made to order; and in grace and beauty as well as in comfort and durability the representative Lynn shoe will hold its own in any company, and crowd out any shoe that is not strictly first-class when it is offered in open competition before intelligent and experienced buyers. We say "the representative Lynn shoe" because some of Lynn's leading manufacturers make shoes which are known in every part of the country where first-class footwear is in demand, and which are especially popular among those to whom "money is no object," and who insist upon having the best that capital and skill can produce. But Lynn by no means devotes itself exclusively to the production of high-priced footwear; in fact its leading specialty is the manufacture of medium grade shoes, and it is an open secret among the trade that this city leads the entire country in the production of lines which cost the retailer from $1.60 to $2.50, and which not only sell rapidly but give that lasting satisfaction to consumers which results in the building up of an extensive and regular patronage. There is no mere "bluff" about this, it is a simple statement of fact, made in the interest of no one manufacturer or clique of manufacturers, but stating the condition of things as they actually are. Hence it is not to be wondered at that the demand for Lynn shoes is constantly increasing, and that the manufacturers are encouraged to continue their policy of steady improvement in style, in fit and in durability. They concentrate their attention upon the production of special lines; they win a reputation for those lines by general distribution and persistent advertising, and they maintain and add to that reputation by not only keeping the goods fully up to the standard, but by raising that standard every season. Just as long as that policy is adhered to Lynn will easily maintain her present leading position among the shoe manufacturing centers of the country.

THE ELECTRIC INDUSTRY.

The name "city of shoes," although eminently appropriate for a city that manufactures shoes by the hundreds of thousands and is greatly increasing her output every year, still does not tell the whole story by any means, for modern Lynn is not only a "city of shoes" but a "city of electricity," and her name is borne to all parts of the world as that of the birthplace of the most efficient electric machinery that is produced. Just about ten years ago the Thomson-Houston Electric Company began operations in Lynn, and the wonderful growth the enterprise has made since that time shows that the world demands first-class electrical machinery and that Lynn is admirably located for the manufacture and distribution of it.

The business was started in 1880, at New Britain, Connecticut, under the style of the American Electric Company, but its early development was very slow, although the company produced the best electric lighting plants then on the market. In fact so superior were these plants that a rival corporation found it expedient to purchase a controlling interest in the company, for the purpose of practically retiring it from the field, but certain restricting clauses in the contract with Professors Thomson and Houston rendered this scheme impracticable, and the only things that hindered the development of the business were lack of capital and poorness of location. In June, 1882, a small arc light plant was brought to Lynn, for the purpose of lighting some of the principal stores. Lynn men know a good thing when they see it—the result was that a number of them united, bought the stock held by the rival company and proceeded to re-organize the American. Its name was changed to the Thomson-Houston Electric Company, its capital was increased to $250,000, and its factory was removed from New Britain to Lynn. This was in the fall of 1883, and the company then gave employment to about seventy-five hands. The records show that January 1, 1884, the company employed 144 hands, and that the total pay-roll for 1884 was $92,591.20. Just eight years later, on January 1, 1892, the company employed 3,492 hands, and the pay-roll for the year 1891 amounted to $1,518,186.02. These figures tell their own story of phenomenal development, and it goes without saying that an enterprise which now affords employment to about 4,000 people is a most important factor in Lynn's prosperity. The manufacture of electric lighting machinery is now but one of several great industries carried on by the company, the most important of which is the manufacture of electric dynamos and motors for

ELECTRIC FOUNTAIN AND COMMON.

street railway service. By far the larger part of American electric railways are equipped by this company, and some idea of the magnitude of the demand may be gained from the statement that in January, 1890, there were 80 railway companies using electricity; in January, 1892, there were 204, using 2,769 cars with 2,363 miles of track. The business of the company in 1883 amounted to $426,000. The business during the latest fiscal year exceeded $12,000,000. The amount of material used in a year will also show the magnitude of the business, and indicates that Lynn is well up to the times as regards transportation facilities. There was used, of iron of all kinds 18,000,000 pounds, at a cost of $500,000. Of copper, 6,000,000 pounds worth $1,000,000. Of brass, 2,000,000 pounds, worth $320,000. The total purchases of material equalled $3,500,000.

Every piece of machinery leaving the great factories of this company is marked "Lynn, Mass., U. S. A." and as shipments are constantly being made, not only to every state in the union but to every country in the world, this is certainly a well advertised city. And the best of it is, it is advertised by the quality of the goods also. Lynn-made electric machinery is the best of its kind in the world, just as surely as Lynn-made shoes are conceded to be superior to the best that are produced elsewhere and are offered at the same prices. A combination of quality and quantity is what succeeds in this busy world, and there is no room for doubt of the prosperous future of Lynn as long as she has the ability to produce the best goods the market affords, and the facilities to promptly meet all demands.

"BAPTISM BY FIRE."

Lynn was very fortunate in escaping severe loss from fire until the end of 1889, when she was visited by a conflagration that would have almost ruined a less energetic city and have put it far behind in the race for supremacy in a national industry. But this great fire, although regarded at first and for a long time as a terrible calamity, was really the great turning point in the modern history of this city. It brought the people more closely together; induced union of effort, inspired mutual confidence, and out of the ashes and ruins has risen a fairer and more progressive city.

The origin of the fire was almost as insignificant as that of the great Chicago conflagration, for it was set by an oil stove used to heat irons in a glove-kid shop. The flames spread with lightning rapidity and hardly seven hours had passed before thirty acres of the very heart of the city were covered with smouldering ruins. These represented thirty-two brick blocks, including some of the finest shoe factories in Lynn; 158 wooden mercantile and manufacturing blocks, and 129 dwelling houses, twelve stables and one church, making a total of 332 buildings destroyed The direct consequences of this was that 162 families were rendered homeless; eighty-seven shoe firms burned out, and shoe machinery valued at $275,500 destroyed. The total damage to buildings was $1,659,014, and to contents was $3,301,117. More than sixty per cent. of the shoe and leather houses were burned out, and many outsiders believed that the shoe industry of Lynn had received its death blow but they reckoned without their host, for when the Lynn people came to cast up the account they balanced it so quickly that it was soon hard to realize that any disaster had visited the city.

At sunrise the morning after the fire the work of preparing for rebuilding was begun and was prosecuted with such vigor that the cost of the buildings erected during the following year exceeded the value of those burned.

The appearance of the city was greatly improved by this cleansing fire. Some of the old buildings were small, many were shabby, and not a few rickety, but the new buildings are all of good size, are massively built of stone and brick, and contain the most improved apparatus for the supply of heat, light, steam and water.

It was supposed that the heavy losses in stocks in trade occasioned by the temporary removals of many concerns from the city would greatly reduce the total valuation, and that the population of the city would diminish or, at least, show no increase, but such was far from being the case, for the report rendered by the assessors on the first day of August, 1890—barely nine months after the fire—showed that the gain in real estate during the past year amounted to $1,805,346 and the loss in personal property amounted to $1,109,185, so the total valuation was increased about $700,000, and amounted to $40,721,028. Nor was the gain in real estate due entirely to the erection of manufacturing and mercantile buildings to replace those consumed; on the contrary there was an average of one dwelling house per day built during the year, and instead of the population decreasing it increased so that there was a gain of 925 polls.

Of course, no one can say whether Lynn will be visited by another great fire or not, for experience has proved that even the best built and best equipped city is far from being positively secure against conflagrations, but so far as precautions are concerned, so far as comprehensive and thoroughly enforced ordinances relating to the erection of buildings will prevent the building of "fire-traps;" so far as a thoroughly efficient fire department, supplied with the best apparatus and backed by an abundant and reliable water supply can afford insurance against the spread of fire—Lynn is certainly well provided for and can safely challenge comparison with any city in the state.

And, if a great fire should occur, the record made by Lynn men during their former experience would do much to maintain confidence in the city and the public would be sure that she would "pull through" all right.

LYNN WOODS.

A visit to Lynn Woods is a delight to everybody, a surprise to every new visitor and a perfect revelation to those who previously knew Lynn only as the "city of shoes"—an enterprising bustling municipality that contains more thoroughly modern shoe factories than any other city in the country and is too busy to spare time to bother over scenic beauty and pastoral recreations. The time has gone by when a public park was the exception instead of the rule and when a diminutive "common" was considered all that was necessary even in a typical New England city, but notwithstanding the great progress that has been made in the matter of public parks there is no other city in the Republic that has a park like Lynn Woods. To begin with, think of the area of it!—1650 acres. Or, to put it another way—for the Eastern man is not used to such great areas of land and cannot estimate them correctly—think of a public park forty times as big as Boston Common. And the bigness of Lynn Woods is by no means the greatest of its attractions, for these are many and varied, and present so many inducements that it is perfectly safe to say that one who cannot enjoy himself here cannot do so anywhere. Do you enjoy rambling about a wild forest, covering hill and dale, unchanged from its original condition and as quiet and secluded as the most remote spot in the White Mountain region? Do you enjoy views of ocean and shore; of city and town; of farm and factory; of lakes and streams? Do you enjoy driving over smooth and curving roads, through heavy woods, up and down hills; one moment commanding a magnificent view and the next moment being apparently as shut off from the world as if you were far from civilization? If you enjoy any or all of these things you will need no urging to induce you to repeat your visit to Lynn Woods, for all of them are there besides many others that are really too numerous to mention. The greatest charm of this great park is that it is natural—it is not a more or less painful attempt at picturesque ornamenting by would-be landscape artists but it stands to-day as it came from the hands of Nature—and "Nature unadorned is adorned the most." Those entrusted with the care of the land for park purposes have wisely made no attempt to improve upon the architecture of nature, and the only changes made are those that were necessary in order to make the different parts of the park more accessible; to add to the safety of visitors, and to improve views by the removal of underbrush and the judicious pruning of dead branches. Excellent roads have been made through the most picturesque parts of the territory, and the exposed points along them are provided with rustic fences which add to the security of the traveler without marring the beauty of the scenery. Benches are placed on the various points of view and in the favorite resting places; plain but inconspicuous signs tell the names of each locality and point out how to reach adjacent points of interests—in fact on every side may be seen evidences that this is a park for the people and that those in charge of it wish to make it as pleasant as possible.

Besides the carriage roads, there are foot-paths extending in every direction; each plainly marked and each offering attractions which can be offered by no carriage road no matter how skillfully laid out. The mere names on some of the signs are enough to arouse pleasant expectations—such names as "Glen Dagyr," "Fern Dell," "Dungeon Rock," "Echo Cliff"—and those expectations will most surely be realized, for Lynn Woods is romantic, picturesque and mysterious enough to stimulate the imagination of even the most prosaic. The principal eminence in the park is called "Mt. Gilead," and its name seems most appropriate to one who has visited it at the end of a week's hard toil and been wonderfully refreshed by its cool and bracing air; its far reaching views of sea and shore and its thoroughly "natural" appearance, for this is certainly a most efficient "balm of gilead" and one that well deserves unstinted praise. The greater part of Lynn Woods consists of rugged oak trees but there are many noble specimens of the evergreen varieties here and there in the tract,

DUNGEON ROCK ROAD, LYNN PARK.

and around "Hemlock Ridge" are some of the most beautiful hemlocks to be found in the state. Great rocks are scattered about here, there and everywhere, and the uppermost of the great ledges in these woods bear evidences of glacial action which make them as interesting from a scientific as from an æsthetic point of view.

But the most interesting thing in the park, the thing which interests young and old, romantic and prosaic, imaginative and sternly practical, is Dungeon Rock. There are many interesting legends associated with Lynn's history, but that of Dungeon Rock surpasses them all, for this rock is a monument to the faith, courage and perseverance of one who was laughed at by all; who expended all his means in an effort to accomplish what he considered his pre-ordained task; and who was confident to the last although he had not received the least encouragement. He searched for treasures which he believed to have been buried in Dungeon Rock two centuries before he began operations, and he was an ardent spiritualist, who was sure that he was ordered by spirits to begin the excavations, and was guided by them in his hunt for the treasure.

The tradition is that about 1656 a pirate vessel anchored off the mouth of Saugus River and four of the crew came ashore and entered the woods for the purpose of concealing their ill-gotten gains. Then they set sail again and were gone for months, but finally returned and built a hut in a glen in Lynn woods that was very secluded and yet was so located that from a cliff near by the land and sea for miles around could be watched. It is hardly necessary to add that the pirate chief was accompanied by a beautiful woman, for a romantic story without a woman connected with it would be as incomplete as a fisherman's equipment without a bottle. But she did not live long nor did the pirates long survive her, for shortly after she died they were captured, taken to England and executed, excepting one—Thomas Veale—who had escaped capture and who made his home in a cave which had been used as a pirate storehouse. But he was destined not to escape divine justice, for during a terrific earthquake the cave was forever shut up, and the entire face of Dungeon Rock shattered so that a great heap of jagged stones was all that remained of it. No more was seen of the pirate, and it was generally believed that his body lay under the ruins of Dungeon Rock together with vast wealth in gold and precious stones, but no persistent effort was made to find the treasure until Hiram Marble began to search about half a century ago. Receiving his instructions through spirit mediums he directed his excavations accordingly and drilled and blasted for year after year, progress being slow because the rock is very hard and without seam or break of any kind. There was not the slightest indication of any cave ever having been there and so there was nothing to direct the course of the cutting but the advice of the spirits, and as this varied from time to time the direction of the shaft is somewhat irregular. Marble soon had the help of his son, who continued the work alone after his father died, but although father and son continued the search from morning till night for almost thirty years they found nothing but death. As a result of their work Dungeon Rock is penetrated by a gallery about 150 feet long, but so winding that it is but about 100 feet in a straight line from its entrance to the end. The entrance is guarded by a locked iron door and the cave is not open to the public, but this is no loss, for it is a dark, wet, dreary and dangerously slippery place, and even the most emotional and imaginative would find it hard to take any pleasure in visiting it. The end of the gallery is about 40 feet lower than the entrance, and one must descend a flight of steps before reaching the level of the tunnel.

A goodly part of the beauty of the Lynn woods region is due to the extensive artificial lakes which furnish the city's water supply. These afford a most happy illustration of the combination of utility and beauty, for, of course the primary object of forming them was to secure an adequate supply of water, and yet they could not have been more artistically arranged had beauty been the only aim of those who planned them. The expediency of guarding against the contamination of Lynn's water supply had much to do with the creation of the present beautiful park, as the land surrounding the lakes was placed under public control in order to avoid the establishment of any enterprise that would tend to impair the water. Certainly there is now no reason why it should not always remain pure, for the storage basins lie in the midst of a great tract of virgin woods and every provision is made to prevent contamination from any source.

The father of the Lynn Park system was the late Cyrus M. Tracy, for to his efforts was due the purchase of about 160 acres of forest land by private subscription. Much had previously been said on the subject of preserving Lynn Woods and securing them for the use of the people, but it was Mr. Tracy who took the first decisive step in the matter and who showed that "actions speak louder than words" by arousing the people by energetic action. A few years later the city made use of the "Park Act" and appointed trustees for a public park. The result is that Lynn has the largest municipal forest park in the country, and the largest municipal park of any kind with the exception of Fairmount Park, Philadelphia. Its maintenance will not call for much expense as it is essentially a "natural" park and about the only expenses will be the maintenance of the roadways and the providing of the few necessary protections and conveniences.

The park is situated in the northwesterly part of Lynn about two miles from the centre of the city, and is reached by three lines of street cars, all of which use electric power and are capable of transporting thousands easily and swiftly. A more accessible and yet more remote and picturesque park could not be imagined, and the people of Lynn are to be congratulated on having such a pleasure resort and on having the necessary determination and public spirit to secure it for the use of the public. Lynn common is another "institution" of which the people have good reason to be proud, for although it is of course but very small when compared with the Lynn Woods park still it is large as commons go and is a very pleasant resting place in the very heart of the city. Beautiful flowers, a gleaming fountain, velvety turf, hospitable benches, a spacious band stand—all of these are features of Lynn common, and it is a favorite gathering place for the people and the scene of many animating and instructive open-air meetings. The common has an area of 21 acres; Meadow Park, of 30 acres; Goldfish Pond Park, of 3 acres, and Washington Square and Highland Square a quarter of an acre each; so when we add the 1,650 acres of Lynn Woods it will be seen that there is no lack of public grounds in the city of shoes

LYNN AND ITS POINTS OF INTEREST.

There are also a number of cemeteries, among them being Pine Grove Cemetery which has an area of 133 acres and is one of the most beautiful in the country.

There are many ponds in Lynn, nearly all of which are beautiful, and several of which are quite extensive, but it is a notable fact that about all of them are artificial. The largest is Walden Pond which has an area of 128 acres and is one of the sources of the water supply. The scenery about this pretty sheet of water is beautiful and a drive along its shore is an experience not soon to be forgotten. There are ten more Lynn ponds, varying in size from 1½ to 84 acres

LYNN AND NAHANT BEACH AT HIGH TIDE.

and having an aggregate area of 380 acres. One which should be visited by all is "Floating Bridge Pond," for the floating bridge is a veritable curiosity, it being the only bridge of the kind in the country. It was built in 1803 and is to-day as sound as ever, although the only repairing done has been the renewal of the upper planking. This is not a floating bridge merely in name, for it rests upon the water and was designed to serve the purposes of a bridge at a point where it was well-nigh impossible to secure a firm foundation. It is a raft 511 feet long, moored at the ends and made of solid timber. The lower part is made of trunks of trees, covered by four thicknesses of timber hewn one foot square, laid crosswise and secured by great tree nails. The roadway is made of planks laid crosswise, and is six inches higher in the middle than at the rails. The bridge is five and a half feet in thickness and is capable of bearing up a very heavy weight, although it is a curious fact that no elephant can be induced to cross it. It is on Western avenue or Salem turnpike, near the Salem and Swampscott lines and will repay a visit.

SUMMARY OF LYNN'S ADVANTAGES.

An attempt to "sum up" the advantages of Lynn is rendered very difficult by the vast amount of material which is available. Some cities are excellent places to do business in but not very desirable places to live in ; others are delightful as places of residence but offer very few inducements to manufacturers or merchants ; and others are too far "out of the way" to combine the advantages of healthful and comfortable living with the conveniences of a metropolis. But there is not one of these objections that can be reasonably made in the case of Lynn, for she offers almost unequalled advantages to manufacturers, an excellent field for the operations of merchants, and is as truly desirable a place of residence as can be found in the entire country.

The school system is admirable ; the school houses are many and well equipped ; the churches of Lynn are a credit to the city, and the fraternal and charitable associations are many and liberally supported. An abundance of beautiful and varied scenery ; pleasant roadways ; an almost endless variety of enjoyable drives, walks and sails—all these things go to make up an almost ideal place of residence from an æsthetic point of view, and the showing from a practical point of view is even more favorable if possible.

Lynn is an extremely healthful city ; it is admirably equipped with "all the modern improvements" including an adequate water supply, ample facilities for gas and electric lighting, and an efficient fire department; the national and savings banks of the city are as strong as any in the state and are very ably managed; and the street railway system is superior to that enjoyed by any other city in the country.

The rate of taxation is low and the city debt is very small in comparison with the valuation and resources of the municipality.

Under such conditions it is but natural that Lynn should steadily continue her rapid growth and should not only hold but make more and more evident her supremacy as the shoe manufacturing centre of the country.

But shoe and leather manufacturing and the great electrical business are by no means the only important industries ; many other branches of manufacture are carried on, and the present indications are that the great industries of the future Lynn will be as varied as they will be important.

The Lynn Board of Trade is an association of more than 300 of the leading business men of the city, and is active, earnest and successful in promoting the best interest of the community. It is prepared to welcome and assist by all reasonable means, any serious or legitimate firm or corporation that desires or could be induced to locate in the Shoe City, but it is not at all disposed to favor any unnatural "boom," and it cannot be induced to lend its name or its influence for the introduction of any enterprise that is doubtful in its ultimate end. In the future, as in the past, the people of Lynn, both individually and collectively, will refrain from any attempt to "boom" the city into abnormal growth but will remain content with that very rapid but still thoroughly natural growth that has been characteristic of Lynn during the past score of years and has raised her to her present high position.

REPRESENTATIVE BUSINESS MEN

OF

LYNN.

LYNN GAS & ELECTRIC CO., 8 Central Square, Lynn, Mass. Store, 82 Exchange Street.—President, Charles H. Newhall; Treasurer, Charles C. Frey; General Superintendent, Charles F. Prichard; Superintendent Electrical Department, W. P. Hazletine. Gas as a Fuel: One of the most important developments of recent years has been the use of gas as a fuel. It has had even a greater effect upon domestic economy than electric lighting, although its progress has been more quiet. Several patent and easily tested facts underlie the growing popularity of gas for this purpose. These are its cleanliness, the great saving of labor, its economy—as it costs less than coal, prompt and effective work, the fact that it is always ready so that a meal can be prepared in from twenty to thirty minutes, the better and more even results obtained by the use of gas in cooking, and the absence of fuel or ashes to carry. Such a combination of advantages is bound to win the day, and no sensible housekeeper can fail to be gratified by trying this great labor saving and economical substitute for coal and wood. In recognition of the growing demand for gas in this direction, the Lynn Gas and Electric Company have both reduced the price of gas to $1.30 per thousand feet, and also have opened a special store at 82 Exchange Street, for the sale of gas appliances. These include the "Perfect Cooking Stove" in different styles and sizes, with all the attachments for complete cooking purposes ; also water-heating stoves, gas radiators for general heating, the Yale gas heater, the Backus heater, the Fire-King and the Otto gas-engine. They also keep on hand tin and Russia-iron ovens, iron-heaters, boiler-heaters, gas-hose of all kinds and a complete line of gas-heating and cooking appliances. These are sold at cost figures to the public of Lynn and vicinity, and the number in use is increasing every month. A competent man is in charge of the Exchange Street store, and can explain all details to those desiring to introduce into their homes this new and valuable method for the purposes indicated. The company is also largely engaged supplying electricity for light and power, and have just completed a new station near their gas works. Recognizing the fact that if the electric business is to be satisfactory to the public it must be free from interruptions the company has supplied their new station with the most improved appliances, duplicating wherever possible, and thereby reducing to a minimum the liability to accidental delays.

LAKE SHORE IMPROVEMENT CO.

= SPECIAL OPPORTUNITIES IN REAL ESTATE. =

Room 14, CURRIER BUILDING.

333 Union Street, LYNN, MASS.

Mr. T. W. GRAVES, Manager.

Suburban development is one of the greatest facts in the growth of our American cities. Nothing is more solid than the sure and steady increase in the value of eligibly situated building property within easy distance of a growing city. Some of the greatest fortunes in the country have built up on this fact alone. Judgment in selection is the great point necessary, and with electric cars to the business centre, good drainage and water supply, graded streets, shade trees, and electric lights, there can be no question of unrivalled eligibility. On the shores of the Lake, the company have reserved seven acres of beautifully wooded land, as a public park for "all time." The houses fronting the lake will always have an unobstructed view of woodland and water. Combine with these advantages, which are all possessed by the property at Lake Shore Park, on the suburbs of this city, the fact also that lots are being sold at very low prices and on liberal terms, and it would take a very obtuse person not to see that a rare opportunity was presented for investment. There has been so much foolish speculation in Western and Southern lands, that many have closed their eyes to better advantages near at home. These exist, however, and are coming to be more thoroughly appreciated. The Lake Shore Improvement Co. has for some time been completing the development of this property now thrown open to all. The low prices and easy terms on which lots are sold make them exceptionally attractive for homes to working people. They can easily be secured now at prices which can never be repeated, by a small first payment and yet smaller weekly installments. A good foundation for a life's fortune can be laid at once. Titles and guarantees are protected by the most solid security. A very liberal offer made by the company is that all taxes will be paid by them until the payments are complete. The offices of the company are at room 14, Currier Block, 333 Union Street, Mr. T. W. Graves being the general manager. All those desiring to examine the advantages now open in Lynn's most beautiful suburb, will here receive courteous and thorough attention. No sensible working man or general investor can regret the time necessary to convince themselves that the opportunity here presented is one indeed of a lifetime. Lynn has not hitherto seen so liberal an opening, nor is it likely that such will occur again.

KINGMAN GURNEY,
DINING ROOMS
FOR LADIES AND GENTLEMEN.
52 MONROE ST., ALSO 48 SPRING ST.,   **LYNN, MASS.**

Open 6 A. M. to 8 P. M.   Sundays, 8 A. M. to 8 P. M.

One of the principal reasons why so many of us think "there's no place like home" is because it is generally pretty hard to get a "square meal" away from home, without paying a big price for it, for many dining-rooms seem to be run on the principle of getting as much, and giving as little as possible. But some are more liberally managed, and among them that of which Mr. Kingman Gurney is proprietor must be given a high position for here you can get a good, hearty meal of well cooked food promptly and neatly served, at a very reasonable price. Mr. Gurney is a native of Maine and has carried on his present business in Lynn since 1881, since which date he has built up a large business. His establishments are popularly known, and located at No. 52 Monroe Street and 48 Spring Street, they having a capacity for seating a large number of guests at a time. Sufficient assistance is employed at both places to avoid all annoying delays in the filling of orders, and we would advise our readers in this vicinity who have not already done so to make trial of the service offered by Mr. Gurney, for he caters to both ladies and gentlemen, and his Dining-Rooms are open from 6 A.M. to 8 P.M.; Sundays 8 A.M. to 8 P.M., and patrons are assured prompt and courteous attention at all hours.

A. K. ADAMS & CO., Painters and Paper-Hangers, and Dealers in Paints, Oils, Brushes, Artists' Supplies, Picture Frames, Paper-Hangings, Mouldings, etc., 730 Western Avenue, and 9 South Street, Lynn, Mass.—The advantages gained by placing orders for painting and paper-hanging with a responsible firm that not only does such work but deals largely at wholesale and retail in paints, painters' materials, paper-hangings, etc., are so obvious that there is no need of mentioning them in detail; and conclusive evidence that the people appreciate them is afforded by the success of the enterprise carried on by Messrs. A. K. Adams & Co., for they are painters and paper-hangers, and dealers in paints, oils, brushes, artists' supplies, picture frames, paper-hangings, mouldings, etc., and they do a business so large as to require the employment of ten assistants. The enterprise was inaugurated by Mr. George H. Colley, and in 1888 came under the control of Messrs. George H. Colley & Co., who were succeeded by the present firm in 1890. The premises utilized are located at 730 Western Avenue and 9 South Street, and comprise one floor and a basement, 50x30 feet in dimensions. A very large and complete stock is carried, made up of the productions of the leading manufacturers, and including the latest novelties in artistic paper-hangings, and artistic supplies of guaranteed excellence. Estimates on the exterior and interior painting and decorating of houses will be cheerfully made on application, and the facilities are such that commissions can be executed at short notice, all work being carefully supervised, and no pains being spared to attain the best possible results. No inferior stock is used by this firm, and as they employ competent help and are moderate in their charges it is not surprising that they do an extensive business, and are called upon to fill many important orders.

G. M. TUCKER & CO., Wholesale and Retail Dealers in Cigars, Pipes and Tobaccos, 335 & 337 Union Street, Lynn, Mass.—It is comparatively easy to get good smoking and chewing tobacco, for there are many reliable brands on the market and at least one or two of them are handled by about every storekeeper who sells tobacco at all, but getting good cigars at moderate prices is quite another thing, as the market is fairly flooded with brands that are apparently made only to sell to "transient" customers—at all events they are so poor that they are not worth half the money they cost at retail, and when once a man has tried a cigar of this kind he won't ever get another if he can buy some other brand. Still, it is easy enough to get good cigars at fair prices if you know where to place your orders; and many residents of Lynn know from experience that the store carried on under the style firm of G. M. Tucker & Co., at 335 and 337 Union Street, and managed by Mr. C. Harry Hooper for the estate (Mr. Tucker having died some years ago), is headquarters for the Little Bee, Little Wonder, Pastime, 4-50-1, American Eagle, Manzinilla, 5 cent; B. B. Conchas, B. B. Perfectos, B. B. Loudre, Palestine, Pennants, Handmade, 10 cent. A specialty is made of the 4-50-1, which is unrivalled by any in the market as a 5 cent cigar. You can here buy cigars singly, by the quarter's worth, or by the box, and be perfectly sure of getting excellent value for the money you pay out, and have so carefully chosen and varied an assortment to choose from that you can find just what you want. Messrs. Tucker & Co.'s stock includes not only a full line of imported and domestic cigars, but also a complete assortment of manufactured tobacco, both plug and fine-cut, and a great variety of smokers' articles in general. Bottom prices are the rule at this popular store, and it is also the rule here to give prompt and polite attention to every caller. Employment is given to four assistants, and an extensive wholesale and retail business is done.

J. F. DERMODY & CO., Desirable Clothing, Hats and Furnishings, 31 Central Square, Lynn, Mass.—It is a nuisance to have to buy your clothing in one place, your hats in another, and your neckwear and other furnishings in another; but many do it because they believe they can save money and get more variety of choice by so doing. But that is not the opinion of those who have tested the facilities of Messrs. J. F. Dermody & Co.'s establishment, for they know from experience that here you can always find fashionable and perfect fitting clothing, the latest novelties in hats and furnishings, and a sufficient variety to admit of all tastes being suited. But how is it as regards price, for that is certainly a most important factor to be considered? Well, call and see for yourself, and compare goods and prices with those offered elsewhere, and if you know where you can get equally desirable goods at prices that are a bit lower you are certainly in luck, for we have yet to find such a place. Messrs. J. F. Dermody & Co. don't make any extravagant pretensions—they simply announce that they offer "desirable clothing, hats and furnishings"—and they couldn't describe their stock better if they used all the words in the dictionary, for the goods composing it are most certainly "desirable" in every sense of that much abused word, and the more thoroughly you examine them the better you like them. The store is located at No. 31 Central Square; four competent assistants are employed and callers may depend upon receiving prompt and courteous attention.

JAMES H. CURRY,

• PLUMBER •

STEAM AND GAS FITTING,

HOT WATER HEATING A SPECIALTY.

TELEPHONE 231-2.   **45 ANDREW ST., LYNN.**

Whatever is worth doing is worth doing well, especially anything in the line of plumbing or steam and hot water heating, for inferior plumbing is not only unsatisfactory, but is apt to be dangerous to health; and poor steam or hot water heating is wasteful, inefficient and troublesome. Hence "the best is the cheapest" in every respect, and one sure way to get the best is to place your orders with Mr. James H. Curry, whose office and shop are located at No. 45 Andrew Street, for he has experience, skill, and excellent facilities; he is fully up to the times in every detail of his business; he employs thoroughly competent and reliable help, and he gives personal attention to the filling of every order of any importance. Mr. Curry is not a "cheap plumber," that is to say, he is not one who depends entirely upon underbidding his competitors to get orders—but on the other hand he makes no fancy charges, and is prepared to furnish and put up first-class plumbing and heating apparatus in first-class style, at as low rates as can be named by any house doing equally good work. In fact, he is prepared to figure very closely on contracts for any work in his line, and parties will best serve their own interests by communicating with him before placing an order.

NOVELTY POP-CORN WORKS, Mrs. Charles A. Andrews, Proprietress, Manufacturer of Fancy and Flavored Pop-Corn Goods for Wholesale and Retail Trade. Beach Trade a Specialty. 37 & 39 Market Street, Lynn, Mass.—Residents of Lynn take a well-founded pride in their city and its "institutions," and one of the most popular establishments among them is the Novelty Pop-Corn Works, located at 37 & 39 Market Street, of which Mrs. Andrews is the proprietress. There is ample reason for the favorable manner in which this enterprise is regarded, for there is not a similar undertaking in this vicinity that is more liberally or progressively conducted, and the well-arranged store and extensive stock are certainly worthy of the highest encomiums. The premises made use of comprise one floor and basement 2,700 square feet each in dimensions, and the business done includes manufacturing, wholesaling and retailing pop-corn goods; about every description is made and sold, and the delicious flavoring of Mrs. Andrews' productions is so well known that we only need give it passing mention. Great care is exercised in the selection of material and in its after handling, and we can confidently recommend the fancy and flavored pop-corn goods made here as being not only palatable but healthful as well. The proprietress is in a position to quote bottom prices on her goods, and the very heavy trade she carries on is proof that the inducements she offers are generally understood, and as four competent and polite assistants are employed at her Market Street store, prompt and courteous attention is assured to every caller. Her experience has been large, having also conducted a branch at Point-of-Pines for ten years, and is also proprietress of a variety booth at Crescent Beach, where lunches, ice cream, soda, confectionery, etc., are served, and another branch at Salem Willows, where a specialty is made of pop-corn goods and confectionery. In all her enterprises a specialty is made of high grade confectionery, a fresh assortment always being on hand of the famous chocolates and bonbons made by the Walter M. Lowney Co., of Boston and Chicago; her ice cream and soda trade is very extensive, so great pains are taken to excel in quality and superior flavors. In the summer season she employs about thirty assistants in her entire business.

OXFORD LADIES' AND GENTS' DINING ROOMS, Open from 6 A.M. to 10 P.M., 155 Oxford Street, Lynn.—There is no surer way to gain the good will of the average man than by directing him to an establishment where he can get what is popularly known as "a square meal" at a moderate price, for if the service there offered prove satisfactory to him he will remember you gratefully every time he repeats his visit. Therefore, we feel that we are bound to make many friends among our readers by bringing to their attention the "Oxford Ladies' and Gents' Dining Rooms," conducted by Mrs. Susan A. Miller. She treats her patrons so liberally that we do not see how it would be possible for any reasonable man to find fault with the accommodations offered. The premises, which are located at 155 Oxford Street, comprise one floor, 70x25 feet in size, and afford a seating capacity for quite a number of guests at a time. Three competent assistants are employed, and Mrs. Miller feeds a great many people every day, and feeds them well, too. She is a native of Massachusetts, and began her present enterprise here in 1892, and is now proprietress of a first-class restaurant and dining-hall. The bill of fare is varied, the cooking good, and the service is prompt, polite and intelligent, while the prices are low enough to suit the most economical person. Open from 6 A.M. to 10 P.M.

WILLIS L. SNOW, Real Estate Agent. Collecting Rents a Specialty. Office, 132 Central Avenue, Lynn, Mass.—One of the most active, energetic and busy of the various real estate agents doing business in the populous shoe city is Mr. Willis L. Snow, whose office is at No. 132 Central Avenue. He is a native of Orleans, Cape Cod, Mass., and founded his present business in 1888. Mr. Snow makes a specialty of the collection of rents; and some idea of the satisfactory manner in which he discharges the responsible duties incidental to such work may be gained from the fact that he now collects for 55 estates, and has about 350 houses to rent and 500 tenants to collect from. It is hardly necessary to add that Mr. Snow's time is pretty fully occupied, especially as he does not employ assistance but gives personal attention to the work of collection; but he has things so systematized that no time is lost, and collections are made and accounts rendered with a promptness and regularity that might profitably be imitated at many an office doing a much smaller business. His office hours are from 8 to 9 A. M., 1 to 2 P. M., and 5 to 6 P. M., and real estate owners wishing to secure a competent and reliable agent, and persons wishing to secure a desirable house or tenement, would do well to avail themselves of the service which Mr. Snow is so well prepared to render.

PINE GROVE MARBLE AND GRANITE WORKS, Marble and Granite Monuments, Tablets, Curbings, Posts, etc. Carving, Lettering, etc., a Specialty. Frank McHugh, Cor. Washington and Boston Streets, Lynn, Mass.—The Pine Grove Marble and Granite Works are very popular under their present management, and it is not at all difficult to account for their popularity, for the public appreciate prompt, skillful and faithful service and reasonable prices, and they have learned that these are assured to patrons of this establishment. The business was founded nearly a quarter of a century ago, operations having begun in 1870, by Mr. E. Hayden and the present proprietor, Mr. Frank McHugh, assumed control in 1887. Mr. McHugh is a practical stoneworker who has had long and varied experience, so he knows what the public want and he knows how to supply that want at the lowest possible cost. No extravagant charges are made for work entrusted to him, and all designs of monumental work from the most simple to the most elaborate, are executed carefully and skillfully. Quite an extensive assortment of finished work is always to be found at the Pine Grove Marble and Granite Works, including marble and granite monuments and tablets, and a specialty is made of carving, lettering, etc., work being delivered at a few days' notice in cases where haste is desired. All cemetery work, including the making and setting up of curbings, posts, etc., is done in first-class style, and an ample force of experienced workmen is employed, so that the prompt and satisfactory filling of orders can be safely and unreservedly guaranteed.

F. W. SKINNER, Dealer in Confectionery, Cigars and Tobacco, Fruits, Wholesale and Retail, 2 Union Street, Lynn, Mass.—It is said that Americans consume a larger amount of confectionery in proportion to population than any other people in the world, and it is easy to believe this when we think of the many confectionery stores in every city and large town, and remember that drug stores, grocery stores, and many other establishments are also more or less largely devoted to the sale of candies. But it is generally better to buy them at a store where a specialty is made of this class of goods, and in this connection we may properly make mention of the store carried on by Mr. F. W. Skinner, for not only does he make a specialty of confectionery but he quotes positively bottom prices, and carries so large and complete a stock that all tastes can be suited, especially as the goods are the best the market affords, they being guaranteed pure and wholesome and being very carefully made and delicately flavored. Confectionery, cigars and tobacco are handled, also foreign and domestic fruits of all kinds which are sold at both wholesale and retail, uniformly low prices being quoted on all goods dealt in. Mr. Skinner is a native of Lynn and very well known throughout the city. He has been identified with his present business since 1891, and now occupies premises located at No. 2 Union Street, where his trade is steadily increasing and will doubtless continue to do so as long as such decided inducements to purchasers are offered as is now the case.

F. A. BURNSVILLE, Dress and Cloak Maker, 2d story, 46 Market Street, Lynn, Mass.—As it is the aim of the publishers to make this book interesting and valuable to all classes of readers, and as much of its circulation will be among families, we take pleasure in calling attention to the enterprise conducted by Miss F. A. Burnsville, for this is of especial interest to the ladies. This lady being a well known and fashionable dress and cloak maker, is prepared to fill all orders in a most satisfactory manner. Miss Burnsville is a native of Swampscott, Mass., and established her present business here at Lynn in 1888 under the firm name of Morse & Burnsville, which was continued until 1890, when Miss Burnsville assumed entire management of affairs. She is a first-class artistic dress and cloak maker, and the productions of her establishment are as attractive in style and finish as her prices are reasonable. Miss Burnsville does an extensive business, and now occupies premises located in the second story of 46 Market Street, and as she employs six to eight thoroughly competent assistants, is prepared to assure the prompt and accurate filling of every order, and that the results attained shall prove satisfactory to the most fastidious customer, for Miss Burnsville not only has excellent taste but is very thorough in her methods, and considers the interests of her customers as being identical with her own.

ELMER E. BOYNTON, Clothing Cleansed, Pressed and Repaired. Pants creased while you wait. Goods called for and delivered. Towel Supply. 311 Union Street, Room 2, Blake's Block, Lynn, Mass.—A first-class suit of clothing can often by thorough cleaning and pressing be made to present a more handsome appearance than it did at the very first. One great advantage is that the clothing has become adapted to the form of the body, and as every one knows no clothing feels so comfortable as the old suit we have become thoroughly accustomed to. It is a great mistake to leave this work unattended to until the power of restoring clothing in the best manner is entirely past. This is a marked instance where a stitch in time will save the whole cloth. Sensible people in this section of the country who want to secure the best satisfaction in these matters, will do well to send clothing or leave orders at the reliable establishment of Mr. Elmer E. Boynton, 311 Union Street (Room 2, Blake's Block), Lynn, telephone 338 4. Mr. Boynton makes a specialty of the cleaning, pressing and repairing of clothing at very reasonable prices. He guarantees the most thorough and complete satisfaction. Pants can be creased here on short notice and in the best style. Goods called for and delivered promptly. A specialty is also made of furnishing towels. First-class reliable service, courteous attention and liberal prices make this an attractive and satisfactory establishment with which to deal. Personal examination will prove convincing on this point and ensure the saving of much labor and expense.

S. J. WEINBERG, Dealer in Tailors' and Dress-Making Trimmings, G. A. R. Building, 56 Andrew Street, Lynn, Mass.—Experienced buyers do not need to be told that it is not always the most pretentious stores that offer the biggest bargains, and those who have made purchases at the store conducted by Mr. S. J. Weinberg, in the G. A. R. Building, 56 Andrew Street, will heartily endorse our statement that no better value in trimmings, etc., can be obtained in the city than is there offered. This is a very neat and well-kept establishment, and always contains a seasonable and carefully selected stock; and an exceptionally complete assortment of tailors' and dress-making trimmings, of which Mr. Weinberg makes a specialty. The goods are sold strictly on their merits (they being guaranteed to prove just as represented), and the prices quoted will bear the closest comparison with those named elsewhere on goods of equal merit, for Mr. Weinberg is a close buyer and he does business on the "quick sales and small profits" system. Employment is given to three competent assistants, and callers are assured prompt and courteous attention; goods being cheerfully shown and prices quoted at all times.

MARKET STREET.

FRED. F. DOW & CO., Successors to Boston Hat Store. Dealers in Hats, Caps, Furs, Trunks, Bags, Umbrellas, and Gents' Furnishings, 158 Market Street, Lynn, Mass.—Those who judge of the value of a garment entirely by the price of it, will probably not think much of the productions of Messrs. Fred F. Dow & Co., when we say that they quote very low rates, being satisfied with a small margin of profit, but those sensible people (and we are happy to say Lynn has its full share of them) who look at things as they really are, and are no more impressed in favor of a garment because a big price is put on it, than they are prejudiced against one that is quoted at a low figure, will examine the goods this house turns out—and that is all they ask any one to do, being confident that the result will be more business for them and a larger circle of regular patrons. This enterprise was founded some years ago by the "Boston Hat Store," they being succeeded in 1892, by the present proprietors, the individual members being Messrs. Fred F. Dow and D. H. Remick, both natives of this State. The premises occupied are located at 158 Market street, comprise two floors in two stores 40 x 20, and 40 x 80 feet in size, respectively. Four competent assistants are employed and callers are assured prompt and courteous attention. Hats, Caps, and Furs, Trunks, Bags, Umbrellas and Gents' Furnishings are largely dealt in while this house is prepared to fill all orders at short notice and at the lowest prices.

JUSTICE OF THE PEACE.   **NOTARY PUBLIC.**

ISRAEL AUGUSTUS NEWHALL,

◁ GENERAL INSURANCE ᴬᴺᴰ REAL ESTATE AGENCY, ▷

112 MARKET STREET, LYNN.

Specialty:— Fire Insurance in the best Mass. Mutual Fire Insurance Cos. Returning to the Policy Holders good Dividends on all Policies.

ANDERSON HOTEL, J. H. Anderson, Manager. Special rates to the profession. Corner Andrew Street and Central Avenue, Lynn, Mass. It is safe to say that very few of the theatrical profession think of Lynn without also thinking of the Anderson Hotel, for not only is this one of the very best hotels in the city, but it is especially attractive to the profession, for the genial proprietor and manager, Mr. J. H. Anderson, has made a special study of their needs and how best to satisfy them, and he also quotes special rates, so that it is but natural that the Anderson Hotel should be *the* hotel of Lynn, so far as the profession is concerned. Commercial men also have a tender regard for the house and its manager, for they appreciate good rooms, good living and good management, and experience has taught them that all these are sure to be found at this popular hostelry. It is most eligibly located at the corner of Andrew Street and Central Avenue, and occupies three buildings, one of which is used exclusively as a café. The latter is very largely patronized by those who appreciate excellent food, good cooking and neat and efficient service; and we cannot help saying that a man who would kick at the accommodations given and the charges made at this cafe must either be a chronic kicker or else not be able to appreciate a soft snap when he gets one. The Anderson Hotel was opened in 1881, but has been so greatly enlarged and improved of late years that its accommodations and comforts have been more than doubled. Mr. Anderson is constantly trying to improve the service: he spares no pains to make every guest feel perfectly "at home," and probably one reason why he is anxious to do so is because he has knocked about the world a good deal himself, and knows how greatly a really homelike hotel is appreciated by sensible people. He has visited one or more ports of nearly every country in the world; for he began seafaring life at the age of thirteen, and has served in about every capacity. He entered the United States navy in 1860, and during the next four years he took an active part in convincing our friends down South that this was a nation and not a collection of States, and that they had no right to dissolve partnership no matter how badly they wanted to. Mr. Anderson was in the hotel business for years before he came to Lynn, and as clerk of the Central House and proprietor of the Farragut House in Salem he got a good deal of the knowledge that is now being used in the management of the popular Anderson Hotel. A man of such extended and varied experience (and we have mentioned only some of the more prominent features of Mr. Anderson's career) should certainly be a "man of the world" in the true sense of that much abused expression, and it is not at all surprising that Mr. Anderson should be in touch with the people and find no difficulty in making everybody feel at home.

J. C. BAILEY, Designer and Maker of Women's, Misses' and Children's; also Men's, Boys' and Youths' Boot and Shoe Patterns, 479 Union Street, Libby's Block, up one flight, Lynn, Mass.— Long experience, natural ability and first-class facilities make a strong combination, and as Mr. J. C. Bailey possesses all of these it is perfectly natural that he should meet with success as a designer and maker of boot and shoe patterns. Mr. Bailey is a native of London, England, but is certainly an American by adoption if not by birth, for he has carried on business here in Lynn for more than a quarter of a century, having begun operations in 1867. His shop is located at No. 479 Union Street, in Libby's Block, up one flight, and is excellently equipped for the manufacture of women's, misses' and children's, also of men's, boys' and youth's boot and shoe patterns. As a designer Mr. Bailey is highly commended by those familiar with his work as being both original and practical; and as a manufacturer he has the reputation of producing patterns that are uniformly accurate. Competent assistance is employed, and orders are assured prompt attention, and can be filled at short notice.

W. J. YOUNG, Manufacturer of Moulded Counters and Moulded Counter Machinery, 416 Union Street, Lynn, Mass.— There is a saying to the effect that it takes a practical man to invent a practical machine, and there is a good deal of truth in that as all experienced manufacturers will admit. Certain it is that most of the really successful machines were devised or improved by men who know from experience just what work had to be done, and this can be said of the moulded counter machinery manufactured by Mr. W. J. Young, for he is a manufacturer of moulded counters as well as machinery, and his machines embody the results of long experience and close observation. They are thoroughly practical from start to finish—in other words there is nothing "fancy" about them but they are "built for business," and are strong, simple, rapid working and accurate. Hence, it does not require an expert mechanic to run them; they are not liable to get out of order; they are very easy to adjust; they don't waste power, and they do work that can be depended upon for accuracy. Mr. Young's shop is located at No. 416 Union Street, and employment is given to about thirty assistants. The facilities are ample, and orders for moulded counters or for moulded counter machinery can be filled at short notice, and satisfaction can safely be guaranteed.

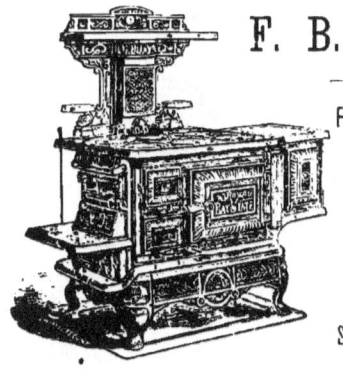

F. B. STEVENS,

—DEALER IN—

FURNACES, RANGES, CROCKERY

—and—

FURNISHING GOODS.

Sanitary Plumbing and Ventilating a Specialty.

93 MARKET STREET, LYNN, MASS.

Among those homely New England sayings which contain more common sense to the square inch than the prettiest modern proverbs is one, "Don't fish for horn pouts in a trout brook," and we commend it to the careful attention of those who seem to have a positive genius for looking for the right things in the wrong place. Such people would be sure to visit a furniture store or some such establishment, when wanting to buy a stove or range, and yet it would seem to be plain enough that the place to buy an article of that kind is at a stove store, for if an establishment which makes a specialty of such goods can't furnish what you want, what chance is there of finding it elsewhere? Go direct to such a store as is carried on by Mr. F. B. Stevens, at No. 93 Market Street, and you will not only get what you want, but will get it at bottom figures, for he deals in Stoves, Furnaces, Hardware, Crockery, Etc., and can furnish anything in these lines at the lowest market rates. Mr. Stevens employs eight competent assistants, and occupies premises covering an area of 3,500 square feet, where, in addition to dealing at both wholesale and retail in the above named goods, he is prepared to fill orders for Plumbing and Stove Work of all kinds in first-class manner and by competent workmen at short notice. Mr. Stevens is a native of Portsmouth, N. H., and has carried on his present business in Lynn long enough to become an acknowledged leader in his line of trade, both as regards the reliability of his goods and work, and the uniform lowness of his prices. For many years Mr. Stevens has been sole agent for the celebrated Barstow Furnaces and Ranges, which for service, durability and economy are unrivalled. Mr. Stevens was formerly connected with the manufacturers of these goods and thoroughly understands his business in every detail. Mr. Stevens has the valuable assistance of Mr. Wm. J. Larrabee who has sold this line of goods to the Lynn public for the last forty years, and also of Mr. W. S. Babbit, who has also been in this line of business since boyhood. All callers are assured prompt service and courteous treatment.

FRANK W. ATKINS, Real Estate, Deeds and Mortgages Written, House Lots in all Parts of the City. For Sale on Easy Terms, Newhall Building, Room 2, 34 Central Square, Lynn, Mass.—There are very few cities in the entire country that can approach Lynn in healthfulness and beauty, and it is gratifying to see that the development of the suburbs of the city is being carried on by men who have the ability and the determination to guard against the mistakes which have seriously injured many another growing city. The important work which has been done in connection with the development of Lynn's suburbs by Mr. Frank W. Atkins, is even more remarkable for character than for magnitude; and yet the magnitude of this operations in such that in a single season he sold house lots aggregating in area more than a million square feet. This success was due to a careful study of the needs of the public; to a thorough acquaintance with Lynn territory and Lynn facilities, and to close adherence to the principle embodied in the saying: Not cheap land, but land cheap." Mr. Atkins is a Maine man by birth, but has resided in Lynn ever since 1871 and is one of the best-known business men in the city. Mr. Atkins has improved and disposed of hundreds of house lots; his operations include " Lakeside," " Orchard Park," " Glenwood," Pleasant View, and Swampscott besides numerous small parcels of land in different parts of this city. " Lakeside," on the northerly shores of beautiful Flax Pond, is the latest of Mr. Atkins' enterprises and it is also the most popular, for Lakeside is almost an ideal place of residence as it combines all the advantages of city and country, and the advantages it offers are within the means of the people looking for homes in a genteel neighborhood. The territory includes about 43 acres of beautifully undulated land and has been " improved " in the true sense of that much-abused word. Broad streets and sidewalks; numerous shade trees, electric lights and water service—these are a few of the many attractions at Lakeside, and as the land is offered at moderate price and on easy terms, it goes without saying that this charming new suburb is very rapidly building up. The Lynn and Boston "electrics," pass through the main avenue of the property; so that not only any part of Lynn but also all the neighboring cities and towns are easily accessible. Mr. Atkins' office is in the Newhall Building, No. 34 Central Square, and certainly no one should neglect giving him a call if they wish to build, to buy a house, or to purchase a house lot, for he has house lots in all parts of the city for sale on easy terms; and is in a position to render valuable assistance to those who are ambitious to own a home.

DOWLING & CO., Merchant Tailors, No. 408 Union Street, Room 9, Earl Building, Lynn, Mass.—A garment that doesn't fit well doesn't look well—no matter how costly and handsome the material of it may be; a garment that isn't made well won't wear well, no matter how strongly it may be sewed together; and a garment that neither fits well nor wears well is dear at any price, so it most emphatically "pays" to wear custom clothing made by a skillful tailor. There you have the whole philosophy of the clothing question, and therefore when you hear that a man is "extravagant" or is "putting on style" because he is having his clothing made to order, don't you endorse the statement unless you know that the tailor he patronizes is unsatisfactory in his work or extravagant in his prices. If you wish to get strictly first-class clothing at strictly reasonable rates, place the order with Messrs. Dowl'ng & Co., whose chambers are in the Earl Building, No. 408 Union Street. This firm are merchant tailors who carry a large and most skillfully chosen stock of foreign and domestic fabrics, and you can feel sure that a garment or a suit made by them will be made from fabrics and patterns that everybody wears but will be correct in style, thoroughly satisfactory in material and in every detail of workmanship, and will be so designed, cut and put together as to " fit " you in the true sense of that much-abused word. Messrs. Dowling & Co. began business in 1893 and have already built up an extensive patronage as their work suits the most critical tastes and their prices suit the most careful buyers. Employment is given to an adequate force of skilled assistants, and orders are assured prompt and careful attention and early delivery.

BENJ. PITMAN, Real Estate and Fire Insurance, Mortgages Negotiated. Agent also of the State Mutual Life Insurance Company. Justice of the Peace and Auctioneer, 408 Union St., Earl's Block, 9 Exchange St., Rooms 10 and 11, Lynn, Mass.—Mr. Benjamin Pitman is one of the best known real estate and insurance men in the city, and not only does a large business, but is steadily increasing it from year to year. If you wish to buy, sell, exchange, rent, or lease real estate, the chances are that you can save time and trouble by making use of the facilities he offers; and if you wish to negotiate a mortgage you will also do well to utilize his services, for Mr. Pitman has placed many mortgages, is very favorably known to investors, and is in a position to execute commissions promptly and satisfactorily. As agent of the State Mutual Life Insurance Company, he is prepared to furnish "insurance that insures" at the lowest possible rates; and he also places a great deal of insurance against fire, as he represents the leading companies and can place insurance in large or small amounts at bottom rates. Certainly there is no excuse for anyone allowing his house or furniture to remain uninsured when he can have it done at a cost of only $3.75 for $500 for 5 years, and that is just what the cost will be if you make use of Mr. Pitman's services. His offices are at No. 408 Union St., Earl's Block, and No. 9 Exchange St., Rooms 10 and 11, and all orders are assured prompt and careful attention.

HARRY KATZES, Dealer in Cigars and Tobacco, Box Trade a Specialty, Union Square Cigar Store, 267 Union Street, Lynn, Mass.—This establishment which ranks among the leading enterprises of its kind in this section of the State, is one of the most popular dealing in cigars. This establishment was founded in 1892, by its present proprietor, and to his enterprise, skill, able management and untiring industry, is due in a great measure the progress and success which has been attained since the establishment of the business. Mr. Harry Katzes is a wholesale and retail dealer in fine cigars and tobacco, and possesses every facility for giving his patrons and friends extra inducements, both in low price and excellent quality of goods sold. The business is being rapidly developed and its growth is very gratifying to the proprietor. The premises occupied are popularly known as the Union Square Cigar Store, and located at 267 Union Street. Mr. Harry Katzes is a native of Pennsylvania, and is very well known in Lynn and vicinity. He does an extensive wholesale and retail business, making a specialty of box trade. He is enterprising and energetic, and his business standing and general reputation as well as the liberal manner in which his business is conducted is a subject of the most favorable comment.

THE L. A. MAY CO.,
Tin, Sheet Iron and Copper Smiths,
Dealers in House Furnishing Goods, Drain Pipe, Fire Brick, Kaolin and Contractors' Supplies.

281, 289, 293 UNION STREET, - - - - LYNN, MASS.

This large, influential business house has for more than half a century been the recognized leader in its department of trade throughout this part of the state. It was established in 1838, and the immense trade built up has been founded upon the rock basis of solid reliability and unvarying enterprise. The house was incorporated under its present name in 1883. The business premises occupied comprise four floors 160x75 feet in dimensions, and a large basement 100x90 feet. The largest and most complete stock of goods between Boston and Portland in its line is carried here. It includes crockery and glassware of all kinds, cutlery, silverware, china, gas and kerosene goods, baby carriages, refrigerators, ice-cream freezers, agricultural tools, woodenware, hardware, brushes of all kinds, hydrant hose, drain pipe, fire-brick, cement, steam, hot air and water heating goods, tin and sheet-iron ware, and general plumbers' supplies. A special feature of large importance is the supply of rope-fire escapes, which are furnished and put up at short notice. These have won wide approval for their economical, and at same time thorough, service. The house employs from seventy-five to one hundred men throughout the year, and handles an immense wholesale as well as retail trade. It can furnish the most modern and skilled workmanship in every feature of sanitary plumbing, and heating by hot-air, hot water, or steam. Its unrivalled facilities commend themselves to all intelligent people desiring the most complete satisfaction, and those aware by thorough experience, that in these lines nothing is so economical as the best.

MANUFACTURERS' SHOE STORE, 159 Union Street, Phelan's Block, Ladies' and Gents' Fine Footwear, Custom Work and Repairing a Specialty. Agent for Boston St. Laundry. J. B. Emery & Co., Managers. John B. Emery, Isabel B. Stone.—The methods followed and the general management of the business, conducted at the "Manufacturers' Shoe Store" cannot fail to be perfectly satisfactory to every reasonable patron. To begin with, the stock carried is large, varied and complete. An entire family may visit the establishment and each member find footwear precisely suited to his or her needs. Tiny shoes for the baby, stronger ones for the young child, school shoes for those a few years older; street, dress and working boots and shoes for youths, and young men and young ladies; easy and durable footwear for the parents; warm and comfortable slippers, etc., for the aged—all these things and many others are to be found at this store, and so we may say that every reasonable patron can be satisfactorily suited at this store without any exaggeration. Then the prices are popular, too. Messrs. J. B. Emery & Co., the proprietors, do not as a rule sell goods "away below cost," that is not what they are in business for, and they do not insult the intelligence of their patrons by pretending differently, but they have had long experience in the shoe trade, enjoy the most favorable relations with producers, and are in a position to quote bottom prices on dependable footwear. It don't make any difference whether you know a good shoe when you see it or not, you can buy at the Manufacturers' Shoe Store and be sure of getting your money's worth every time. That's the way this company does business, and guarantee that everything they sell shall prove as represented and honor that guarantee to its full extent. This establishment is under the able management of J. B. Emery & Co., who are too well known to require an extended mention, having been engaged in the shoe trade for twenty-five years from shoe cutter to manufacturer and retailer. The establishment, popularly known as the Manufacturers' Shoe Store, is located at 159 Union Street (Phelan's Block), where callers are assured prompt and courteous attention at all times, and special attention is given to custom work and repairing. John B Emery, Isabel B Stone, managers.

DR. J. KENNEDY, D. D. S., 94 Market Street, 2d story, Lynn, Mass.—The old saying has it, "A man convinced against his will is of the same opinion still," and here, perhaps, may be found the reason why so many persons persistently neglect and abuse their teeth, in spite of all that has been said and written concerning the folly of such practice. We Americans, as a nation, have never been accused of not being open to conviction, and we have long had the reputation of being quick to perceive and prompt to follow any line of conduct that will be apt to "pay," but nevertheless, we unquestionably abuse and neglect our teeth, although we have long since been convinced that it "pays" to keep them in the best possible condition. Probably the explanation of this apparent contradiction lies in the fact that we feel that we have not the time to give them proper attention, but we manage to find time for much less important things, for all that. But "it is never too late to mend," and therefore, if your teeth have become impaired, visit a competent dentist, have them put in as good condition as possible, and then keep them so by proper care. One of the most thoroughly competent dentists in town is Dr. J. Kennedy, who has practiced his profession in Lynn, since 1884, and has won an enviable reputation for skill and thoroughness. His premises which comprise three rooms are located on the second story of 94 Market Street, and handsomely fitted up, and have the most improved appliances for the practice of dentistry in all its branches while no trouble is spared to make the work durable and satisfactory.

C. H. KENT, JR. F. P. SMITH.

KENT & SMITH,
ENAMEL ⊗ STAINS,
62 OXFORD STREET, COR. ALMONT. - - LYNN, MASS.

The firm of Kent & Smith was formed in 1890, and is composed of Messrs. C. H. Kent, Jr., and F. P. Smith, the former a native of Massachusetts, and the latter of New Hampshire. Both these gentlemen are well known to the shoe trade and they are becoming better known every day, for as manufacturers of and dealers in Enamel Stains, they supply the trade with goods that win their way wherever introduced, and that stand the test of practical use so successfully, that they need only to be tried to be commended by any practical shoe manufacturer. The line carried by Messrs. Kent & Smith includes Liquid Enameline stain for red leather; shank, edge, and heel polishing inks; Acme polishing wax, etc., and their specialties are improved enamel stains for the bottoms of ladies' boots and shoes, and burnish stains for edges, heels and shanks. They make stains for all kind of stock, including The American Oak tanned leather, they furnishing the only stain on the market that can be successfully used on that make leather. The firm claim that their light shades of bottom stains have no equal, and there seems to be no room for doubt that their claim is fully justified by the facts, for the manufacturers who try those stains speak very highly of them and show their opinion of them by using them exclusively. The factory and salesroom are located at No. 62 Oxford Street, corner of Almont, and the firm are prepared to fill all orders, large and small, at very short notice.

WM. A. FAULKNER & CO., Dealers in Ladies', Misses' and Children's Soles and Leather, 139 and 141 Oxford Street. Lynn, Mass., Wm. A. Faulkner, Wm. A. Bacheller.—The enterprise, skill and business ability, so markedly characteristic of the manufacturers of Lynn, have fitting representation in the energetic firm of Messrs. William A. Faulkner & Co.,the extensive dealers in soles and leather for ladies', misses' and children's shoes. This firm, which is one of the foremost in its line of business in the great shoe and leather section of the old commonwealth of Massachusetts, was established just twenty years ago, under the title which it bears to-day, and during the intervening years, the industry,energy and ability of the gentlemen composing it, Messrs. William A. Faulkner and William A. Bacheller, have brought it into great prominence, and gained for it an enviable and well-earned reputation. Messrs. Faulkner & Co. employ the services of five men in their store,at 139 and 141 Oxford Street, and carry an extensive line of the goods they have made a specialty of. As to the quality of the stock they handle, there is no need to go into particulars, the name of the firm and the high place it holds in the business community being a sufficient guarantee of its uniform excellence and superiority. The business of the firm, which is strictly wholesale, is constantly increasing, as the firm is in a position to fill all orders promptly, and with thorough satisfaction to the buyer. To those who are consumers of the class of goods sold by Messrs. Faulkner & Co., and who are not as yet numbered among their customers, we commend the house. Those who purchase soles and leather for ladies', misses' and children's shoes from this firm consult their own interests.

GEORGE E. BARNARD CO., Manufacturers of Fine Hand Made Shoes, Lynn, Mass., Boston Office, 97 Lincoln Street.—Among the representative manufacturing houses of Lynn, the George E. Barnard Co. at Nos. 703-705 Washington Street, holds a prominent and merited position. Few houses in the country do so large and valuable a business in their special lines of fine hand made shoes. The two large and modernly equipped buildings occupied are three stories in height, and are respectively 150x80 feet and 50x100 in dimensions. The house employs on an average three hundred and fifty hands. Their trade reaches throughout the United States and also to foreign countries. This house has the reputation, based upon actual and demonstrated facts, of making the finest grade of ladies' shoes in New England. These are entirely hand-made and the Barnard special styles have obtained wide recognition as superior both in point of beauty and adaptability to the normal shape of the foot. Being hand-made and of guaranteed A1 material throughout, the wearing power of these shoes stands the severest tests. The Boston office of the Company is at 97 Lincoln Street. All orders receive prompt attention and the large stock carried secures to patrons at all times the best of service. The thriving condition of the trade of this company during the dull seasons is striking testimony to the superiority of its goods. The demand for them continues steady at all periods of the year. (Mr. George E. Barnard the founder of the business and of the special styles manufactured is one of the best known and progressive among New England leaders in the shoe trade. The immense business now handled is a sufficient monument in itself to his ability as well as to the expert skill of Lynn shoemakers, who can safely hold their work up favorably in comparison with that of the world at large.)

JOHN A. WOOD, Horseshoeing and Blacksmithing, 253 Broad Street, Lynn, Mass.—The importance of having a horse shod with the greatest care is appreciated by all sensible people. Damage which can never be repaired is often done to valuable animals by inferior service in this department. The business of Mr. John A. Wood, at 253 Broad Street, Lynn, is one of the best known and popular local establishments in this line. It was started here by Mr. Wood in 1886 and from the first has been recognized as executing the most careful and reliable class of work. Mr. Wood served seven years' apprenticeship in the old country and took a two years' veterinary course. He employs two competent assistants and gives prompt attention to all demands upon his time and skill. The most delicate and high-spirited horses can be safely entrusted to his charge. He also carries on a general blacksmith business and guarantees thorough satisfaction in all work of this kind. His charges will be found uniformly reasonable and fair. We can assure our readers that they can nowhere obtain a finer grade of service and satisfaction in this line than at Mr. Wood's establishment. He has given many years to perfecting his facilities in every detail of the business—and they represent the very latest and most advanced methods. The shop occupied is a convenient one (35x20 feet), and equipped with every needed appliance for their work. Be sure to call upon this reliable and first-class place when desiring the best work in this line.

1893.

That popular song "Oh; what a difference in the morning," might be altered so as to begin "Oh; what a difference in the wearing." and then it would be applicable to the footwear made by some manufacturers. It is a notorious fact that some footwear is made simply to sell—it looks pretty enough, it feels well enough, and its price is low enough to suit even the most economically disposed—but it very soon loses its beauty, and soon becomes utterly unfit to wear. Of course such footwear is the bane of dealers who cater to regular patrons, and when they come across such goods as are made by Messrs. Harris & Story they need no persuasion to induce them to repeat their order. The misses' and children's fine foot wear made by this firm is carefully designed and carefully put together, and can be depended upon to compare favorably with any goods of similar grade in the market. And it is always good. It is not good to-day and inferior to-morrow but it as uniform in merit as careful selection of material and close supervision of workmanship can make it. No firm quotes lower prices of *equal merit*, or is more prompt and accurate in the filling of orders; their specialty is from medium to fine grade goods and thus the popularity of Harris & Story's fine footwear is not at all difficult to account for. Both members give the business undivided attention and in their spacious premises located at 587 Washington Street, employment is given to an adequate force of experienced and thoroughly competent assistants.

T. B. REARDON,

Steam and Hot Water Heating,

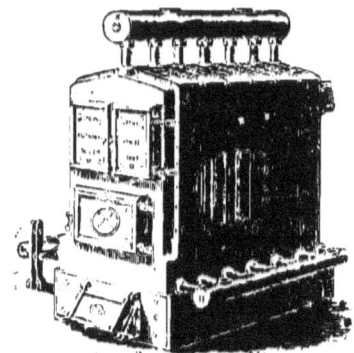

Sanitary Plumbing

AND

Drain Laying.

Manufacturer of

Shoe Dryers.

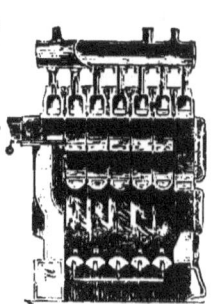

Basement of 29 Central Avenue,

LYNN, MASS.

Residence, 595 Western Avenue.   TELEPHONE CONNECTION.

Lynn is a thoroughly modern city and hence it is perfectly natural that such an enterprise as is carried on by Mr. T. B. Reardon should be liberally patronized, for he is an expert in steam and hot water heating, sanitary plumbing and drain laying, and therefore is fully qualified to equip churches, public buildings, houses, factories and stores in first-class style and in accordance with the most advanced principles of scientific heating, plumbing and draining. He makes a specialty of churches and schools, and out-of-town work. Mr. Reardon has had extended experience and is well qualified to give valuable counsel in the matter of economic and successful heating of churches, halls, large blocks, public buildings, as well as residences. He makes a specialty of large jobs, and has successfully fitted up many blocks in this city with first class steam heating equipments, a few of them are as follows: the Pevian Block, Mowers Brothers Block, E. E. Stroat's Block, P. B. Magrane's entire block, also the steam heating, plumbing and gas fitting, the Hurley Blocks—one on corner of Spring and Broad Streets, the other on Washington and Railroad Avenues. Also Harney Bros. Shoe Factory, Consolidated Adjustable Shoe Company's Factory, Flagg & Breed's large block, N. Weber & Son's large block, St. Mary's Church, Lynn, Rev. A. J. Tuling Parochial School, Peabody, Rev. M. J. Martin, Parochial School and Church, Chelsea, Rev. J. McGlen, two Parochial Schools and Convent, Roxbury, Rev. H. P. Smith, Catholic Church, Plymouth, Rev. J. J. Buckley, Catholic Church, Whitman, Rev. E. J. Patterson, Parochial School, East Boston, Rev. M. J. Clark, and a large number of others. His shop is located at No. 27 and 29 Central Avenue and his residence at No. 595 Western Avenue, both having telephone connection, so that orders can be given without delay from any part of the city. Employment is afforded to from 15 to 30 competent assistants, according to season, and all important work is done under Mr. Reardon's personal supervision; so it is not surprising that entire satisfaction is guaranteed to every customer and that all orders, large and small, are assured prompt and careful attention. Mr. Reardon is a manufacturer of shoe dryers and does a large business in that department alone for shoe manufacturers have learned by experience that his drying plants work well, wear well, and are economical of steam, they being thoroughly practical and "built for business" in every part. Estimates on all work in Mr. Reardon's line will be promptly furnished on application, and such of our readers as are thinking of placing contracts for heating, plumbing, or draining apparatus would do well to communicate with him, as he is prepared to figure very closely and to execute even the largest commissions at short notice.

LYDIA E. PINKHAM MEDICINE COMPANY,

No. 271 Western Avenue,

LYNN, - MASS.

Although Lynn is called the Shoe City, and the footwear made here is so extensively and favorably known that there is an extensive demand for it in every section of the Union, the most famous and the most popular of Lynn's products are those prepared by the Lydia E. Pinkham Medicine Company, for the demand for these is not only national but international, and the solid basis upon which it is founded is that of unequalled merit—hence it is inevitable that the enormous demand for the Lydia E. Pinkham medicines should be steadily increasing. There is not the slightest need of our describing the character and the effects of these medicines in detail, for they are so universally known that the simple mention of Lydia E. Pinkham's Vegetable Compound, Lydia E. Pinkham's Blood Purifier, Lydia E. Pinkham's Liver Pills, and Lydia E. Pinkham's Sanative Wash, is all that is necessary. The Vegetable Compound is by far the most famous and the most popular proprietary medicine in the world, for it occupies a field peculiarly its own, and it has alleviated more suffering and done more towards substituting joy for sorrow, and healthfulness and vigor for illness and weakness than any other remedy ever placed before the public. That familiar signature—"Yours for health, Lydia E. Pinkham," has been read by many hundreds of thousands in all classes of society, and very many of them know from practical experience that "Yours for health" is not merely a "catching" phrase, but a literal statement of fact. The company utilize a very extensive and most elaborately equipped laboratory, located at 271 Western Avenue, and employ a large force of skilled assistants in the preparation, packing, and shipping of their products; which are handled by every druggist and every dealer in proprietary medicines, and unanimously pronounced to be (to use a trade expression) "the best selling goods in the market."

E. E. WINKLEY & CO., Mechanical and Electrical Engineers and Practical Draughtsmen. Designing, Pattern Making and Patent Office Drawings a Specialty. All Work Warranted. 416 Union Street, Brown Building, (Opposite Item Building) Lynn, Mass. It has been said that it requires almost as much ingenuity and patience to get an invention properly protected by patents as it does to devise it, and although that of course is overstating the case it is nevertheless a fact that it "pays" to secure the best possible expert assistance in the preparation of drawings and models for the patent office. In this connection it is fitting that we should make mention of the firm of E. E. Winkley & Co., for they make a specialty of what may be called "patent office work" and are admirably qualified to attain the best possible results, as is proved by their record. The firm is composed of Messrs. E. E. Winkley and W. J. Young, and began operations in February, 1891. Mr. Winkley is a mechanical and electrical engineer and practical draughtsman; has thorough knowledge of pattern making, machine work, and foundry work, and is entirely competent to superintend the construction of work in any of these branches. Mr. Young is a skillful machinist. He has invented several machines which are in successful operation; and the prevailing opinion among the many who have done business with this firm is that Messrs. Winkley and Young form a "strong combination." Mr. Winkley should certainly be well-schooled in both the theory and practice of his profession, for he has worked for several years as pattern maker; was in charge for a year of the woodwork and repairing department of the Newmarket Mfg. Co. which operates 40,000 spindles, and has been employed by the Thomson-Houston Co., as draughtsman and designer. He had a two years' course at the Massachusetts Institute of Technology and (to use a somewhat slangy but very expressive phrase) is thoroughly "up to date" in every detail of his work. He makes a specialty of designing, pattern making and patent office drawing, and orders can generally be filled at short notice; while all work is warranted. Well equipped premises, located at 416 Union Street, opposite Item building are occupied, and the firm also utilize premises located at 747 Washington Street, where pattern making is extensively carried on; skilled assistants being employed and no trouble being spared to ensure absolute accuracy in every detail of the work.

WILLIAMS BROS., Dealers in Fresh, Salt, Smoked and Pickled Fish of Every Description. Canned and Bottled Goods, Cod Liver Oil, etc., 157 Union Street, Lynn, Mass. No firm can carry on a retail fish Market for nine years in one location without becoming widely known themselves; and when at the time we have specified their business is larger than ever before, and they are held in the highest esteem, it is evident that their business methods must be honorable and liberal and their goods first-class in every respect; and a visit to Messrs. Williams Brothers' market will show that they are prepared to meet the demands of their customers. The individual members of this firm are J. J. and F. J. Williams, both of whom are natives of Massachusetts, and have been identified with their present business here at Lynn since 1884. The premises utilized comprise one floor and basement each 1,080 square feet in dimensions, also a storage room for stock 120 square feet in size, located at 172 Union Street. Messrs. Williams Brothers employ three active and intelligent assistants, and thoroughly understand their line of business in all its branches. They deal largely in fresh, salt, smoked, and pickled fish of every description, as well as lobsters, oysters, clams, also canned and bottled goods, cod liver oil, etc. These goods are selected expressly for first-class family trade and consumption, and are fully guaranteed as to their freshness and qualities for such purposes. They are careful to offer only such articles as they can confidently recommend, and by keeping faith with their customers, have built up an enviable reputation in this section of Lynn.

J. T. SUTHERLAND & CO.,

Manufacturers and Dealers in

◁ CUT TOP PIECES, INNER SOLES, STIFFENINGS, HEELS, &C. ▷

TELEPHONE 315-4.

416 Union Street, LYNN, MASS.

It is said that success in shoe manufacturing is largely a matter of machinery, and no doubt it is to a certain extent, but it is also a matter of making it a point to secure supplies from reliable sources, for even the best equipped shoe factory receives some proportion of its material in a manufactured state and if that is not made as it should be, the use of best machinery in the world won't make it up into perfect footwear. Enterprising manufacturers understand that, of course, and doubtless that is one reason why there is a large and constant demand for the productions of Messrs. J. T. Sutherland & Co., for this firm are manufacturers of and dealers in cut top pieces, inner soles, stiffenings, heels, etc., and it is known that they sell goods strictly on their merits, and are prepared to meet all competition in prices. This business was founded in 1884, and has steadily increased until it now requires the employment of from thirty to forty assistants, according to condition of trade. Very spacious premises located at No. 416 Union street, are occupied, and the shop is equipped with an elaborate plant of improved machinery, the capacity of the establishment being large and the firm being prepared to fill the largest orders at short notice, while all orders—whether large or small—are assured prompt and careful attention.

HENRY G. BREED, Dealer in Daily and Weekly Papers and Magazines, Cigars and Tobacco, Confectionery, Varieties etc., Pool and Billiard Room Connected, 33 Market Square, Lynn, Mass. This enterprise, though not necessarily occupying very extensive premises, is one that interests about as many residents of this neighborhood as any other which is within its limits. The proprietor, Mr. Henry G. Breed, has been identified with the business since 1877, and now occupies premises at 33 Market Square. His stock consists of Daily and Weekly Papers, Magazines, etc., also Cigars, Tobacco, Confectionery, Variety Goods, etc. Mr. Breed also runs a Billiard Room in connection with his other business having both Pool and Billiard Tables which are kept in excellent condition at all times. It is perfectly safe to say that this is a familiar place to a very large number, who are daily patrons, and to whom it is a great convenience to have just such a place where one can run in and be sure of getting a good cigar or tobacco if their own supply has given out and then the papers, how convenient to be able to buy them here, also pure confectionery of all kinds, and the numberless articles coming under the head of variety goods. Mr. Breed employs two capable and courteous assistants, and his establishment enjoys a first-class reputation and he has always maintained the most favorable relations with his patrons and the public in general.

G. W. ARROLL, Bakery, 168 Franklin Street, Lynn, Mass.—Probably the first store ever in existence was a baker's shop, as this certainly is the oldest kind of food universally made and dealt in. Although new methods may improve some details of preparation, it is still a fact that those establishments are the most popular, which follow the old fashioned styles and afford patrons the same carefully made and wholesome goods our ancestors enjoyed. Such has been the plan of the well-known bakery establishment conducted by Mr. G. W. Arroll, at 168 Franklin Street, this city. It has now been in successful operation for ten years past,and has built up a wide, thriving trade. Mr Arroll employs six experienced hands. Every feature of the business is executed with energy and promptness. Prices have been reduced to the most reasonable basis, and no pains spared to secure the finest material and most thorough, homelike methods. Indeed, the leading attraction of the "Home Bakery" has been the fact that it is impossible to distinguish its goods from those of the best housekeepers. Equal satisfaction and greater economy can thus be secured, to say nothing of saving exhausting labor in the household. Mr. Arroll's store and bakery are handsomely equipped in every particular. Families can be supplied with all kinds of breads, rolls, crackers, pastries, cakes and general cooking. A first class catering business is handled by this house. Ice-cream in all popular flavors furnished for parties or domestic use on short notice and wholesale rates. The reliable goods and services of the "Home Bakery" commend its facilities to all who appreciate the best.

W. J. BURTON, Harness Manufacturer. Constantly on Hand a Good Assortment of Blankets, Robes, Whips, Travelling Bags, Etc. Trunks Repaired. Headquarters for the Alger Hitch, Marcus Bodge, Prop. and Man'fr. Repairing in all its Branches Promptly Attended to. 129 Central Avenue. Lynn, Mass.—Although there is no sense in paying fancy prices for harnesses, still it is as sensible to do that as to buy so low-priced an article that it is impossible that it can be honestly made from reliable materials, for such a harness is hard on the horse, is dangerous to use, and, if kept in repair, will prove the most expensive to buy in the long run. The fact is, it is good policy to avoid extremes one way or the other,and the best way to do is to pay a fair price and get a harness that will do good service for years and require little or no repairing unless improperly used. Mr. W. J. Burton is a manufacturer of, and dealer in, Harnesses of all kinds, and is prepared to furnish a thoroughly dependable article of this kind at moderate price. He is native of Nova Scotia, began business at Lynn in 1886, and is now located at 129 Central avenue, where he does quite an extensive business, not only in the manufacture of harness, but also by dealing in blankets,robes, whips, horse furnishings, etc., a fine assortment of these goods constantly being on hand. Mr. Burton's establishment is also headquarters for the Alger hitch, (Marcus Bodge being proprietor and manufacturer). Repairing of all description is done by Mr. Burton in a neat and durable manner at short notice, and the charges made are low enough to suit even the most economically disposed. Mr. Burton has a store located at 42 Main street, Amesbury, and devoted to the harness business where he does an extensive business in manufacturing and repairing harness, and employs three men. He also carries a fine stock of trunks, traveling bags, etc., in addition to a full line of harnesses, horse furnishings, etc., and has gained there a reputation equal to that enjoyed by him throughout the business circles of Lynn.

H. HARDY, Dealer in Choice Provisions, Fruits and Vegetables, 212 Union Street, Lynn, Mass.—Although there are some people who seem to "want the earth" and as they are satisfied with nothing less are "chronic kickers" at all times and under all circumstances, the great majority of the public have more common sense and are quick to appreciate fair and liberal treatment. A proof of this is afforded by the popularity of the enterprise carried on by Mr. H. Hardy, who retails provisions, fruits, and vegetables, at 212 Union Street, Lynn, for although Mr. Hardy did not begin operations here until 1893, he has already built up quite a trade in spite of the great competition in his line of business. The stock handled by Mr. Hardy includes Beef, Mutton, Poultry, etc., also Fruits and Vegetables of all kinds in their seasons, and which are sold at the lowest retail prices. These goods are carefully selected, and especially adapted for family use, and are offered in great variety. Competent assistants are employed, and all orders are assured prompt and careful attention. Mr. Hardy is a native of New Hampshire, and well known throughout Lynn and vicinity as a thoroughly reliable, and progressive business man.

BROAD STREET, FROM NEWHALL STREET.

HARNWER & QUINBY, Plumbing done as it should be. Jobbing of all kinds, rear 141 Broad Street, Lynn, Mass.—True economy always is secured by having work done in the most thorough manner at the very outset. In no department is this more important than in that of sanitary plumbing, where even a slight mistake is the source of constant annoyance, and often of serious danger to health. One of the most thorough and reliable plumbing firms of this section is that of Messrs. Harnwer & Quinby, rear 141 Broad Street, Lynn. Their business is now recognized as first class in every feature of equipment, promptness and accurate service. Their store at above address is 40x25 feet in dimensions and contains a complete stock of plumber's supplies and tinsmithing goods. The firm employ a competent force of assistants at all times; they execute every kind of copper, tin and sheet iron work; also gas and hot water piping, as well as other branches of sanitary plumbing. The terms of this firm will be found equal to the very lowest in the trade, and when combined with their uniform first class service, deserve the careful attention of all our readers. Those desiring the best results in these important matters will do well to call upon this firm.

DUFFY & OULTON. Machine and Steel Forging, and Tool Dressing, Light and Heavy Carriage Work. Horseshoeing. Superior Workmanship and Prompt Delivery, 296 to 300 Broad Street, Lynn, Mass.—A long established and leading business house of its kind in Lynn is that conducted by Messrs. Duffy & Oulton, at Nos. 296-300 Broad Street. It was first started by Mr. Duffy in 1880 and Mr. Oulton became a member of the firm in 1887. For the past year the business has been under the general management of Mr. Oulton. A very extensive and valuable business is conducted, the influence of which is felt in all parts of the city. This house makes a speciality of machine and steel forging, also tool dressing, light and heavy carriage work and general horseshoeing. They have special facilities in all these lines, employing ten men and using the latest machine appliances throughout. They guarantee a prompt delivery and superior workmanship in every detail. No establishment of the county in its line has so complete all-around facilities as this old and enterprising house. Their machine forgings are marked by the most thorough and exact mechanical execution. Carriages and wagons made here are used by many of the leading houses of this section. As practical horseshoers also the firm can secure for its patrons the very best results. Every kind of difficult work handled with thorough care and satisfaction. The prices of this firm will be found uniformly low and reasonable. Our readers will do well to examine their figures and equipment when desiring the best class of work in the lines indicated. Since the decease of Mr. James B. Duffy in 1893, the interests of his heirs have been represented by Mr. Oulton. The shop (now 60 x 40 feet) has been newly fitted up throughout. They have an improved power hammer, fan-blowers, etc., and carry on the old business with even greater success than has been uniformly achieved in the past.

C. R. LINDSTROM, D. D. S., No. 130 Market St., cor. Oxford. Office hours, 8.30 A. M. to 12.30 P. M. and 1.30 to 5, Lynn, Mass.— In the rapid improvements of the last quarter of a century every branch of business has seemed to move forward, but in no profession has improvement been more marked than in that of Dental Surgery, which would seem to be at its height, especially as we view the appliances and improvements at our best dental rooms. Dr. C. R. Lindstrom stands high among the men engaged in the profession in this section, and no pains or money is spared to provide every modern invention, and all branches of dentistry, including crown and bridge work, are conducted in a thoroughly skillful and scientific manner. Dr. Lindstrom is a native of Stockholm, Sweden, and studied there his profession for three and one-half years before entering the Philadelphia Dental College, of which he is a graduate, and has been identified with his profession in Lynn since 1891, and has obtained a reputation for first-class services and reasonable prices. He is thoroughly conversant with the dental art, and conducts it in all its varied and difficult operations. All operations in dental surgery carefully performed. Special attention is given to the care and preservation of the teeth of children. Dr. Lindstrom's office is located on the second story of the building, No. 130 Market street, corner Oxford, is beautifully fitted up, and supplied with every convenience for the comfort of his patients. So we recommend his establishment to our readers.

TROY LAUNDRY. C. F. Howes, Proprietor, 20 Albany Street, Lynn, Mass.—If it be true that "cleanliness is next to godliness," then first class public laundries must rank next to churches as public benefactors, for they are doing more to make cleanliness universal than any other agency. But, unfortunately, all public laundries are not first-class. The average is high, and the laundry business engages the attention of some of our most reliable and progressive men of affairs, but some laundries do poor work, some use destructive means of cleansing goods, and some are unreliable, especially in their delivery service. Therefore it is well to use discretion in the choice of one; and many of our readers need not be told that the Troy Laundry, located at No. 20 Albany Street, offers unsurpassed inducements to those who appreciate excellent work, prompt and careful service, and reasonable prices. The proprietor, Mr. C. F. Howes, has had long experience in the laundry business, and he knows how to carry on a laundry so as to attain uniformly satisfactory results at the least possible expense. The business is very thoroughly systematized; the loss or exchange of articles is of rare occurrence; mistakes are promptly and cheerfully corrected, and the delivery service is regular, reliable and comprehensive. Of course, such a laundry is very popular; but the facilities are ample and the business is promptly and easily handled.

E. S. & E. M. McELHINNEY, Manufacturers of Fine Harnesses and Dealers in Whips, Brushes, Curry Combs and Blankets. Repairing a Specialty. 208 Essex Street, Lynn, Mass.—It is very difficult to accurately judge the value of a harness from examination alone; for even the poorest stock can be so finished as to look all right before it is put to practical use, and so the only sure way to get full value for every dollar you pay for a harness is to buy from a reputable dealer, who is satisfied with reasonable profits and who knows that the best way to get and keep your trade and that of your friends is to treat you squarely and liberally. Such dealers are Messrs. E. S. & E. M. McElhinney, who carry a full assortment of harness and stable requisites in stock and can supply you with what you want at the lowest market rates, quality considered. Messrs. McElhinney are well-known in Lynn, for they are natives of this place. Mr. E. S. McElhinney has been identified with this enterprise since 1885; his brother, Mr. E. M. McElhinney, entering the firm in 1893. This store and shop are located at 208 Essex Street, and callers are assured prompt and courteous attention; order work, including harness making and repairing in all its branches, being done skilfully, thoroughly, at short notice and at moderate rates, and no pains are spared to deliver all work promptly at the time promised. The premises utilized cover an area of 40x15 feet and a large stock is carried including whips, brushes, curry combs and blankets, all at reasonable prices.

EDWARD H. SMITH, Civil Engineer and Surveyor, 145 Munroe Street, Room 33, Lynn, Mass.—There is a great deal of sound common sense embodied in that familiar old saying,—" Whatever is worth doing is worth doing well," and it applies with especial force to the doing of that class of work which comes under the head of civil engineering, and particularly to that branch of it which is known as surveying, for so serious and so expensive are apt to be the mistakes which arise from inaccurate surveying that as a rule it is doubtless better not to have surveying done at all than to have it done by incompetent or unreliable hands. But fortunately there is no lack of skillful and trustworthy civil engineers and surveyors in Lynn, so there is no difficulty in having commissions satisfactorily executed; and in this connection we may fittingly make mention of Mr. Edward H. Smith, whose office is located at 145 Munroe Street. Room 33, for he certainly spares no pains to insure absolute accuracy in every detail of the work with which he is entrusted, and to protect and advance the interests of his clients in every legitimate way. Mr. Smith, who is a native of Massachusetts, is a thoroughly competent and reliable civil engineer and surveyor, having had fourteen years' experience both in public and private work. He is also Justice of the Peace, and is therefore well-known throughout this vicinity, not only professionally, but also socially, he having a large circle of friends.

J. NICKERSON, Manufacturer of and Dealer in Men's, Women's, Misses' and Children's Inner soles, stiffenings, &c. All kinds of stiffenings and taps, 127 Market Street, basement, Lynn, Mass.—Mr. J. Nickerson has been prominently identified with Lynn's commercial history for the past fourteen years, having begun operations here in 1879, and has so continued without interruption ever since. He is a native of this State, and so well known in this city as to require no personal extended mention. Mr. Nickerson is a manufacturer of and dealer in men's, women's, misses' and children's inner soles, stiffenings, etc., and all kinds of taps. The premises occupied are located at 127 Market Street, in the basement, 50x22 feet in dimensions. The trade is by no means confined to this section or even to this State, but extends throughout other sections. The employment of competent assistants and the careful supervision given by the proprietor in every department of the business, assures the prompt and accurate filling of all orders, and it is obvious that so old established a house must be widely and favorably known to manufacturers, and excellently fitted and prepared to meet all honorable competition by quoting the lowest market rates on standard goods, and no pains are spared to fully maintain the high reputation the product of this factory has so long enjoyed while Mr. Nickerson's long experience in this business has made him thoroughly conversant with the needs of the public.

GEORGE C. HIGGINS,

ROOM 4, PEVEAR BUILDING.

113 MONROE STREET, LYNN, MASS.

PROBATE BUSINESS A SPECIALTY,

WILLS, MORTGAGES, DEEDS AND LEASES CAREFULLY WRITTEN,

RENTS COLLECTED AND ESTATES CARED FOR.

NOTARY PUBLIC.   JUSTICE OF THE PEACE.

W. T. BOWERS, Photographer, 15 Market Street, Lynn, Mass.—It is safe to say that knowledge of photography has been more popularized during the past twelve years than in all the preceding years since the discovery of the art, for the introduction and perfection of "dry plates" has worked radical changes in apparatus and in methods of work, and made amateur photography so popular that about every fourth man knows something of the art from practical experience. Under such circumstances it is not surprising that the standard should have been greatly raised, so that poor or even passable photographs are difficult to sell at any price and some competent artists have taken advantage of the popular demand for excellent work, by quoting fancy prices on all that leaves their studios. But it is by no means necessary to pay fancy rates in order to get really excellent work, and in proof of the assertion we would refer to the results attained and the prices quoted at the studio of W. T. Bowers, at 15 Market Street, for really the work done here is equal to the best, while the prices will compare very favorably with those usually quoted on work of an equal degree of merit. Mr. Bowers became identified with his present profession about 1850, and has thus had a long and varied experience. He has kept up with the times and has always been the first to introduce into Lynn every new discovery and useful improvement in photography, and has the facilities and the skill to do any work usually done in a first-class photographic studio. Orders will be filled at very short notice and entire satisfaction is guaranteed to every customer.

H. C. FENNING, Druggist, 205 Franklin Street, corner Boston Street, Lynn, Mass.—There are many important advantages gained by having prescriptions compounded at an establishment where a leading specialty is made of such work, and where an exceptionally large patronage is enjoyed, for not only is extra assurance afforded that the prescriptions will be accurately and promptly prepared, but there is much less liability of any of the ingredients used being impaired by long keeping, not to mention other advantages too obvious to need demonstration. A prominent Lynn druggist, giving particular attention to the important duties under consideration, is Mr. H. C. Fenning, whose store is located at 205 Franklin, corner of Boston Street. He carries a complete and carefully selected stock of the best and purest drugs, medicines and chemicals the market affords, and is prepared to compound prescriptions with the nicest accuracy at short notice and at very reasonable rates. Mr. Fenning also carries in stock and deals at retail in toilet and fancy articles, choice domestic and imported cigars, and such other goods as one is accustomed to find at a first-class city pharmacy. Employment is given to only thoroughly reliable assistants, and callers are assured immediate and courteous attention at all times.

JAMES H. CURTIS, Kalsomining, White-washing, etc., 117 Broad Street, Lynn, Mass.—The only way to get the best results in any line of work is to employ the service of one who has made a specialty of that particular line. In the hurry and competition of modern trade, perfection of detail can be secured only in this way. The business of Mr. James H. Curtis at 117 Broad Street, has built up a wide and enviable reputation for the excellence of its service and liberal prices. Mr. Curtis is a thorough master of kalsomining, white-washing, and every sort of work in this line. His shop at above address is well fitted up and contains a full line of materials necessary for the successful prosecution of this work. Long and thorough experience enable Mr. Curtis to give his patrons uniform first-class service. Our readers will find his terms very liberal and fair. Prompt attention given to all orders. Those desiring the best of workmanship and satisfaction in these lines will do well to patronize Mr. Curtis.

CHICAGO BEEF MARKET, Groceries and Provisions, wholesale and retail, E. J. Johnson & Co., proprietors, 55 Market Square, Lynn, Mass.—Everybody is thinking of Chicago nowadays because it is the home of the World's Fair, and hundreds of the residents of Lynn and vicinity are thinking daily of the Chicago Beef Market, for that is where they get their groceries, provisions, tea, coffee, etc. And they show good judgment in patronizing that establishment, as it caters successfully to all classes of trade and furnishes satisfactory goods at bottom prices. The proprietors, Messrs. E. J. Johnson & Co., assumed control in 1891, and the first year business was over $80,000, and the second year over $50,000, while the present year bids fair to exceed $65,000, and now requires the employment of 7 assistants, the above facts showing that the business is steadily increasing. The store is located in the West Lynn Hotel Block, at No. 55 Market Square, and has an area of about 1,250 square feet. The stock includes Chicago dressed beef, pork, hams, tripe, sausage, lard, butter, cheese, eggs, fruit, vegetables, canned goods, etc., also a full assortment of staple and fancy groceries, teas and coffees. Messrs. E. J. Johnson & Co. are receivers of butts, rolls, strips and tenderloins, and are also receivers of butter and eggs direct from Maine, New Hampshire and Vermont. The business is conducted on strictly cash principles, and the prices quoted to wholesale and retail buyers are as low as the lowest. Boarding houses are supplied at wholesale rates, and all orders amounting to one dollar or more are delivered free. Mr. E. J. Johnson is sole proprietor and gives close personal supervision to the business, and customers may depend upon receiving prompt and courteous attention.

THOMAS F. MURPHY, Hacking and Herdic Stable, 439 Boston Street, Lynn, Mass.—There are a good many stables in Lynn, considering the size of the city, and as a natural consequence the competition between them is quite keen, although as a rule it is honorably conducted. Competition is an excellent thing when not carried to excess, but its consequences are not always agreeable to the public and an example of this is to be found in the unsatisfactory accommodations provided by some stable keepers who say they "can't afford to do any better at prevailing rates." Certainly the margin of profit in the stable business here is small, but the more enterprising proprietors don't allow that fact to impair the efficiency of the service they offer, and such is the policy pursued by Mr. Thomas F. Murphy, for he furnishes first-class hacks and herdics at short notice, although his charges are uniformly moderate. The stable in question is located at 439 Boston Street, being well fitted up throughout. It has been under the control of the present proprietor since 1891, who has endeavored to serve the public in a most liberal manner. Mr. Murphy has made many friends in Lynn and vicinity, while his hack and herdic stable is steadily and rapidly gaining in popularity and patronage.

P. R. MURPHY, Manufacturer of Cutting Dies, for Cutting Leather, Cloth, Paper, etc., 176 Oxford Street, Lynn, Mass.—In these days of close competition and extensive use of machinery, no manufacturer can afford to be at all careless in the choice of machines and appliances, for not only is it true that the best is the cheapest, but it is so much the cheapest that inferior tools are dear at any price. Cutting dies are tools that are exceptionally dependent upon excellence of material and workmanship for value, and hence intelligent manufacturers exercise special care in the ordering of them and carefully note how the dies furnished by different makers stand the test of practical use. Hence the fact that a very large proportion of the orders received by Mr. P. R. Murphy are from regular customers who have done business with him for years is convincing proof that his work is equal to the best, for as a manufacturer of cutting dies for cutting leather, cloth, paper, etc., he fills orders for many houses that require the very best and most accurate dies obtainable. All new work is fully warranted by Mr. Murphy, and his facilities are such as to enable him to execute extensive commissions at short notice and to quote the lowest prices consistent with the use of selected material and the employment of skillful and reliable assistants. His shop is located at 176 Oxford Street, and has an area of about 1,750 square feet. It is very thoroughly equipped, and its capacity is such as to ensure the prompt filling of orders even during the busiest season.

F. H. FRIZZELL, Real Estate and Insurance Agent, Room 4, Lee Hall, City Hall Square, Lynn, Mass.—Among the reliable business agencies that contribute to the growth and prosperity of this portion of Lynn may be mentioned that of Mr. F. H. Frizzell, located in Room 4, Lee Hall, City Hall Square. His extended acquaintance and general knowledge of real estate makes his services valuable to any party wishing to buy, sell or exchange anything in that line, and his list of real estate for sale can be depended upon to comprise some of the best bargains in the city. Mr. Frizzel also does a life and fire insurance business, representing the Manhattan Life, St. Paul Fire Insurance, Buffalo German, Albany, British America, Employes' Liability and Plate Glass Insurance Company also in Mutual Companies, the Norfolk, Dedham and Essex, and is prepared to place small or large risks in these or other first-class insurance companies at standard rates, and will attend to the prompt settlement of all claims incurred by losses and all business entrusted to him will receive prompt attention. Mr. Frizzel employs an assistant who attends to the details of the business when he is away from his office, and the public are therefore assured of able and intelligent service at all times.

KELLEY & GREEN, Successors to Thomas Green & Co., Manufacturers of Dull and Bright Dongola, Pebble Morocco in all Colors a Specialty. Factory, 627-637 Summer Street, Lynn. Salesroom, 132 Summer Street, Boston. Office, 129 Market Street, Lynn, Mass.—Favorable location, extensive and first-class facilities, and careful management guided by long experience will go far to assure the success of any enterprise, and as that carried on by Messrs. Kelley & Green has all of these, it is but natural that this firm should hold a leading position in their field of industry. The business was founded by Messrs. Thomas Green & Co., in 1880; the firm consisting of Messrs. Thomas Green, Thomas A. Kelley, and William H. Green, and in 1885, Messrs. Kelley & Green assumed sole control. The factory is located at Nos. 627-637 Summer Street, on tide-water, the wharfage facilities being excellent, and the factory being a great 4½ story building, in which employment is given to 100 assistants. It is equipped with the most improved machinery for the manufacture of their celebrated French glazed kid. This is their sole production; the output is very large. An office and salesroom are maintained at No. 129 Market Street. The demand for Messrs. Kelley & Green's productions is very extensive, they being shipped to many distant points as well as having a large local sale. Orders are filled at short notice, and no firm is better prepared to quote bottom prices on goods of standard merit.

STEPHEN R. KEARNEY, Hack, Livery, Boarding and Sale Stable, Public Carriages Nos. 25 and 26. Stand at Central Depot. Telephone 305-3. 22 Union Street, Lynn, Mass.—The public stables of New England average well in quality, but still there are some which are far superior to others, and it is rare to find one that is not deficient in some important respect; for instance, in the accommodation, in the management, or in the cost of the service rendered. There are exceptions to all rules, and the hack, livery, boarding and sale stable, carried on by Mr. Stephen R. Kearney, at 22 Union Street, may be cited as an exception to the rule of deficiency in some department of stable service. Not that this stable is absolutely perfect, but, still it comes so near to perfection, that it satisfies the most critical customers. This business was founded by its present proprietor, who is a native of New London, Ct., and very well known in Lynn and vicinity. The premises occupied are spacious, well arranged and well equipped, containing forty-one stalls for horses, and as employment is given to seven competent assistants, reasonably prompt service can be guaranteed in every department of the business, which includes the furnishing of hacks for funerals, parties, weddings, and all public and private uses; the boarding of horses, they being assured comfortable quarters, proper food and kind treatment; and the supplying of teams for livery purposes, the horses being good, free and safe drivers, and the carriages being correct in style, excellent in quality, and well and neatly kept in every way. The stable is connected by telephone 305-3, and teams will be brought to and called for at houses in any portion of the city. Mr. Kearney does a large livery, boarding baiting, and sale business, and also has public carriages Nos. 25 and 26, stand at the Central Depot which are largely patronized, and evidently a great public convenience.

UNION STREET, FROM CENTRAL SQUARE.

J. M. HARRIMAN & CO., Pharmacists, 248 Union Street, Lynn.—There is one piece of information which should be possessed by every person, and that is, the whereabouts of a pharmacy at which prescriptions are carefully and skillfully compounded of first-class ingredients at moderate rates. So long as drugs and medicines maintain their present importance in the treatment of disease, so long will the chances of cure be greatly influenced by the quality of the supplies furnished, and it is "illogical to take great pains to choose a skillful and experienced physician and then exercise no care in the matter of having his prescriptions properly prepared. Without for a moment asserting that J. M. Harriman & Co. are the only firm of pharmacists worthy of confidence, it may still be truthfully said that no pharmacy in this city is more carefully conducted than theirs, or offers more reliable, prompt and economical prescription service. The stock of drugs, medicines and chemicals is complete, and of the best quality the market affords, while no precaution is neglected to ensure absolute accuracy in the filling of every order. The store utilized is located at 248 Union Street, its proprietors being too well-known throughout Lynn, to call for extended personal mention. Suffice it to say, they know their business and give it very close attention, employing sufficient assistance to ensure prompt service to all, and drugs, medicines, chemicals, and druggists' sundries are well represented in the stock carried.

H. W. COOK, Builder and Real Estate Dealer, 319 Union Street, Residence, 169 Essex Street, Lynn, Mass.—The name of Mr. H. W. Cook, can by no means be unfamiliar to the residents of Lynn and adjoining towns, for he is prominently connected with the public as a builder and real estate agent, and has long since developed a very important business. Building and Real Estate are given prompt and faithful attention in any locality in the State if desired. Mr. Cook is an acknowledged leader in his special line. He is a first-class and thoroughly reliable builder, and also buys, sells, rents or exchanges real estate in Lynn and vicinity, cares for property, collects rents, secures or rents residences, and his reputation being ample guarantee that in the future as in the past, he will carefully guard the interests of his patrons. He is prepared to take entire charge of the building of houses, stores, etc., furnishing everything desired, and attending to every detail, thus relieving the owner of all care and anxiety. Mr. Cook's office is located in Room 9, No. 319 Union Street, and his residence at 169 Essex Street, where all orders left will receive immediate and courteous attention, and his charges will always be found moderate. In conclusion we will simply say that we think the foregoing remarks sufficiently indicate how prominent and important a factor Mr. Cook and his enterprise has been to the growth and development of the city of Lynn.

AMERICAN DYE HOUSE, Frederick A. Simms, Prop'r. Not connected with any other Dye House. 207 Market Street, Lynn, Mass. French Cleaning and Dyeing, Mackintoshes, ladies', gentlemen's and children's clothes cleansed, dyed and finished without taking to pieces, Camels' Hair and all kinds of Shawls, Fine Laces, Lace Curtains, Blankets, Feathers and Gloves Cleaned and Dyed.—Somebody has said that in order to get rich it is only necessary to make money like an American and spend it like a Frenchman, and it must be confessed that there is a good deal of sound sense in that way of putting it. Most Americans have the money-making gift, but few know how to use their money to the best advantage, whereas a Frenchman can make every dollar count, and can enjoy himself on a comparatively small income. We were reminded of this fact when visiting the American Dye House establishment conducted by Mr. Fred. A. Simms at No. 207 Market Street. The character of the work turned out here is unexcelled, and many a hard earned dollar may be saved by sending soiled or slightly worn garments here to be cleaned and dyed. Care is taken not to injure the fabric or to cause undue shrinkage, and we saw garments that had gone through the process, and had been made for all practical purposes as good as new at a merely nominal expense. Ladies,' gentlemen's and children's clothes are cleansed, dyed and finished without taking to pieces, camel's hair and all kinds of shawls, fine laces, lace curtains, blankets, feathers and gloves cleaned and dyed. Mr. Simms has had long experience in his present line of business. The premises utilized comprise one two-story building, 25x49 feet in dimensions, and a large business is done, many having discovered the advantage of patronizing such an establishment. Four assistants are kept busy all the time.

JOHN C. WILLIAMS, Merchant Tailor, 106 Market Street, over Baker's Millinery, Lynn, Mass.— An accepted and prominent authority on matters of dress has said, " Material is nothing, fit is everything," and although this, like all general statements is not to be interpreted too literally, still, the leading idea it conveys is worthy of careful attention. The richest and most tasteful material can never make a thoroughly presentable garment unless it be skillfully cut, perfectly fitted, and carefully put together, while on the other hand, comparatively inferior material, if its pattern be not absolutely offensive, can be so treated as to make an effective and attractive garment. Of course the object to be striven for is to combine good material, skillful workmanship and a perfect fit, and one of the surest methods we know of to attain this highly desirable result is to place the order with Mr. J. C. Williams, doing business at No. 106 Market Street. This gentleman is a native of England and has carried on his present enterprise here since 1892, and has already built up a well deserved reputation for producing artistic and well made clothing at moderate prices. The premises occupied comprise two rooms on the second floor of No. 106 Market Street. A large and carefully chosen stock of foreign and domestic fabrics for gentlemen's wear is carried, thus enabling him to suit all varieties of taste and to make garments suitable for all occasions at short notice. Employment is given to five competent assistants and every order is assured immediate and painstaking attention, entire satisfaction being guaranteed both as regards the quality of the work and the prices quoted.

C. E. SHOREY, Studio, 40 Market Street, 2d story, Lynn, Mass.—There are not a few people who think it necessary to visit the largest cities in order to obtain a first-class portrait, and would laugh at the idea of being able to get an equally faithful and handsomely finished likeness at home, yet expert photographers are not confined to the important cities by any means, and we have an instance of this in the firm of C. E Shorey whose studio is located on the second story of No. 40 Market Street, occupying four rooms. Mr. Shorey has had an experience of many years in his profession. The generous patronage bestowed upon him by the residents of Lynn and vicinity shows that his work is equal to the best that can be procured. We do not hesitate to recommend Mr. Shorey to all who appreciate fine portraits, nor do we ask anybody to take our word for it. Visit his studio, examine the finished work there on exhibition, compare it with that turned out at establishments of much greater pretensions, and see if you can find its superior. Three competent assistants are employed, and photographs of all kinds are produced at short notice, and at as low prices as can be named on work of this character, and no work is allowed to leave the studio that is not fully up to the high standard established by Mr. C. E. Shorey.

FARMER & LEMMON, Retail Dealers in Boots, Shoes and Rubbers. Fine Goods a Specialty, 150 Market Street. Lynn, Mass.—Many persons pride themselves on being good judges of boots and shoes, but as a matter of fact, it is practically impossible to accurately determine the real value of a made up boot or shoe, for the simple reason that many important details of workmanship cannot then be examined. Of course, it is generally safe to assume that if the stock is good, and the workmanship, so far as it can be seen, is all right, the entire shoe is properly made from suitable materials, but there is no certainty about it, and, therefore, the only way to be sure of getting your money's worth is to patronize thoroughly reputable dealers. Messrs. Farmer & Lemmon are such and during the ten years that they have sold boots, shoes and rubbers in this town they have established an enviable reputation for skill, fair dealing and enterprise. They established their present enterprise in 1883, and the store occupied at No. 150 Market Street measures (60 x 2) feet in dimensions, and contains a large stock of boots, shoes and rubbers, fine goods being a specialty, while every facility is at hand for the doing of first-class repairing. The assortment is complete, the goods are fully warranted to prove as represented, and the prices are uniformly moderate in every department.

GEO. C. HERBERT & CO., Stationers and Booksellers, Account Book Makers, Printers and Lithographers, Plate Printing, Book Binding. 10 Central Avenue, 470 Washington Street. Lynn. Mass.—An enterprising manufacturing and trade centre is an excellent field for the operations of such a house as that of George C. Herbert & Co., for a business community that is really up to the times insists upon having first-class stationery, artistic cards, bill-heads and circulars, and also account books that are especially designed to meet the requirements of individual houses. All these things and many more including miscellaneous books can be furnished by the concern we have mentioned, and therefore they do an extensive wholesale and retail business and one that is steadily increasing. Spacious premises located at 10 Central Avenue, and 470 Washington Street, are occupied, and they are excellently equipped for the carrying on of the many operations incidental to a business which includes the manufacture of stationery, account books, etc., and printing, lithographing, plate printing and book binding. Employment is given to fourteen experienced assistants, and orders can be filled at short notice, and at the lowest rates consistent with the use of suitable material and the production of work that is fully guaranteed to prove as represented in every respect.

REPRESENTATIVE BUSINESS MEN OF LYNN.

F. L. SPINNEY & CO., Manufacturers of Ladies' Boots and Shoes, No. 311 Union Street, Lynn, Mass.—The principle of progress as applied to the making of boots and shoes, while it has received marked illustration in this section, has not yet reached the maximum point. New inventions and ideas constantly modify and cheapen the production of these important staples of trade. The house of F. L. Spinney & Co., manufacturers of ladies' boots and shoes at 311 Union Street, Lynn, was established in 1891, and by introducing new and valuable features has already built up a wide influential trade in this line. Their goods are distinguished by a combination of finest quality of material and stylish workmanship with a price which commands attention and respect. They have in two years created a large business, extending throughout the New England and Middle States, and their fine ladies' shoes are steadily increasing in popularity wherever introduced. A thoroughly equipped factory building is occupied, 80 x 60 feet in dimensions, and four stories high. The company employs forty-five trained and first-class workers, and every department is carefully conducted on modern principles. All orders receive prompt and energetic attention. An examination of price lists and samples will convince wide awake dealers that they can secure exceptional satisfaction in handling the attractive and uniform high-grade goods of this house. Our lady readers should take an early opportunity of assuring themselves of the fact that the easy and stylish fit, high-quality material and low price of these shoes, make them desirable beyond many higher priced goods. The members of this progressive company are Mr. F. L. Spinney, Mr. W. A. Burrill and Mr. T. D. Morse. The two former gentlemen are natives of Massachusetts, and Mr. Morse of Maine. The entire company believe in energetic, untiring enterprise, combined with the most thorough and conservative business methods. Upon this basis they have built up a prosperous business, which has as fine an outlook as any in the city.

T. J. READY, New and Second Hand Furniture, 67 Munroe Street, Lynn.—There are many careful housekeepers to be found in Lynn and vicinity, and not a few of them have discovered that the establishment conducted by Mr. T. J. Ready at 67 Munroe Street, is a most excellent one to visit when anything in the shape of crockery ware, bedding, stoves, or other house furnishing goods are wanted, new or second hand. This business was established forty years ago; in 1883 the present proprietor, who is a native of this State and thoroughly familiar with every detail of his business, assumed control. Mr. Ready is a large dealer in new and second hand furniture, paying the highest market prices. The premises made use of comprise one four story building 200x40 feet in dimensions, together with two floors 20x40 and 20x30 feet respectively, and a large trade is done in new and second hand furniture, also repairing, bedding, crockery, lamps, stoves, tinware, wooden ware and housefurnishing goods, etc., together with a complete assortment of the latest fashionable novelties, so that all tastes and purses can be suited. Ten competent assistants are employed and all orders for either branch of the business will be promptly attended to, and we need hardly say that a merchant having Mr. Ready's long experience and ability should be in a position to quote the lowest market rates on all his goods.

A. H. SISSON, Gunsmith, Locksmith and Bell-Hanger, 35 Munroe Street, Lynn, Mass.—There is one bit of information so useful that it should be stowed away in the minds of all our readers, and that is the whereabouts of a first-class practical locksmith and gunsmith. You may not have occasion for the services of such a man for years, it may even happen that you might never require them, but the contrary is much more apt to be the case, and no little trouble, not to say expense, will then be saved by knowing just whom to apply to. Therefore, we take pleasure in calling the attention of our readers to the facilities possessed by Mr. A. H. Sisson, at 35 Munroe Street, as he is a practical locksmith, gunsmith and bell-hanger, in the fullest sense of the word. He is prepared to undertake anything in his line of business, with the assurance of carrying it out to the satisfaction of all parties concerned. Locks will be repaired, keys fitted, and guns or anything pertaining to them in the way of general repairing will be done in a thorough and workmanlike manner, moderate charges being made in every instance. Special attention is given to bell-hanging and repairing of all kinds, while all orders for such will be promptly attended to and carefully done. The shop utilized comprises one floor, 30x20 feet, which has all the facilities necessary for conducting the business.

JOHN J. MOLONEY, Wholesale and Retail Dealer in Foreign and Domestic Fruits, No. 126 Market Street. Residence: 515 Boston Street, Lynn, Mass.—There is no doubt that the greatly increased demands for fruits, so noticeable of late years, is due in a great measure to the spreading of hygienic knowledge among the people, for although the most of us eat fruit because we like it, we would not consume nearly so much as we do, were we not convinced that it is healthful as well as palatable. The growth of the trade in foreign and domestic fruits during the past decade has been truly wonderful, and by its extension their price has been so reduced that bananas, oranges, etc., are about as cheap as apples, pears and other domestic fruits. Mr. John J. Moloney of 126 Market Street, handles a large proportion of the foreign fruits received in Lynn, for he is a leading wholesale and retail dealer in these commodities, and also in domestic fruits of all kinds. The business was founded by the present proprietor. The premises utilized comprise one floor 60 x 25 feet in size, and a large and varied stock is constantly carried so the heaviest orders can be filled at short notice. Three competent assistants are employed and fruits of every description are dealt in, and Mr. Moloney is always prepared to quote the lowest market rates, and ship goods without delay. His residence is at 515 Boston Street and well known in Lynn.

FLEXITY STAIN CO., Manufacturers of Bottom Stains, and Burnish Colors for Heels and Edges, Flexible, Durable and Elegant Easily Applied and Quickly Finished. No. 13 State Street, Lynn, Mass.—The Flexity Stain Company began operations in 1892 and have already built up a large business that is still steadily increasing. And it is not at all difficult to account for the immediate and decided success of this company, for they are manufacturers of bottom stains and burnish colors for heels and edges that are flexible, durable and elegant; are easily applied and quickly finished—and that is just what the trade want and just what they insist upon having after they have learned that such stains and colors are on the market. The proprietor of this business is Mr. W. F. Dee, who is a thoroughly practical "shoe man" and is well-known in Lynn and vicinity. The factory is located at 13 State Street, and the facilities are such that all orders, large and small, can be filled at short notice. The work of production is carefully supervised; carefully selected materials are used, and the Flexity stains and burnish colors are as uniform in merit as they are unequalled in convenience and appearance.

J. A. COOK, Manufacturer of Hand Turns, Boots and Slippers. White Slippers a Specialty. Custom Work a Specialty. Second Story, 30 Summer St., Lynn, Mass.—The most successful buyer is one who discriminates the most successfully between "goods cheap," and "cheap goods," and it is just such a buyer who will find the most to admire in the assortment of boots and slippers offered by Mr. J. A. Cook, for this gentleman carries on a business on the "quick sales and small profits" system, and both his goods and his prices combine to form a powerful argument in favor of patronizing his establishment. This enterprise was started here in 1892, by the present proprietor. He is a manufacturer of hand turns, boots and slippers, custom work and white slippers being made a specialty, and as may be guessed from the inducements he offers is thoroughly conversant with his business in every detail. He does a wholesale business and gives personal attention to customers, and employs six efficient and skillful assistants to enable him to fill all orders without delay. The premises occupied are located on the second story of 30 Summer Street, being 75x22 feet in dimensions. The products of this establishment, as named above, though made in great quantities, in workmanship and finish are not in any degree slighted, and we have no hesitation in saying these goods are equal to any in the market, and Mr. Cook will do everything in his power to maintain the reputation already established.

C. A. HODGES, Apothecary, 18 Market St., Lynn, Mass.—It may seem a strange assertion to make to say that the carrying on of a large number of drug stores argues well for the public health, but there is ground for the statement for the simple reason that many drugs depend greatly upon their freshness for their effect, and the existence of a large number of drug stores has the result of causing each dealer to carry but a comparatively small stock of any one article, the consequence being that physicians can depend upon having their prescriptions filled by the use of ingredients much fresher than would otherwise be possible—a fact which we commend to the consideration of the few who think that now as formerly that every doctor should compound his own medicines. This enterprise was founded in 1857 by the present proprietor, Mr. C. A. Hodges, who is a native of Vermont, and very prominently known throughout Lynn and vicinity. The premises occupied are located at 18 Market Street, comprise one floor 70x25 feet in size, and contain a fine assortment of all that is usually to be found in a first-class apothecary store. Two assistants are employed, and great care and attention is given to the compounding of physicians' prescriptions. Many of the residents of Lynn can testify to the merits of this pharmacy, and a careful examination of the methods pursued will convince any one of the value of such an establishment. A fine selection of toilet articles and druggists' sundries can always be found here while the prices are always moderate.

DEARBORN & BLANCHARD, Tailors, 58 Munroe St., Lynn, Mass. Ladies' and Gents' Clothing Cleaned, Dyed and Repaired in First-Class Shape. Kid Gloves Cleaned in one Day. Goods Called for and Delivered Without Extra Charge.—" Good wine needs no bush," says the proverb, and good clothing needs no commendation in order to attract the attention of those really appreciative of such garments, for really artistic clothing is not so common as to cause it to be passed by unnoticed, and if proof of this assertion be needed it may be found in the development of the business carried on by Messrs. Dearborn & Blanchard since its inception. They are first-class tailors, and cater to the most fastidious trade and yet quote prices considerable below those usually named in connection with first-class tailoring. No better fitting, better trimmed, or more thoroughly made garments are produced in Lynn than those furnished by this firm, and we have no hesitation in guaranteeing satisfaction to all who may favor them with an order, for their work is equal to the best and prices are moderate enough to suit the most economically disposed, and in addition to doing tailoring work in all its branches, ladies' and gents' clothing will be cleansed, dyed and repaired in first-class shape. The premises occupied are located at 58 Munroe street, and are equipped with the most improved facilities for the doing of work in all departments in the best manner possible, and only thoroughly competent assistants are employed. Mr. Fred C. Dearborn is a native of Massachusetts and Mr. Peter Blanchard was born in the Provinces. They are prompt and reliable business men.

AGNES LEE, Dealer in Boots, Shoes and Rubbers, 275 Essex Street, Lynn, Mass.—There are very few people but what are anxious to get shoes that both look well and feel comfortable, and it is not to be wondered at that this is the case, for while an ill-fitting or shabby boot or shoe will spoil the appearance of the finest costume, a neat and stylish article of footwear will do much to atone for any deficiencies in the other details of the apparel. When this establishment, of which Agnes Lee is the proprietress, was opened in this city during the current year, it was evident that the stock had been very carefully and skillfully chosen with an eye to the requirements of all kinds of customers. There were goods for adults, goods for children, shoes for dress purposes and shoes for ordinary street and business wear; and last but by no means least, the prices were right. A specialty is made of reliable shoes from Lynn manufacturers, made for first-class New England trade. Small hosiery and dry goods are also carried and the prices are the lowest that can be placed on reliable goods. The trade is steadily increasing and no efforts are spared to make this a first-class family shoe store, especially catering to ladies' trade. The premises utilized are 25x18 feet in dimensions and are located at 275 Essex Street between Fayette & Chestnut streets. All grades of goods are sold strictly on their merits, no misrepresentation being allowed in the slightest particular. The proprietress is a native of Massachusetts and has hosts of friends in this vicinity.

E. J. WATSON, Dry and Fancy Goods, Ladies' and Gents' Furnishings, Small Wares at Wholesale and retail. Domestic Sewing Machines and Patterns. 277 Union Street, Lynn, Mass.—The high standing of the establishment carried on by Mr. E. J. Watson is indisputable, and its popularity is also too evident to admit of its being denied, this store being largely patronized by the best informed and most careful buyers. The business was founded over forty years ago, operations having been begun in 1852, and the enterprise has attained its present importance by long continued and skillfully directed public service. As a wholesale and retail dealer in dry and fancy goods, ladies' and gents' furnishings, small wares, sewing machines, etc., etc., Mr. Watson carries a large and carefully selected stock, which includes the latest novelties as well as the most staple articles, and as the productions of the leading manufacturers are handled, the goods are "reliable" in the true sense of that much mis-used word. The premises occupied are located at 277 Union Street, and comprise one floor, 1,250 square feet in dimensions, so that ample room is available; and the size and completeness of the stock, and the facilities for promptly and satisfactorily serving many customers, are correspondingly adequate, employment being given to three efficient assistants. We need hardly say that Mr. Watson is in a position to sell as low as the lowest, quality considered, and even the closest buyers find his prices satisfactory.

C. L. ROSS,

FAMILY BAKERY,

Manufacturer of Ice Cream —Wholesale and Retail. Dealer in Confectionery, Etc.

211 ESSEX, Cor. CHATHAM ST.

BRANCH:—163 UNION STREET. **LYNN, MASS.**

Among the varied industries pursued in Lynn, the bakery of which Mr. C. L. Ross is proprietor, holds a prominent place in the trade centre. This enterprise was started in 1889 by its present proprietor, who during the time since elapsed has most ably managed his establishment. The premises are located at No. 211 Essex, corner of Chatham St. and are 90 x 20 feet in dimensions. The energies of the house are devoted to the manufacture of Bread, Cake and pastry of all kinds, also Ice Cream in large or small quantities. Postal orders promptly attended to. A fine line of choice Confectionery. This extensive business is both wholesale and retail, Mr. Ross also running a branch store at No. 163 Union Street, employing seven experienced assistants in both stores. The proprietor, Mr. C. L. Ross, is very well known throughout Lynn, and we feel justified in commending both the establishment and its wide awake proprietor to the favorable attention of all housekeepers and others desirous of finding a first-class bakery, whose products can be implicitly relied on.

JOSIAH B. BLOOD & CO., Dealers in Staple Groceries, Country Produce, Fresh Eggs and Choice Butter, 103-109 Summer Street, Lynn, Mass.—The business of which Messrs. Josiah B. Blood & Co. are proprietors was founded by them in 1879, and has steadily developed until it has reached quite extensive proportions. They are both wholesale and retail dealers in staple groceries and country produce, fresh eggs and choice butter, being well prepared to furnish first-class goods at reasonable prices. The premises utilized are located at Nos. 103-105 Summer Street, comprise one floor 100x30 feet in dimensions, and are very conveniently fitted up, enabling orders to be filled at short notice and in a thoroughly accurate and satisfactory manner. The stock is so uniformly good that it is difficult to single out certain articles for individual mention, but we may at least call attention to the assortment of teas, coffees and spices, these being of standard purity, of fine and delicious flavor and of comparatively low cost, and those who appreciate good butter and fresh eggs should certainly test the goods offered by this house. Five competent and reliable assistants are employed, and all callers are treated with courtesy. The individual members are Messrs. J. B., E. H., and A. J. and L. K. Blood, all natives of Lynn, and well-known in this community as honorable business men. They have built up a large trade, on the basis of *cash grocers* and advertise their business as follows: "J. B. Blood & Co., cash grocers, 103 to 109 Summer Street. Our system: Cash! no books! no bad bills! no sleepless nights! no delivery teams. This grocery team once, twice a day, costs money; you pay it. We send a bbl. of flour, express paid, other goods with it if you wish, or allow for delivery if you take it. Any goods without flour, 10 cents anywhere in Lynn. You can save a large per cent. by trading with us, we won't say how much. Try it on a week's supply. We have done business this way for ten years, and grown steadily. We can do more, and want to extend our trade in your direction.

HOFFMAN HOUSE. P. W. Cloran, Proprietor, 59 Andrew Street, Lynn.—It may be putting it a trifle too strong to say that *everybody* in Lynn and vicinity knows Mr. P. W. Cloran, either personally or by reputation, but it would not be much of an exaggeration, for Mr. Cloran has been a prominent hotel man for years; is manufacturer of the " P. W. C." cigar (a famous ten cent cigar that has not only " caught the town" but is gaining in favor yearly—) and is a prominent society man who is almost universally known in social circles. Mr. Cloran began to "run a hotel" at the age of 22, when he was proprietor of the Railroad House, at Beverly. At the end of two years he removed to Gloucester, where he remained six years. In 1881 he came to Lynn, and assumed control of the hotel he now carries on, but it was then known as the Crawford House. Mr. Cloran sold out, but in a few years resumed possession of the hotel, and under the name of the Hoffman House it is now known as a most excellent place for those who think more of comfort than they do of mere "style," and who appreciate the advantages of stopping at a centrally located, well kept and comfortably furnished hotel where the board is excellent, and the prices are very reasonable. The Hoffman House is a brick structure; contains 24 sleeping rooms, and dining rooms that will accommodate 150 people a day. Mr. Cloran's cigar factory and store are located at No. 39 Central Square, and whether you want the best ten cent cigar on earth (which is, of course, the " P. W. C.") or anything else in the line of cigars, tobaccos and smokers' articles it will pay you to visit this establishment, for it contains a large and complete stock, and the prices are low enough to suit even the most economically disposed. Some idea of the popularity of Mr. Cloran's productions in the cigar line, may be gained from the simple statement that the output averages about a million and a quarter per annum.

WILBUR C. LAMPHIER, Dealer in Photographic Supplies, Rooms 21 and 23, Bergengren Block, 343 Union Street, and 19 Central Square, Lynn, Mass.—In the sixty years since Daguerre laid the foundation of modern photography, this new science and art has made tremendous strides. It has now become an important feature of social life, has revolutionized astronomy and at the same time has provided a most pleasant and instructive occupation for many having leisure time upon their hands. Amateur photography has become one of the great features at this end of the century, and has already produced not a few valuable results. The leading center in Lynn for the supply of photographic materials will be found at the establishment of Mr. Wilbur C. Lamphier, rooms 21 and 23, Bergengren Block, 343 Union Street and 19 Central Square. This business has been conducted very successfully by Mr. Lamphier for the past two years. He has made a specialty of the finest and best class of photographers' supplies, and by securing special prices has built up a select and valuable trade. Plates, lenses, chemicals of all kinds necessary. Kodaks and the best amateur cameras are among the articles which Mr. Lamphier has always on hand. It will be a saving of time and money to all interested in these lines to make an inspection of his attractive goods and prices. They will find that they can secure just as good service here as at any of the largest city establishments. Mr. Lamphier is a native of Massachusetts, and has brought to the development of his business those traits of solid industry, enterprise and foresight which has made the New England of to-day what it is.

C. A. WHEELER, Dealer in Stationery and Fancy Goods of all kinds. Paper by the pound. Dennison's English Tissue Paper a specialty. Exchange Building, 16 Market Street, Lynn, Mass.—Nothing is risked by asserting that Mr. C. A. Wheeler is as widely and favorably known as any of our Lynn business men, for there is no room for doubt on that subject. He founded his present enterprise in 1880. He deals in stationery and fancy goods of all kinds, selling paper by the pound and making a specialty of Dennison's English tissue paper which is always kept in stock. A good assortment of optical goods is carried, and special attention is paid to testing the eyes. The premises occupied are located in Exchange Building, No. 16 Market Street, comprise one floor 40 x 25 feet in size, so that ample opportunity is provided to display the large assortment to excellent advantage, and which is as attractive as it is varied, for it comprises the latest novelties and is selected with unusual care. Low prices are quoted on all the goods Mr. Wheeler handles, and as he is thoroughly conversant with the minutest details concerning the business to which he gives his close supervision, our citizens are sure that they can obtain here the latest fashionable styles of stationery and small fancy goods. The proprietor makes it his study to meet the wants of the people, and give prompt and courteous attention to all callers, while the prices quoted on all goods offered are as low as can be found at any place in the town, and he endeavors to keep the service up so as to maintain his old reputation.

TUPPER & GRANT, Wholesale and Retail Dealers in Fine Cigars and Tobacco, also Smokers' Articles, 42 Market Street, Lynn, Mass.—If all the energy and eloquence that are wasted in this world could only be turned to practical account, only think what reforms might be accomplished, think of the time, money, breath and patience that have been spent in opposing the use of cigars, tobacco, etc., and then think of the few men you know who don't use either in one form or another. Common sense is a hard thing to fight, and the common sense of the people has decided that tobacco used in reasonable moderation is a blessing not to be given up. A cigar is a wonderful consoler (provided it be a good one), and the consolation it affords is cheap at the price. In order to get an article that will console, and not exasperate, you must patronize the right dealer, and we may say right here that Messrs. Tupper & Grant, on Market Street, have the reputation of selling as good cigars, tobacco, etc., also smokers' articles, as anybody could desire. This enterprise was founded some years ago and the present proprietors took possession in 1892. They do both a wholesale and retail business. The premises occupied are located at No. 42 Market Street, comprise one floor 40 x 18 feet in dimensions, and contain a fine stock, always fresh, and for sale at moderate prices. One assistant is employed, and all callers are treated with prompt attention and courtesy.

HANNAFORD & PERKINS, Plumbers, Tin Plate and Sheet Iron Workers, also dealers in Stoves Ranges, Furnaces, Tin Ware, Sheet Lead, Zinc, Lead Pipe, etc., Roofing and Jobbing of all kinds, 753 Western Avenue, Lynn, Mass.—We take pleasure in calling attention to the enterprise conducted by Messrs. Hannaford & Perkins, for a house that does strictly first-class plumbing at the lowest possible rates; that employs thoroughly competent and reliable help; that gives prompt and careful attention to large and small orders and that does sanitary plumbing, that is sanitary in the full sense of that much abused word, is a decided benefit to a community, and that is just what is done by Messrs. Hannaford & Perkins. But plumbing by no means constitutes all of their business, on the contrary they are extensive tin plate and sheet iron workers, do roofing and jobbing of all kinds, and deal largely in stoves, ranges, furnaces, tinware, sheet lead, zinc, lead pipe, etc. Operations were begun about 15 years ago, and some idea of the present magnitude of the business may be gained from the fact that employment is given to 13 competent assistants. The shop is located at No. 753 Western Avenue, and is spacious, well-arranged and well-equipped in every respect. The leading makes of cooking and heating stoves are handled by this firm and they will set them up and guarantee them to do all that is claimed for them, provided they are used in accordance with instructions.

T. J. SEXTON, Dealer in Wood and Coal at Wharf Prices. Hacks furnished for Weddings, Funerals, Etc., 203 Summer Street, Lynn, Mass. So far as quoted prices are concerned, it doesn't make much, if any difference, where you place your orders for coal and wood, for the prices named by all the retail dealers in a given city or town are substantially the same; but, nevertheless, it is well worth while to use discrimination in the placing of orders, for there is decided difference in the quality of the fuel furnished and in the promptness and reliability of the service afforded by different houses. Mr. T. J. Sexton has excellent reason for inviting the closest investigation of his facilities and his record, for he is prepared to furnish coal and wood of excellent quality at wharf prices and at short notice; and since beginning operations here in 1890 he has made an enviable record for enterprise and fair dealing. Mr. Sexton is a native of Lynn and is widely known throughout this neighborhood and the surrounding towns. The premises occupied are located at No. 203 Summer Street comprise one building 60 x 25 feet in size, and as he employs two efficient assistants, orders for wood and coal will be promptly filled and delivered. A five horse-power electric motor is used for the sawing of kindling wood into proper sizes, which saves a vast amount of time and labor. Hacks are furnished for Weddings, Parties and Funerals by this gentleman.

T. W. TYLER, Oak Tanned Belts, Lacings, Oils, Waste and Engine Supplies, Paper, Twine, Oil Cans and Oilers, 93 Central Avenue, Lynn, Mass.—As Lynn is distinctively a manufacturing city there is, of course, an immense demand here for mill and shop supplies, and no one is more prominent in supplying it than is Mr. T. W. Tyler, for he carries on a business founded a score of years ago and he has long held an enviable reputation for furnishing dependable goods at bottom prices, and for filling orders promptly, carefully and accurately. Mr. Tyler was born in Haverhill, and is extremely well-known in industrial circles, not only in Lynn but also in neighboring cities and towns. His relations with the leading manufacturers of oak-tanned belts, lacings, etc., are such as to enable him to quote bottom prices on goods of standard merit, and his facilities are such as to enable him to fill even the largest orders at very short notice. His store is located at No. 93 Central Avenue, and always contains a large and complete stock, including belting, lacings, oils, waste and engine supplies oil cans and oilers, and manufacturers' supplies in general. He carries a full line of Boston Belting Company's Garden Hose. Also best cotton and steam hose, rubber tubing of every variety at lowest prices. Nozzles, hose reels, lawn fountains, couplings, spiral wheel washers, sponges, chamois, castor oil for oiling carriages, light and heavy oil of all kinds for machinery, naptha; benzine and gasoline. Agent for Little Giant St. P. Forcer. Anti-rattle rubbers always on hand. A full line of paper bags, wrapping paper and twine. The store has telephone connection, and all orders are assured prompt and careful attention, ample assistance being employed.

CENTRAL AVENUE AND WILLOW STREET.

WM. F. EMBREE, Machinist and Millwright, Shafting, Hangers and Pulleys Always on Hand, Shoe Machinery Moved and Set Up. Agent for the Sturtevant Blowers and Exhaust Fans. Machine Jobbing of all kinds done at short notice. 22 Central Avenue, Lynn, Mass.—It is more true now than ever before that "time is money," for the use of rapid moving machinery has so increased the speed of production that more can be produced now in an hour than could be turned out in double that time comparatively few years ago, and hence the breaking down of machinery during the busy season is apt to have much more effect upon the total output of a factory than it would have had when both machinery and men moved much more slowly than they do to day. But a good deal of time and trouble can be saved by making use of the services of a thoroughly competent machinist and millwright who makes a specialty of the repairing and re-arranging of machinery, and is in a position to give prompt attention to all orders; and as Mr. William F. Embree has gained an excellent reputation among Lynn manufacturers in connection with such work it is hardly necessary to say that he is called upon to execute many commissions, large and small. Shafting, hangers and pulleys are always on hand at this shop; and shoe machinery will be moved and set up, and machine jobbing of all kinds done at short notice and in a thoroughly workmanlike manner. Emery wheels and emery wheel stands are carried in stock and sold at bottom prices. A well-equipped shop, located at 22 Central Avenue, is utilized, and employment is given to four experienced assistants. Mr. Embree is agent for the famous Sturtevant blowers and exhaust fans, and is prepared to set them up, guarantee their performance, and to execute all such commissions at very short notice, and at manufacturer's rates.

MISS JOSIE E. CATE, Dry and Fancy Goods, 161 Chestnut Street, Lynn, Mass., Agent for Boston St. Laundry. F. C. Cheever, Elder's Block, Washington Street, Lynn, Mass.—One of the best known stores in this section of Lynn is that conducted by Miss Josie E. Cate and the exceptionally high reputation it enjoys is the best proof that could be given that its management is, and has been all that could be desired. Miss Cate is a native of New Hampshire and has been identified with her present line of business for some time. The premises occupied and which are located at 161 Chestnut Street, comprise one floor 45x20 feet in dimensions, and a very extensive stock is carried, made up of dry and fancy goods, hosiery, corsets, gloves, notions, ladies' and gents' underwear. There is also a department devoted to dressmaking, where first-class work as regard fit, etc., is guaranteed at reasonable prices. Miss Cate is also the agent in this section for the Boston St. Laundry. From four to seven competent assistants are employed and an extensive retail business is done. A special feature in this store is a circulating library of about four hundred books. The high esteem in which Miss Cate's store is held is easily explained, for the policy pursued by her, is as simple as it is satisfactory, consisting merely of giving every customer full value for money received, and offering such a variety of desirable goods that all tastes can be suited. Miss Cate gives her close personal attention to the business, and keeps the service at the very highest standard of efficiency.

TUCKER HOUSE, A. S. Cole, Proprietor. Two minutes from Depots and Theatres. Steam heat and all modern conveniences. Transients accommodated at moderate rates, 36 Munroe Street, Lynn, Mass.—The Tucker House has been a favorite Lynn hotel for many years, but it is safe to say that it was never more popular than at present. Mr. A. S. Cole, the popular proprietor, is a born hotel keeper and has made the Tucker House one of the most thoroughly comfortable and homelike hotels in this city. It is located at 36 Munroe Street, and contains 35 guest rooms. The building is well arranged and excellently fitted up, its equipments including steam heat and all modern conveniences, while its furnishings is equally satisfactory, the beds especially deserving favorable mention as they are equipped with the most efficient type of springs, etc., and afford a refreshing contrast to the comfortless couches far too common in even the most pretentious hotels. The terms of the house are very low, and transients are accommodated at moderate rates, and as the table is bountifully supplied with the best the market affords, it is no wonder the hotel is very popular among the best informed portion of the traveling public. The Tucker House is located only two minutes' walk from depots and theatres, and as an efficient force of competent assistants are constantly employed, it is a most convenient and comfortable house to patronize while staying in Lynn.

BLANCHARD & CURRY, Clothing Cleaned, Dyed and Repaired, 205 Union Street, and 140 Liberty Street, 2d door from Central Avenue, Lynn, Mass.—No man should be, and no one but a fool is, ashamed to wear shabby clothes during working hours when the work is of a nature that makes the wearing of good clothing unadvisable, but when circumstances permit proper self-respect impels one to present a neat and attractive appearance, and while clothing is as cheap as it is now, there is no reason why every man should not be comfortably and fashionably clad. A little money will go a great ways in this line nowadays, especially if you have your clothing cleansed and repaired, once in a while, and if you doubt this statement we would advise you to avail yourselves of the facilities offered by Blanchard & Curry, who carry on business at two places, one at 140 Liberty Street, 2d door from Central Avenue, and one at 205 Union Street: their premises are ample, and have every requisite facility at hand to enable them to fill all orders for cleaning, dyeing and repairing gentlemen's clothing of all kinds, being agents for the Salem Dye Works. They employ two thoroughly competent assisstants, and quote prices that are away down to the lowest notch—so low in fact as to make one wonder "where the profit comes in" but that is no concern of the public's, for they certainly have no reason to complain at a policy which enables them to save money and dress neatly and well at the same time. The firm of Blanchard & Curry, was formed in 1891. They assure prompt and polite attention to every caller and fully warrant that every order shall be satisfactorily executed in every particular.

FRANK E. FLINT, Pharmacist, 44 Market Street, Lynn, Mass.—The pharmacy conducted by Mr. Frank E. Flint, was established by him in 1872. Mr. Flint is a native of Massachusetts and is very well known throughout Lynn, and vicinity. Premises having an area of 1,200 square feet are occupied, they being located at 44 Market Street, and are fitted up in the most convenient and complete manner, especial attention having been given to the facilities for accommodating the prescription trade,which is one the most important and popular departments of the business. The stock of drugs, medicines, chemicals, etc., is deserving of particular and favorable mention as it comprises a full selection of such commodities, obtained from the most reputable dealers, and the articles composing it may therefore be safely depended upon for freshness and purity. Four competent and thoroughly reliable assistants are employed,and prescriptions are compounded with the most scrupulous care and accuracy, at short notice and at moderate rates. Toilet articles, and druggists' sundries of all kinds are largely dealt in, and as the goods are uniformly desirable, and the prices strictly in accord with the lowest market rates on articles of equal merit, this store is one of the most popular of its kind in the city.

S. RYAN, Groceries, Provisions, Fruit and Vegetables, Dry and Fancy Goods. Nos. 86 and 88 Lewis Street, Lynn, Mass.—An admirably equipped store in its department of trade, and a recognized leader throughout Lynn and vicinity,is that conducted by Mr. S. Ryan at Nos. 86 and 88 Lewis Street. It has now been in successful operation here, under Mr Ryan's management, since 1863. The trade is one of the most select and valuable in the city, including groceries, provisions, fruits and vegetables ; also dry and fancy goods of all kinds. The store building occupied is 40 x 30 feet in size, handsomely furnished and equipped. Four experienced and courteous assistants are employed, and all visitors to this popular store receive immediate, thorough attention. The grocery and provision department enjoys a very high reputation for the uniform purity and freshness of its goods. In the dry and fancy goods department, great enterprise is shown in constantly presenting customers with the latest popular novelties. Prices are maintained at the lowest notch, and in standard of service, Mr. Ryan's store can afford trade advantages unexcelled anywhere. A prompt delivery system is also maintained. Our readers in search of A1 goods and moderate prices should be sure to call here. We deem it beyond question that they can thus secure a grade of satisfaction which they will find conducive to both pleasure and economy.

MISS G. L. GERRY & CO.,

DEALERS IN
FANCY GOODS AND NOVELTIES,
Sole Agents for THE EQUIPOISE WAIST.

135 BROAD STREET, - - - **LYNN, MASS.**

Among the popular houses in Lynn, it is a pleasure to call attention to the enterprise conducted under the firm name of Miss G. L. Gerry & Co., at No. 135 Broad Street. The partners are sisters—Mrs. A. E. Megquire and Miss G. L. Gerry, both natives of Maine but long residents of this city, having for years been engaged in business here, before succeeding to this business in 1892, and hence both are very well known in Lynn and vicinity and have built up a very important business by close attention to details, and giving patrons the benefit of a choice and carefully selected stock at prices that cannot be discounted elsewhere in goods of equal merit. They carry a full line of fancy goods, novelties, etc., which under these heads embrace so endless a list of articles that we have not the space to attempt any specification of them, only that they have been selected with the greatest care to meet the most exacting demands, and are of the very latest and most desirable styles, which cannot fail to suit every taste, as they are offered at the lowest prices, and are guaranteed to prove as represented. The store is always well stocked and ample assistance is employed, so that prompt and obliging service is assured to every caller.

CAPE COD FISH MARKET, Wholesale and Retail Dealers in all Kinds of Fresh and Salt Fish, Oysters, Clams, Crackers, Pickles, etc. Canned Goods a Specialty. Salad Oils and Dressing. Lobsters Fresh every Day. All Orders promptly Delivered. Finest Oyster Bar in Lynn. All Lobsters Boiled on the Premises. Charles H. and John M. Leach, Managers, 45 Munroe St., Lynn. Telephone 27-4.—Prominent among the enterprising business houses of Lynn, is the "Cape Cod Fish Market," of which Messrs. Leach Bros. are proprietors. The business was established by them in 1892, has rapidly and steadily grown from its inception. The firm are wholesale and retail dealers in all kinds of fresh and salt fish, oysters, clams, crackers, pickles, etc. Canned goods a specialty. Salad oils and dressing. Lobsters fresh every day, while everything is of the best quality which can be selected by the experience and thorough knowledge of the proprietors. These goods, which comprise every variety of fish in their season, are purchased from first hands, and on such advantageous terms as to enable them to furnish their customers with good supplies at reasonable prices. The finest oysters only are handled, while all lobsters are boiled on the premises, and five boats are kept employed fishing for them. A lunch counter and tables are run, giving a fine variety with hot tea or coffee. Charles H. and John M. Leach compose the present firm, they are natives of this State, and highly esteemed in this city for their industry, enterprise and sterling business qualities. Six competent assistants are employed, while all customers are attended to with promptness, and all orders accurately delivered to any part of the city. Special rates to hotels and boarding houses. A specialty is made of opening oysters at residences for evening dinners, the furnishing of lobster salads and lobsters and oysters in any form, their boiled lobster being a very popular dish; their fried clams are also a favorite, and their lunch counters are well patronized.

HATCH & FERNALD, Carpenters & Builders, Jobbing promptly attended to. 44 and 46 Marshall's Wharf, Lynn, Mass.—One way to demonstrate the high standing of the firm of Hatch & Fernald would be to mention some of the buildings with whose construction they were identified, for they had a hand in the erection of such structures as the new Lynn High School; the residence and also the manufacturing plant of Mr. Chas. H. Pinkham; the residence of Mr. T. P. Richardson; Holder & Breed's building; Sawyer & Chase's factory, and one of the Thomson-Houston factories, besides many other buildings for residential, manufacturing, or mercantile purposes. But perhaps the best way would be to enquire anywhere in Lynn and vicinity, for everybody knows this representative concern, and everybody agrees that for integrity, ability and facilities, Messrs. Hatch & Fernald need not fear comparison with any building firm in the county. Mr. A. A. Hatch is a native of Marshfield, Mass., and Mr. J. Furnald of Kittery, Maine. Both are thoroughly practical men, who had long and varied experience in the carpentering trade before becoming associated in 1878; and much of the success of this firm is due to the close personal attention given by the members of it to the execution of all commissions with which they are entrusted. Their plant at Nos. 44 and 46 Marshall's Wharf includes improved facilities for the manufacture of doors, windows, turned work, carving and house finish of all descriptions, and the firm are prepared to figure very closely on building contracts and to execute even the most extensive commissions at short notice. Employment is given to twenty five experienced assistants, and jobbing is promptly attended to, all important work being done under the personal supervision of one of the proprietors.

BOSTON NOVELTY STORE, G. T. Andrews & Co., Proprietors, 83 Market Street, Lynn Mass.—An establishment which is attractive in a variety of ways is the "Boston Novelty Store," located at No. 83 Market Street, Lynn, and there are few people in this city but what might visit it with profit to themselves. The premises cover an area of 1,200 square feet and are pretty thoroughly occupied, a large stock being constantly carried, and including tinware, fancy goods, music, stationery, and full line of novels by all popular authors at less than half price. A specialty is made of sheet music; you can find any piece at half-off the regular price. We give half-off on all sheet music published. Ask for catalogue of 4,043 pieces at five cents per copy; ordered music at half-off; no excuse for paying high prices; special attention to mail orders. The proprietors, Messrs. G. T. Andrews & Co., are very well known in the trade circles of this city, and opened the Boston Novelty Store in 1893. The public will find much to interest them at this general variety store, and will also find that the proprietors are in a position to furnish any desired article in their line, a large and varied assortment always being carried in stock. Employment is given to three efficient assistants, and the prompt and courteous attention given to customers is of itself a great inducement to trade at this establishment. G. T. Andrew's motto is "best goods at low prices," and it certainly is a pleasant task to chronicle a success won by such legitimate and well considered methods.

OLIVER F. JEPSON, 76 Union Street, Lynn, Mass.—It is difficult to do justice to the establishment carried on by Mr. Oliver F. Jepson, at 76 Union Street, within the limited space at our command, for it really embodies two lines of business, each of which is important and merits detailed description. In other words, this is a confectionery store, and ice-cream saloon; and the service rendered in each department is so satisfactory that it would be unjust to single either one of them out for special mention. Suffice it to say here you can get fresh and pure confectionery; in flavor, in quality and in general excellence equal to the best the market affords; here is sold, in quantities to suit, ice cream that cannot fail to satisfy the most fastidious (provided they appreciate ice-cream skillfully made from first-class materials) and the charges made for the excellent commodities served are very moderate. The premises utilized being 1,200 square feet in dimensions and conveniently arranged for the comfort of patrons. Mr. Jepson is a native of Maine, and is extremely well-known here in Lynn, where he has carried on his present line of business since 1893. He employs only competent assistants, and by careful supervision maintains the service at a high standard of excellence.

GEORGE H. NEWHALL, Real Estate and Insurance, Justice of the Peace. Care of Real Estate Solicited. Deeds and Mortgages Carefully Written, 34 Central Square, Room 11, Lynn, Mass.—Such of our readers as are contemplating investment in real estate in the city of shoes would do well to call upon Mr. George H. Newhall—first, because he is exceptionally well-informed concerning realty values and prospects in Lynn and vicinity and second, because he controls some very desirable building lots in various parts of the city and especially some choice lots on the estate of the late Isaac Newhall and is prepared to sell on very easy terms. Mr. Newhall is a native of Lynn and is one of the best known business men of the city. For years he has been actively interested in Lynn's development, and was President of the Lynn City Street Railway Company when it was consolidated with the Lynn & Boston Railroad. He has served two years in the Common Council, and for a year was president of that body; and has also served two years on the Board of Aldermen, and most active service, too, as he was a member of nearly all the important committees, including the committees of Finance, Streets, License, Drainage, Accounts, Education, Fuel and Street Lights, and Water Supply. Mr. Newhall was also a trustee of the Public Library and a member of the School committee. He makes a specialty of the care of real estate, and it goes without saying that a gentleman of Mr. Newhall's ability, experience and training is admirably qualified to perform the responsible duties attaching to that service to the best possible advantage. He is a justice of peace; deeds and mortgages will be carefully written; and insurance can be placed in large or small amounts in reliable companies at the lowest prevailing rates. The office is at 34 Central Square, Room 11.

MERRILL & DURGIN, Dealers in Furniture, Carpets and House Furnishings, 116 Market Street, Lynn, Mass.—There is often considerable difference of opinion as to the standing of a given enterprise in comparison with others of a kindred character, and from the nature of things it is inevitable that such should be the case; but there are individual instances where superiority is so apparent that no chance exists for honest doubt of the supremacy of an undertaking, and a very prominent case in point is that of the business carried on by Messrs. Merrill & Durgin, for this is unquestionably one of the leading enterprises of the kind in Lynn, and it is no discredit to others that such should be the case, for this business has been conducted with marked ability from the beginning. This business was started here by the present firm in 1890. The premises utilized are located at 116 Market Street, and comprise one five-story building, 50 x 84 feet in size, and the house deals largely in all kinds of furniture, carpets and house-furnishing goods, etc., etc., carrying a heavy stock made up of the productions of the leading manufacturers and embracing the very latest fashionable novelties. Eight reliable assistants are employed, while the most intelligent and critical trade is catered to, and bottom prices are quoted all round. The individual members of this firm are Messrs. S. S. Merrill and A. S. Durgin, formerly with Messrs. Titus and Buckley.

ARTHUR A. STINSON, Druggist, Cor. Ocean and Lewis Streets, Lynn, Mass.—Among those odds and ends of information which are to be classed among things that "May come in handy sometimes," perhaps the most important is the address of a skillful and absolutely reliable druggist who makes a specialty of the prompt and accurate compounding of physicians' prescriptions from pure and fresh drugs and chemicals, and such of our readers as will make careful note of the fact that Mr. Arthur A. Stinson may be found at the corner of Ocean & Lewis Streets, will be in possession of the address of just such a druggist as we have described, for Mr. Stinson carries on a well stocked and well equipped drug store, and gives particular attention to the work of maintaining the service in the prescription department at the highest standard of excellence. Mr. Stinson who is a native of Massachusetts opened his present establishment to the public in 1891, since which date he has gained a wide reputation as the most careful and painstaking of pharmacists, and whatever is purchased at this establishment can be thoroughly relied upon as first class in every particular. His pharmacy is conveniently and well arranged, competent assistants being employed, and a fine stock of medicines, chemicals, druggists' sundries, etc., being at hand to select from, and the prices quoted are low enough to suit the most economically disposed.

KOLLOCK & EARP, Manufacturers of Turn Slippers, 458 Union Street, Lynn, Mass.—The shoe trade in Lynn is constantly making new advances and one of the best recent movements in this direction has been the establishment of the firm of Messrs. Kollock & Earp, manufacturers of turn slippers, at No. 458 Union Street. This firm has at once taken a leading position, owing to the special value and excellence of the goods manufactured, as well as to their liberal and straightforward dealings. They employ experienced hands and their trade is steadily on the increase. The building occupied is equipped with the latest machinery. The goods of this house are marked by special care, both in the selection of material and thorough workmanship in every detail. A number of special styles are also manufactured which have commended themselves markedly to the public taste and approval. The goods of the firm will be found to realize an unusual degree of satisfaction for the money, which as in all cases is the only solid basis of success. Those who desire to test these facts can easily do so by examining the samples of this firm. Both dealers and individuals will find it to their advantage to do so. Both members of the firm were recently of the firm of Kollock, Logan & Co. At present it is composed of Mr. F. A. Kollock and Mr. J. B. Earp. Both are wide-awake and progressive business men with a well-earned title to their place among Lynn's successful manufacturers.

F. G. LORENDO,
CONFECTIONERY and CIGARS,

No. 534 Western Avenue.

Agent for F. C. Cheever's Boston St. Laundry,

531 WASHINGTON STREET, ... **LYNN, MASS.**

It is well-known to everybody that the popularity of a store is by no means always in proportion to the pretensions it makes, for the public are pretty sure to form a correct idea of the worthiness of an enterprise if given time to "size it up," and the result of such sizing up is sometimes very unfavorable to a very pretentious undertaking. On the other hand, true merit is recognized even when its claims are not loudly made, and one example of this is afforded by the popularity of the variety store carried on by Mr. F. G. Lorendo, for, although unpretentious, this establishment is a decided favorite with the residents of this vicinity. Mr. Lorendo is a native of Massachusetts, and began his present business here in 1892. He utilizes one floor 25x16 feet in size, at No. 534 Western Avenue, which is also the Street Car Station, and deals in confectionery, smokers' sundries, cigars and tobacco; cold drinks, nuts, fruits, etc., his stock being very carefully selected, and thus being attractive at all times. A fine line of stationery is carried. The assortment of confectionery includes about all the most popular varieties, and is renewed so frequently that the goods are always fresh as well as pure. Pickles, limes, bread, cake, pastry, cookies, crackers, etc., are kept in stock, and seasonable fruits, and the leading brands of cigars and tobacco are also well represented in the stock. Low prices are quoted and callers are assured prompt and courteous attention. Mr. Lorendo is also the agent for the Boston St. Laundry of which Mr. F. C. Cheever is the proprietor.

J. M. RANGER, Dealer in Paper Hangings, Trunks, Bags, Etc., 273 Union Street, Lynn, Mass.—Interior decoration is now acknowledged to be an art by itself, and during the past forty years or so wonderful progress has been made in learning and applying its principles. In order to choose well paper, and similar goods to the best advantage it is essential to visit an establishment where a large and varied stock is carried, comprising the latest novelties as well as full lines of more staple articles, and it is just such an assortment that is offered by Mr. J. M. Ranger, doing business at 273 Union Street. This gentleman is a native of Maine, and has carried on his present business here at Lynn since 1875, it having been originally founded in 1853. The premises occupied by Mr. Ranger comprise one floor and a basement each 100 by 20 square feet in dimensions, and are popularly known throughout Lynn and vicinity. They contain a large stock, so skillfully arranged that the task of selecting from it is easy and pleasant. Artistic wall-papers in great variety are offered at very moderate rates, as well as a choice assortment of mouldings, trunks, bags, etc., the stock being very complete and desirable and in fact the goods included therein are of first-class make, and of the most approved styles and designs. Eight efficient assistants are constantly employed, and customers are promptly and politely served, while every order will be accurately and immediately filled, and the extensive business which is both wholesale and retail in character is most ably managed in every respect.

M. BUTMAN & CO., Dealers in Men's, Boys' and Youths' Clothing, Hats, Caps and Furnishing Goods, Trunks, Traveling Bags, etc. 36 Central Square, Lynn, Mass.—A business that has been carried on for nearly thirty years must have some elements which appeal strongly to the general public, and in the case of the business conducted by Messrs. M. Butman & Co. (which was founded in 1866), it is not difficult to trace out those elements, for it does not take much inquiry to demonstrate the fact that people like to do business with this firm, first, because they are given an opportunity to choose from a large, varied and skillfully selected stock of men's, boys' and youths' clothing; hats, caps and furnishing goods; trunks, traveling bags, etc.; second, because they know that the stock always represents the very latest novelties, and is never "behind the times" in any department; and third, because there is no house in the city that quotes lower prices on goods of equal merit. Certainly it is not surprising that such a store should be popular, especially when we add that every article, large or small, low-priced or high priced, sold here is guaranteed to prove precisely as represented in every respect. The establishment is located at No. 36 Central Square, and is admirably arranged and very spacious, the premises being 85 x 24 feet in dimensions. Employment is given to three competent assistants, and prompt and courteous attention is assured to every caller, the business being carefully supervised by both members of the firm—Messrs. M. Butman and D. E. Conner—neither of whom needs introduction to our Lynn readers, for they are widely known throughout the city.

C. T. SHANNON, Dealer in Groceries, Provisions, Poultry, Etc. Fruit and Vegetables in Their Season. 245 Union Street, Lynn, Mass.—The grocery and provision store carried on by Mr. C. T. Shannon, is a very popular establishment and it well deserves its popularity, for if every grocery and provision establishment was like this one, a great deal of the bother and vexation of housekeeping would be done away with. Mr. Shannon is a native of Peabody, Mass., and assumed control of his present business in 1892. He sells at retail and makes a leading specialty of family trade, especially choice table butter, and fresh eggs. The premises occupied are located at No. 245 Union Street, where a large stock is carried, it comprising staple and fancy groceries in great variety, being made up of goods that are fully guaranteed to prove as represented. Choice provisions, poultry, etc., as well as fresh fruits and vegetables, all these and many other things are to be found at this popular store. Mr. Shannon handles only standard and reliable goods, and is prepared to furnish them in quantities to suit, and at positively bottom rates. In fact, low prices are quoted on all the goods handled by him, and as the goods are reliable, the service prompt and efficient, and orders called for and delivered free of charge, it is perfectly natural that this store should be very popular and highly commended by all who patronize it.

C. A. & J. H. BEAN & CO., Dealers in Furniture, Carpets, Ranges, Crockery, Bedding, &c., 153 to 157 Market Street, Lynn, Mass.—There is often considerable difference of opinion as to the standing of a given enterprise in comparison with others of a kindred character, and from the very nature of things it is inevitable that such should be the case, but there are individual instances where superiority is so apparent that no chance exists for honest doubt of the supremacy of an undertaking, and a very prominent case in point is that of the business carried on by Messrs. C. A. & J. H. Bean & Co., for this is unquestionably the leading enterprise of the kind in Lynn, and it is no discredit to others that such should be the case, for this was inaugurated over forty years ago, and has been conducted with marked ability from the beginning. The founder, Mr. J. H. Bean, began operations in 1850, and was succeeded in 1800 by Messrs. C. A. and J. H. Bean, the existing firm name being adopted two years later by the admission of Mr. N. S. Clark to partnership. The present proprietors are natives of this city, and are so well known in business and social circles as to render personal mention unnecessary. The firm deal very largely in furniture, carpets, ranges, bedding, crockery, etc., and carry a heavy stock, made up of the productions of the leading manufacturers and embracing the very latest fashionable novelties. The premises utilized are located at No. 153 to 157 Market Street, comprise the five story building with basement 40 x 65 feet with an ell 40 x 20 feet, three floors, in dimensions. The firm cater to the most intelligent and critical trade, and have a well earned reputation for quoting bottom prices on goods of standard merit, while their assortment is so varied that all tastes can be suited.

BROWN & BALCOM, Successors to Balcom & Young, Manufacturers of Ladies', Misses', and Children's Fine Boots and Shoes, No. 115 Oxford Street, Lynn, Mass.—No higher praise can possibly be given the footwear manufactured by Messrs. Brown & Balcom than to say that in style, quality, grade and workmanship, it is worthy of a firm who are prominent exponents of what may be called the "new era in Lynn shoe manufacturing," for it is a well-known fact that the past Lynn policy of making "cheap" shoes as cheaply as possible has been superseded by one which results in the production of footwear that is stylish, neat, perfect fitting and durable, and yet can be furnished to the trade at prices which enable it to be profitably retailed at popular rates. Messrs. Brown & Balcom are successors to Messrs. Balcom & Young, who founded the business in 1891. They are manufacturers of of ladies', misses' and children's fine boots and shoes, and produce lines of McKay and Goodyear sewed footwear that are conceded by the trade to compare favorably with any goods of similar grade in the market. New and attractive styles are brought out every season, the firm are very successful in furnishing goods that are fully equal to the samples ordered from in every respect, and they are in a position to fill all orders at reasonably short notice, and to meet all honorable competition in prices. The factory is located at No. 115 Oxford Street, and has a floor space of about 10,000 square feet. It is equipped with machinery of the most improved type, and employment is given to a large force of thoroughly competent assistants.

FAULKNER & HOYLE, Apothecaries, Cor. Summer and Church Streets, Lynn, Mass.—Undue conservatism is, of course, not to be commended, but where health and even life itself is in question, it is scarcely possible to carry conservatism too far, and therefore many who make it an invariable rule to have all their prescriptions compounded at the apothecary store of Messrs. Faulkner & Hoyle, located corner Summer and Church streets, have no occasion to apologize for their caution, for here the public are assured no incompatible drugs are mixed by smooth-faced lads whose only credentials are the druggist's linen coat. Since the opening of this business the prescriptions have been compounded and preparations prepared by experienced chemists and pharmacists. Here the public are also sure to obtain fresh drugs of the purest quality, for the stock has not been accumulating for many years, as is too often the case. This enterprise was established in 1892 by the present proprietors who are natives of Lynn. The premises occupied comprise one floor 40x20 feet in dimensions. A full assortment of drugs, medicines and chemicals, etc., and other goods usually found in a first class apothecary store, are always to be found here and customers will receive polite and courteous attention from the gentlemanly clerk employed by this house.

HARNDEN & BLANCHARD, Manufacturers and Commission Dealers in Shoe Stock and Remnant Leather, 449 Union Street. Factory, 20 Albany Street, Lynn, Mass.—The business carried on by Messrs. Harnden & Blanchard was founded a score of years ago, and this firm have long held a leading position among the most prominent manufacturers of, and dealers in, shoe stock and remnant leather, in the state. The office and salesroom are located No. 449 Union Street, and the firm have a Boston office at No. 120 Summer Street, room 4. The factory is at No 20 Albany Street, and is spacious and well-equipped, the machinery being of the most approved type. A specialty with this firm is the manufacture of rock maple wood heels; and the machinery used is so accurate in its operation that each number heel is an exact duplicate of every heel of the same number. Messrs. Harnden & Blanchard are the largest manufacturers of this kind of heel, and fill many large orders, as the rock maple heel is steadily growing in popularity. Parties wishing to buy or sell leather remnants would do well to communicate with this representative firm, as they are in a position to fill orders promptly, and to dispose of remnant leather in large and small quantities at short notices.

MRS. G. A. BOYNTON, Cigars, Tobacco, Fine Confectionery, Fruits, Etc. Daily and Sunda Papers. 201 Franklin Street, Lynn, Mass.—To say that a person deals in periodicals, confectionery, etc., at retail may seem to give a pretty good idea of the store or rather the business, but as a matter of fact it gives a very imperfect idea, as any one will acknowledge who will stop to think of the great difference there is in stores of that kind. Some are well-stocked, well-managed and attractive, others quite the reverse, and therefore to get an adequate idea of Mrs. G. A. Boynton's store which is located at 201 Franklin street, is to accept her cordial invitation to call and examine the goods for yourself. Mrs. Boynton has carried on her present establishment since 1892. She deals in cigars, tobacco, fruits, bakers' supplies, stationery, fancy goods, cotton thread, needles, etc., also all the leading daily and sunday papers. A specialty is made of fine grade confectionery in which a good trade is enjoyed. Her stock is complete in each of its departments, and what is still more important her prices are always in full accordance with the lowest marked rates. She is also agent for J. A. Callahan's Seaside Hand Laundry, all orders in this department being promptly and satisfactorily attended to. Mrs. Boynton furnishes excellent ice-cream by the plate or quantity for family trade, also cold drinks.

W. B. GIFFORD,

CARPETS, ✶ MATTING, ✶ RUGS, ✶ OIL CLOTHS,

AND WALL PAPERS.

Nos. 97 and 99 MARKET STREET,

LYNN, MASS.

The establishment conducted by Mr. W. B. Gifford is one of the most extensive and popular of the kind in this portion of the State, and deserves prominent mention among the representative enterprises of Lynn and vicinity, for it is a credit to both the proprietor and the community, and will compare favorably with many city stores making the highest pretensions. The premises occupied, comprise one floor 100 x 50 feet in dimensions, are located at No. 97 and 99 Market Street. Mr. Gifford carries a very extensive and varied stock made up of Carpets, Matting, Rugs, Oil Cloths, Mats and Wall Papers, etc., etc., and many other articles too numerous to mention. The assortment of house furnishing goods embraces the latest fashionable novelties, and is so complete that all tastes and purses can be suited, the prices being as low as the lowest and the goods being sold strictly on their merits. Many novel and attractive designs are offered. Employment is given to only efficient assistants and callers are promptly and politely served, orders being delivered at short notice. Mr. Gifford makes no pretensions to running a "cheap store," and in fact has not the least desire to establish a reputation for doing so, it is also a fact that he is thoroughly prepared to meet all honorable competition, and does not allow himself to be undersold by any other reputable dealer.

A. S. HOVEY, Dealer in Cigars and Tobacco, Smokers' Articles of all Kinds. Agent for Blake's Laundry. 17 Exchange Street (next to Earl's), Lynn, Mass.—An excellent example of what can be accomplished by enterprise, ability and strict attention to business is that afforded by the success attained by Mr. A. S. Hovey, who carries on a cigar store at 17 Exchange Street, next to Earl's Block, for although Mr. Hovey did not begin operations until 1892 he now has one of the most popular stores of the kind in the city, and his business is still steadily increasing. What makes the store so popular? Well, to begin with, it contains a large and carefully selected stock, including imported and domestic cigars and tobacco, and smokers' articles of all kinds, so you are pretty sure to find just what you want, whether it is strong or mild, high or low priced. Then you can also depend upon receiving prompt and polite attention, for Mr. Hovey carries on the store himself and he recognizes the fact that "time is money" to most of his customers. And there is no cigar store in the city where you are more sure of getting "full value for money received," no matter what you buy or how much you buy of it. The stock is carefully stored and well cared for, and doubtless that is one reason why Mr. Hovey's cigars smoke well and why about all goods bought from him prove uniformly satisfactory. His prices are literally "as low as the lowest"—quality considered -and, in short there is excellent reason for the exceptional popularity enjoyed by this well managed store.

J. A. CROSSCUP, Carpenter and Builder; Office, 10 Central Square, Room 11; Shop, 69 New Chatham Street, Lynn, Mass.—If it be true that a thing well begun is half done it is equally true that success in getting a house built to suit you is largely dependent upon your choice of a builder, and that is one reason why we take pleasure in making prominent mention of Mr. J. A. Crosscup, for he is a carpenter and builder of long experience, and his record proves that he can be depended upon to strictly carry out all his agreements, and to figure very closely on any work in his line. He has executed many important and almost innumerable small commissions in Lynn and vicinity, and as "practice makes perfect" and "experience teaches," it is manifest that he is well qualified to render very valuable assistance to those who contemplate building and wish to have their plans put into practical shape. Mr. Crosscup's office is at 10 Central Square, Room 11, and he has a spacious shop located at 69 New Chatham Street. Employment is given to an adequate force of thoroughly competent assistants, and jobbing orders are assured prompt and careful attention.

ATKINS, HOYT & CO., Dealers in Women's, Misses' and Children's Cut Soles and Leather, 581 Washington Street, Lynn, Mass.—Common fairness demands that mention be made of the enterprise conducted by Messrs. Atkins, Hoyt & Co. in this review of the leading industrial and mercantile undertakings of Lynn, for it is closely identified with the representative industry of the Shoe City, and although of quite recent origin, it has already attained large proportions. The members of this firm are Messrs. W. B. Atkins, J. F. Hoyt, and G. W. Brown, all of whom are Massachusetts men by birth and are widely known in Lynn and vicinity, especially in the shoe trade. They give close personal attention to the filling of orders, and the firm have already gained an enviable reputation for executing commissions both promptly and accurately, and for furnishing cut soles and leather that can be depended upon to "fill the bill" in every particular. Spacious premises located at No. 581 Washington Street are occupied, and employment is given to five competent assistants.

TIN & WOODEN WARE.   CROCKERY & GLASS WARE.

MELVIN A. DAME,
— DEALER IN —

Stoves, Ranges, Furnaces

And Kitchen Furnishing Goods,

PLUMBING, TINSMITHING, GAS AND WATER PIPING,

Stove Repairs and Repairing a Specialty.

29 MUNROE STREET, - - - LYNN, MASS.

LAMP GOODS.   KEROSENE OIL.

The undertaking carried by Mr. Melvin A. Dame is doubtless familiar to many of our readers, for it has been in operation for twenty-five years and has been conducted by its present proprietor since 1868, when it was established. Mr. Dame is a native of N. H., and is thoroughly familiar with every detail of the business with which he is identified, as may easily be seen by the character of the service he offers to the public, for there is not a dealer in stoves, ranges, furnaces, etc., in this vicinity, that is prepared to hold out more genuine inducements to customers. The premises occupied are located at No. 29 Munroe Street, comprise one floor and a basement, each 90x25 feet in size which are well arranged and fitted up with the most improved facilities for the doing of Plumbing, Tinsmithing, Gas and Water Piping, etc., at short notice and in first-class style, and those who appreciate the importance of having work of this kind done in an honest and painstaking manner, can do no better than to place their orders with Mr. Dame. He employs ten assistants and guarantees satisfaction to every customer. The leading makes of stoves, ranges and furnaces are carried in stock as well as a full line of kitchen furnishing goods, and offered in great variety at the lowest market rates. "Honest goods at honest prices" is a very attractive motto, and its spirit is certainly thoroughly carried out at this representative establishment. This is also headquarters for lamp goods, crockery and glass ware.

MRS. H. D. GRAVES, Periodicals and Stationery, Circulating Library, 70 Market Street, Lynn, Mass.—The Lynn Book Store and Circulating Library now conducted by Mrs. H. D. Graves, is one of the best and most popular business establishments of the kind in this town. This enterprise was begun by the present proprietress in 1891. She is a native of New York State, and is so generally known in Lynn both in business and social circles as to render extended personal mention unnecessary. Mrs. Graves is a bookseller and stationer and occupies spacious premises at No. 70 Market Street, 49x23 feet in dimensions. It contains a large and very carefully selected stock, including all the latest popular novels, periodicals and magazines, etc. This lady deals also in fashionable and business stationery, envelopes, pens, and other articles usually to be found in a first-class store of this kind. A full assortment of goods is carried in each department, which embraces the latest novelties. The prices quoted here are always in strict accordance with the lowest market prices, and the goods vary so greatly in style and in cost, that all tastes and all purses can easily be suited. Four reliable and obliging assistants are kept employed so that all callers are promptly attended and assured of polite and immediate attendance.

MISS ALICIA M. FARLEY, Millinery Parlors, Rooms 6 and 8, 130 Market Street, Lynn, Mass.— The question of just what "style" is has never been satisfactorily answered, and probably never will be—at least not in words, for there seems to be some ideas that cannot be properly expressed in words—but all of us know what we mean when we say that a certain garment, or other article of wearing apparel is "stylish," although in many cases it would be impossible for us to explain the difference between it and some other article equally costly, equally rich, and made with equal care and yet not stylish in the least. Therefore, when we say that the millinery work produced at the establishment of Miss Alicia M. Farley at rooms 6 and 8, on the second story of No. 130 Market Street, is "stylish," we give a better idea of its character than could otherwise be given by pages of description, and we need hardly add that it is satisfactory to the most fastidious tastes. Millinery goods of the most fashionable and latest styles are dealt in, while particular attention is given to custom millinery work, and as two efficient assistants are employed, orders can generally be filled at very short notice. Miss Farley gives the enterprise close personal attention and supervision, and as no work in the least degree defective is knowingly allowed to leave the establishment, entire satisfaction can be guaranteed.

JOHN A. DOYLE, Dealer in Meats, Poultry and Vegetables of all Kinds, 56 Ocean Street, Lynn, Mass. A progressive store and one furnishing the very best advantages in its line of trade is that conducted by Mr. Jno. A. Doyle at 56 Ocean Street, Lynn. It has now been in successful operation for many years, and the goods of the Ocean Street market are very favorably known in all parts of the city. Mr. Doyle conducts a select and thriving retail trade. The store premises are 50x30 feet in dimensions, and tastefully fitted up. The large stock carried includes all kinds of fine groceries, fresh and dried meats, poultry and vegetables. No pains are spared to secure to patrons the very latest and best things in the market at bottom prices. Several competent and experienced assistants are employed. In the range of its stock and fine quality of goods, as well as low prices, this reliable market affords facilities equal to the very best anywhere. We can assure our readers of an exceptional degree of satisfaction in trading here. The first-class bargains offered here deserve the careful consideration of all those appreciating the best. The service is of the most modern kind, and all orders are promptly delivered.

HOYT & ROWE, Manufacturers of Ladies' Fine Hand Turn Slippers. Kid and Satin in the Most Popular Styles, 408 Union and 9 Exchange Sts., Earl's Building.—Retailers say that all ladies' slippers can be divided into two classes—those that sell and those that won't sell—and they say that the latter are about the most unprofitable goods that can be carried in stock, for it is almost impossible to "work them off" at any price. Hence they take especial care in the selection of ladies' fine slippers, and that is one reason why there is already an extensive demand for the goods produced by Messrs. Hoyt & Rowe, although that firm did not begin business until 1893, for the ladies' fine hand turn slippers, including kid and satin in the most popular styles, have proved to be very "popular" in fact as well as in name, and the trade like to handle them because there is not only "money in them" but also because they attract very desirable trade to the store which carries them in stock. The firm utilize well equipped premises located in Earl's Building, Nos. 408 Union and 9 Exchange Sts., and are prepared to fill large orders at short notice, and to quote bottom prices on goods that sell on their merits wherever introduced. Mr. Frank N. Hoyt, is a native of Lynn, and Mr. George H. Rowe is a native of New Hampshire. Both these gentlemen are practical shoe manufacturers who understand the business thoroughly in every detail, and they are very successful in producing goods that combine style, beauty and durability, and that will hold their own in comparison with any of similar grade in the market.

SHOE FACTORIES, UNION STREET.

F. L. BARNARD, Optician, Dealer in Diamonds, Watches, etc. Eyes carefully tested and accurately fitted to spectacles and eyeglasses. Special attention given to oculists' prescriptions. 307 Union Street, Lynn, Mass.—If there is one stock of jewelry, watches, and optical goods, in Lynn, which deserves the highest position, when judged from the standpoint of general desirability, it is that to be found in the store located at 307 Union Street, and carried on by Mr. F. L. Barnard, for this assortment is extremely varied, exceptionally well-selected, and remarkably "clean," it containing practically no unsaleable goods whatever. Nor is it surprising that it should be so desirable in every department, for "practice, makes perfect" and the proprietor of this establishment has had ten years experience in the present line of business. Mr. Barnard is a Vermont man by birth, began operations in his present line at Lynn, in 1883, where during his long and honorable business career he has become one of the best known jewelers and opticians in this city. Mr. Barnard is a practical optician and is prepared to test the vision and provide glasses expressly suited to the conditions prevailing, eyes being carefully tested and special attention given to oculists' prescriptions. Jewelry, diamonds, watches, optical goods, sheet music, and musical instruments, etc., are all well represented in the stock, the very latest novelties being obtained as soon as they appear in the market. Orders can almost always be filled at very short notice, the charges being uniformly moderate in every department.

THE BUBIER LABORATORY CO., Manufacturing Pharmacists, 311 Union Street, Room 4 Lynn, Mass.—The remedial and preventive powers of carefully prepared drugs constitutes one of the greatest triumphs of modern medicine. Chemistry combined with progressive pharmacy has gone very far toward solving the difficulties and dangerous features of most diseases, besides providing many valuable preventives. The Bubier Laboratory Co. is a Lynn establishment which, in the manufacture of pharmaceutical specialties, has built up a national reputation. The business has been characterized from the start by exceptional enterprise and thorough scientific ability. The senior member of the company, Nathan G. Bubier, Ph. G., is a graduate in pharmacy, and has enjoyed very wide and thorough experience in the manufacture of this class of preparations devoting his energies to this branch of the business. The other partner Mr. Wm. A. Burrill, is also an experienced manufacturer, and financier, having charge of that branch of the business. The company manufactures all staple lines of drugs, beside its own popular specialties. These include "Laxative Salz" "Litho Seltzer" and "Seltzerina." These preparations have proved everywhere successful and are highly recommended by the medical faculty. The company uses only the most pure and salutary ingredients. The utmost care is taken also to ensure accurate skill in compounding the preparations. A large wholesale trade is conducted and the popular specialties of this house can be found at leading druggists in all parts of the country. Their reliability is of the highest and unvarying standard, and fully merits the confidence of physicians which they so largely enjoy.

JOSEPH C. LEWIS,
SIGN WRITER,
150 MUNROE STREET, LYNN, MASS.

The old maxim, "if you want a thing well done do it yourself," is worthy of careful consideration, for the general principle it embodies is sound and valuable, but it should not always be followed literally for it is obvious that a man who wanted a job of watch repairing done and should do it himself would be very liable to make a bad mess of it. The same may be said of a job of sign painting, for although about everybody (who has not tried it) thinks he can paint all right, the fact is that experience and skill are essential to success in this as in every other trade, and although a green hand may do a job "after a fashion," that fashion is not at all apt to be either useful or ornamental. It not only pays to have your painting done by practical sign painters but it pays to take pains to see that those painters are "as good as they make 'em," and one sure way to get that kind of help is to place your orders with Mr. Joseph C. Lewis, for he is a first-class Sign and Ornamental Painter, using only reliable materials and employing five thoroughly experienced assistants, and can therefore do first-class work, making a specialty of wood, cloth, glass and metal signs. Mr. Lewis is moderate in his charges, too, and has facilities which enable him to execute all commissions, large and small at short notice. Orders by mail or otherwise delivered at 150 Munroe Street, are assured prompt and painstaking attention, estimates being cheerfully made on application.

THEO. H. KELLAM, Dealer in Groceries and Provisions, Coal and Wood, Hay and Grain, Kellam's Corner, Telephone 121-3, Corner North Federal and Boston Streets, Lynn, Mass.—The grocery business has developed remarkably of late years, and an impressive showing of its present condition was made at the late "food and health exhibition" for a more attractive and better exhibition was never given in New England, and it indicated more clearly than anything else could the high average standing of the men now in the trade and their disregard of petty jealousies in the carrying on of their business. Among the well known of our Lynn business men is Mr. Theo. H. Kellam whose store is located at the corner of North Federal and Boston Streets, for he has carried on operations here since 1886, and controls an extensive and very desirable retail trade. The premises utilized comprise one building covering an area of 2,500 square feet and contains one of the most carefully chosen and complete stocks of groceries, provisions, fancy and canned goods, hay, grain, coal and wood to be found in Lynn, the articles all being adapted to the requirements of the best family trade. Mr. Kellam has become well-known in both business and social circles, and represented Ward 6, in the Common Council for two years, and has built up a good substantial business. He has the sole agency for Lynn for the celebrated Bridal Veil flour. He quotes the lowest market rates on all the goods handled, and employs three efficient assistants thus being in a position to ensure prompt and satisfactory service to patrons at all times.

D. K. MILLETT, Ice Cream at Wholesale and Retail, also Water Ices and Frozen Pudding Made to Order of Superior Quality, and no Adulteration. A Specialty made of Supplying Families and Parties, 16 Brimblecom Street, Lynn, Mass.—It was Sam Weller who said: "Weal pie is werry good, provided you know the lady wot makes it," and with equal truth it may be said that ice cream is palatable, healthful and nourishing, provided it is made by one who uses first-class material, has ample facilities, and thoroughly understands his business. Well, that is just what may be truthfully said of Mr. D. K. Millett, and many residents of Lynn will cordially agree with that assertion, for he has carried on business here for over 30 years, and his ice cream is universally acknowledged to be equal to the best and to be unsurpassed if not unequalled for uniformity of merit. His facilities for making ice cream are the best in the city, and some idea of their magnitude and of the extent of his business may be gained from the fact that he utilizes a three-horse steam engine, and has ice chests capable of storing 40 gallons of cream. It is kept in stone jars; everything in and about the premises is kept neat, clean and sweet, and all the material used is carefully selected and skillfully handled, so it is no wonder that the results are uniformly satisfactory. Mr. Millett sells at wholesale and retail, and makes a specialty of supplying families and parties; not only with ice cream but also with water ices and frozen pudding, which are made to order and are guaranteed to be of superior quality and absolutely free from adulteration. Orders are delivered at the residence of customers; and it is hardly necessary to say that one having Mr. Millett's facilities and experience and doing a large business, is in a position to quote as low prices as can be named on cream and ices skillfully made from strictly first-class material.

A. M. TUFTS, Taxidermist, All kinds of Birds and Animals preserved in a superior manner. Glass Shades and Cases of Birds put up to order on the most reasonable terms. Extra Singing Canaries. Brass, Tin and Wood Cages, Bird Seed, Bath Dishes. Fur Skin Rugs Made to Order. 160 Oxford Street, Lynn, Mass.—The taxidermist's art has reached a high state of perfection, and to it the world is greatly indebted, not only for the faithfulness with which it preserves the forms of birds and animals that have become, or are fast becoming extinct, but for fine specimens of the animal life of all climes to be found in our museums; which without the aid of this great art would be forever unknown to those who are unable to visit the countries from which they come. As a master of taxidermy, Mr. A. M. Tufts of Lynn has no superior, and those who have need of his services will receive the utmost satisfaction, as is proved by the many fine examples of his work to be found at his store, 160 Oxford Street. Mr. Tufts is a native of Lynn, and during the twenty years he has been in business here, has by his integrity and ability acquired an enviable and well deserved reputation. His store and workroom is a spacious apartment, its dimensions being 25 by 60 feet, and here will be found, in addition to the specimens above referred to, all kinds of singing birds, especially fine canaries, which are celebrated as beautiful singers. Bird cages of all designs, in brass, tin or wood are procurable here on the most reasonable terms and made in a superior manner. For stuffed animals or birds, Mr. Tufts is prepared to furnish on order and at short notice, glass shades and cases, at prices that are remarkably low. Mr. Tufts also makes a specialty of fur skin rugs, and those who desire work of this kind will be served promptly and in the most acceptable manner.

"WINDSOR CAFE."

W. J. LARGE, Proprietor.

Best of Board Served Promptly. 21 Tickets, Ladies $2.75, Gents $3.50. 6 Dinner Tickets, $1.25; Single Dinners 25 cts.

76 Central Avenue, LYNN, MASS.

There are not so many first-class restaurants in Lynn as to make such establishments too common to call for particular notice, and indeed this city is not exceptional in this respect, for although the United States leads the world in some things, it makes a sorry showing in comparison with other civilized countries as far as public restaurants are concerned. The rarity of attractive establishments where good food, in good variety, well cooked is courteously and promptly served to every caller, has frequently been referred to by strangers traveling in this country, as well as by native writers, and we will not dwell upon it, preferring the much more pleasant task of informing our readers where a restaurant may be found successfully conducted. The "Windsor Cafe" carried on by Mr. W. J. Large, is of course, well known to many of our readers, but to those who are not familiar with it, we have simply to say that it amply supplies the demand for the above conditions and at popular prices, as a trial will conclusively prove. The prices are 21 tickets for ladies, $2.75, 21 tickets for gents, $3.50, 6 dinner tickets, $1.25, single dinners, 25 cents. Since founding the "Windsor Cafe," Mr. Large has developed it by giving careful attention to the wants of the public, sparing no pains to provide an efficient, economical and satisfactory service, giving it his personal attention. It is located at 76 Central Avenue, being central to the business part of the city. The premises utilized cover an area of 1,200 square feet, and as six assistants are employed, and the bill-of-fare being made up of the best the market affords, Mr. Large deserves the success he has labored so faithfully to attain.

L. L. COLBY, Dealer in Choice Groceries, Flour, Molasses, Teas and Coffees, Spices, Etc., Fresh, Salt and Smoked Meats, Butter, Cheese, Eggs and Meats a Specialty, 52 Union Street, Lynn, Mass.—There are many grocery and provision stores in this city and it is by no means an easy task to pick out those which can be truthfully referred to as representative, but there is no uncertainty in the case of the establishment conducted by L. L. Colby, and located at 52 Union Street, for the prominence of this store is evident and indisputable, and both the magnitude and the character of the patronage it receives are such as to remove all cause for doubt of its holding a leading position. From the outset he has catered to discriminating family trade by carrying a full assortment of strictly first-class groceries and provisions and by quoting the lowest rates consistent with the handling of such goods; and the fact that four assistants are required to attend to the orders received, indicate that the policy is generally appreciated. No trouble is spared to ensure the prompt and accurate delivery of orders and to furnish only such goods as will give complete satisfaction; but should mistakes occur they will be promptly and cheerfully rectified, and steps taken to prevent a recurrence of the trouble. Mr. Colby is a native of Brunswick, Maine, and has been located in Lynn since 1888, where is conducted an extensive retail business in Choice Groceries, Flour, Molasses, Teas and Coffees, Spices, etc., also Fresh, Salt and Smoked Meats, Butter, Cheese, Eggs, etc., all of which are selected expressly for family use.

LUDLOW BERKLEY, Tailor, 27 Summer Street, Lynn, Mass.—To many people a suit of clothes is a suit of clothes, and that is all there is to it, they apparently believe that if a certain quantity of material is used it makes no difference how it is put together as long as it takes the shape of a suit, and hence are easily imposed upon by such dealers as are disposed to work off their goods more by their appearance when new than by their real merits. It may be taken as an axiom that the $5.00 spent for superior workmanship and trimmings are invested to better advantage than any other portion of the purchase money, and those who will accept and act on this hint will find their reward in improved appearance and superior durability of their wearing apparel. To assure the best of material put together in the most skillful manner, an establishment of repute must be patronized, and none better can be chosen than that conducted by Mr. Ludlow Berkley, at No. 27 Summer Street. This enterprise was established by its present proprietor in 1890 and has been steadily prosecuted with constantly increasing success. This gentleman is a Merchant Tailor and very well known in Lynn and vicinity and has that thorough knowledge of his business so essential to the highest success. Fine tailoring, repairing and cleaning are done by several experienced workmen. The premises occupied comprise two rooms 20 x 20 feet and a shop 20 x 20 feet in size, and a large stock of cloths is carried while first-class clothing is made to order, a perfect fit and good workmanship being guaranteed.

COLUMBUS HOUSE, Stephen Darcy, Proprietor, 156 Broad Street, Lynn, Mass.—When Columbus discovered this Western Continent, he found, what many people at various times have desired to find, namely a comfortable and attractive place to stop for several weeks while prosecuting the special business which had sent him forth on his long voyage. This present year is called the Columbian year, in honor of the great discoverer, and we know that likewise all our readers in this vicinity will appreciate the value of having their attention called to one of the pleasantest and best places to stop at while sojourning in Lynn. We refer to the Columbus House at 156 Broad Street, Mr. Stephen Darcy, Proprietor, which, established during the present year, has already built up a high reputation for the excellence of its service and accommodations. The Columbus House is finely situated in one of the most attractive parts of the city, convenient to the cars, business streets and places of amusement. The service and table are of the very best kind while the rates will be found uniformly moderate. There are fifteen large and handsomely furnished guests' rooms, in addition to the parlors, dining rooms, etc. In every feature of a first-class house our readers will find the 'Columbus" at the very head of the line. They should be sure to call here when planning to stop in Lynn either for a long or short period. Mr. Darcy is a thoroughly experienced hotel man and has won the thorough confidence of many of the best people and traveling public in this section.

PLEASANT HILLS PARK.

Thirty Minutes Ride from Boston.
Fifteen Minutes from Lynn.

A FEW CHOICE LOTS.

First Payment, $5.00.
Future Payments, $1.00, $1.25, $1.50
per Week.

NO INTEREST. — NO TAXES.

HIGH LAND.   GOOD DRAINAGE.   SIDEWALKS and STREETS.
WATER PIPES ALL LAID.

The Suburban Land Improvement Co.,

--- *CURRIER'S BUILDING,* ---

333 UNION ST., Rooms 12-13, LYNN.

**ELECTRIC CARS WITHIN FIVE MINUTES WALK,
EVERY 15 MINUTES.**

N. D. JOHNSON,

102 MUNROE STREET, LYNN, MASS.

FINE REPAIRING OF

Locks, Keys, Umbrellas, Parasols, Trunks, Traveling Bags, Etc.

ELECTRIC BATTERIES, BELLS, SPEAKING TUBES.

NEXT DOOR TO MUSIC.

SIGN OF GOLD KEY.

Trunks, Locks, Door Locks, Pad Locks, Key Rings, Key Tags, Etc.

If the rank of an enterprise is to be determined by its genuine usefulness to all classes in the community, then that conducted by Mr. N. D. Johnson should most certainly be placed at the head so far as Lynn is concerned, for Mr. Johnson carries on a general repair shop, and has without doubt saved some thousands of dollars worth of articles from being thrown away or disused, and has proved a great public convenience. Mr. Johnson is almost universally known in Lynn and vicinity. His shop is located at 102 Munroe Street, and is easily identified by the sign of the "gold key," and contains all necessary facilities for the repairing of locks, keys, umbrellas, parasols, trunks, traveling bags, etc., also electric batteries, bells and speaking tubes, at short notice and in first-class style, and there are few men in this city equally skillful at this kind of work. He is uniformly moderate in his charges, and spares no pains to deliver orders promptly at the time promised. Trunks, locks, door locks, padlocks, keys, tags, etc., are offered for sale at low rates, and every article bought of Mr. Johnson will surely prove just as represented.

"**NATIONAL POPCORN WORKS,**" Eaton & Hobbs, Proprietors, Manufacturers of Popcorn Goods of all Kinds, 8 Washington Street, Lynn, Mass.—If the comparative importance of manufactured goods are to be determined by their attractive quality, then the product of the establishment carried on by the National Popcorn Works of which Messrs. Eaton & Hobbs are the proprietors, is surely worthy of prominent and favorable mention, for the goods they make are attractive in the highest degree, for they are carefully made from selected materials and guaranteed to prove just as represented in every respect. The assortment includes popcorn goods of all kinds, manufactured from selected grades of pearl corn, put up with pure sugars, and the best of flavors, so it will be seen that The National Popcorn Works are prepared to cater satisfactorily to all tastes, and we may add to all purses too, their prices being low enough to suit the most economically disposed. Messrs. Eaton & Hobbs founded their present business here at Lynn in 1882, and now occupy premises located at No. 8 Washington Street, comprising a three story building fitted up with every facility for the manufacture of popcorn goods, including a four horse power engine and seven horse power boiler. The business is exclusively manufacturing and wholesale, but as five thoroughly reliable assistants are constantly employed, all orders are promptly filled, while the stock is constantly being renewed, and as regards freshness and desirability, will not suffer by comparison with any of a similar kind in the market. They make a specialty of fairs, and sea shore or summer resort trade, and make bids for privileges in such places, while they supply all wholesale demands promptly. Their goods can be obtained during the summer months at the following places: Sea Beach, East Walk, Sea Beach Palace, Feltman's Pavilion, Coney Island, N. Y.; cor. Boulevard and Sea Side Ave., Rockaway Beach, N. Y.; Bath Beach, N. Y.; Plaza Hotel, Schnitzler's Merry-go-Round, Asbury Park, N. J.

DR. DANIEL GRIFFIN, graduate of Boston Dental College, Dentist, Pevear Block, Room 16, cor. Monroe and Washington Sts., Lynn, Mass.—As truly as the character of the work of a mechanic is largely dependent upon the condition of the tools he uses, so is the condition of the food when it enters the stomach largely dependent upon the condition of the teeth, and yet although everybody knows that the teeth are provided expressly to prepare the food for the stomach, many allow them to get into so bad a condition that they are almost worthless for that purpose—and then wonder why they have dyspepsia or some of the many other diseases that almost surely result from the swallowing of improperly prepared food and the consequent overwork and general abuse of the stomach. Of course there are other reasons why the teeth should be kept in good condition—one's appearance; one's comfort, both of these are largely dependent upon the condition of one's teeth—but health is the most important thing of all, and the intimate connection of good teeth and good health should alone be enough to make everybody consult a competent dentist as soon as the first symptom of affected teeth makes itself manifest. There are many competent dentists in this city, and among them is Dr. Daniel Griffin, whose office is located in room 16, Pevear Block, corner of Munroe and Washington Streets and is equipped with the latest improved apparatus and instruments for the practice of dentistry in all its branches. Dr. Griffin has made a specialty of diseases of the gums and has treated the same with marked success. He is a native of Massachusetts, and a graduate of the Boston Dental College and has been engaged in his profession here at Lynn since 1889 and is therefore very generally known, both professionally and socially, throughout the city. His charges are uniformly moderate and we may be permitted to say that his work is durable as well as satisfactory in other respects.

ANDREW WELSH,
DEALER IN
CIGARS AND TOBACCO, NEWSPAPERS AND STATIONERY,
TROY LAUNDRY AGENCY,
No. 45 MARKET SQUARE, - - - WEST LYNN, MASS.

S. G. GUNN, Dealer in Gents' Furnishings, Headquarters for Blake's Custom Laundry, 305 Union Street, Lynn, Mass.—There are probably few of our Lynn readers but what are more or less familiar with the Gentlemen's Furnishing Goods Store carried on by Mr. S. G. Gunn, for this is one of the best known establishments of the kind in the city, having been conducted from its inception with marked ability and success. This establishment was founded in 1890, by its present proprietor, Mr. S. G. Gunn, who is a native of Maine, and has proved himself fully competent to gain and maintain an enviable reputation and wide popularity for his enterprise. The premises utilized are located at 305 Union Street, comprising one floor 50 x 15 feet in dimensions. They contain one of the most extensive and complete stocks of gents' furnishings to be found in Lynn, the latest fashionable novelties being fully represented, and the variety being so great that all tastes can easily be suited. Mr. Gunn cordially invites all interested to call and inspect his assortment, being convinced that it will prove satisfactory to the most critical. In addition to dealing in gents' furnishings Mr. Gunn carries a choice line of umbrellas, and does an extensive laundry business, he being agent, and his establishment the headquarters for Blake's Custom Laundry. He gives close personal supervision to the most minute details of both departments of his business, where the workmanship is equal to the best, moderate prices quoted, and the facilities are such that all commissions can be executed at short notice.

R. F. RUNALS, D. D. S., Graduate of Boston Dental College, 1890, is located at 94 Market Street, three doors from Andrew Street, where he has fitted up dental parlors for the special convenience of his patients. Dr. Runals has been located in Lynn for the past two years, in which time he has been successful in establishing a practice of some considerable extent. He is equipped with the most improved instruments and appliances for all dental operations, being able thereby to save much time and suffering for his patient. After graduating the Doctor was located for a year with one of the largest crown and plate workers in New England. Having gained much experience in this line, he has not only new ideas, but many improved methods in removable bridges, roofless plates, aluminum and gold plates. He makes a specialty of the preservation of natural teeth. Having taken a course in the study of anatomy of the teeth under the microscope, he is enabled to insert fillings permanently, and with little or no pain. Those requiring the service of a skilled dentist should consult the Doctor. Examinations are free, and courteous attention given to all.

RUSSELL & CO., Moulded Counters, Shoe Mfrs.' Supplies, 93 and 95 Oxford Street, Lynn, Mass., U. S. A.—This is a "bustling" concern that is not content with trying to "keep up with the procession," but is bold and enterprising in its methods and does not try to dodge but fairly challenges honorable competition. As wholesale dealers in moulded and manufacturers of two-piece cemented counters, and shoe manufacturers' supplies in general, including straw pattern and leather board, innersoles, linings, shanking, etc., they do an extensive business and operate a factory at Woburn, Mass., besides the one located in Lynn, at 93 and 95 Oxford Street. Employment is given to an adequate force of efficient assistants, and orders are assured prompt and careful attention and can be filled at very short notice, and at prices in strict accordance with the lowest market rates. The business is steadily increasing, and the more closely it is investigated the more evident it becomes that it has a most prosperous future before it if reliance can be placed upon the continuance of present conditions.

GEORGE D. SARGEANT, Pres.   EDWIN H. JOHNSON, Sec'y.   ISRAEL A. NEWHALL, Clerk.

Established 1828.
Lynn * Mutual * Fire * Insurance * Company,
SAVINGS BANK BUILDING.
112 MARKET STREET, - - - - LYNN, MASS.

A review of the leading enterprises of the shoe city that contained no mention of the Lynn Mutual Fire Insurance Company would be sadly incomplete, not only because that organization has been in existence 65 years and is very closely identified with the development of the city but also because it has been so ably managed from the first as to be one of the best examples in the State of the advantages arising from legitimate and conservative mutual fire insurance. It was established in 1828, and it has the record of 65 successive years of business without an assessment. The company now returns 100 per cent. dividend on expiring five year policies, and it is hardly necessary to add that the insurance it offers is in very active demand, as the company is as prompt in the adjustment and payment of losses as it is conservative in the placing of risks. The officers and directors are composed of the leading business men of the city, as will be seen by an examination of the following list: President, George D. Sargeant; Secretary, Edwin H. Johnson; Clerk, Israel A. Newhall. Directors, George D. Sargeant, Alfred Cross, Edwin H. Johnson, Rufus Kimball, Charles H. Newhall, Daniel A. Caldwell, Roland G. Usher, James S. Newhall, Warren S. Hixon.

F. A. EASTON, Newspapers, Blank Books, Stationery of all kinds, Pocketbooks, Card Cases, etc. Subscriptions received for any publication. Cor. Main and Pleasant Streets, Worcester, Mass., Central Square, Lynn, Mass. Mr. F. A. Easton's establishment in Central Square has been described as "a stationery store that is never stationary,"—the idea, of course, being to emphasize the fact that the management is always "on the move," and hence is always "up to the times" in every respect. If you wish to see the latest novelties in writing papers, in envelopes, in ink stands, in pens and pen holders, in writing materials and stationery of all kinds, just drop in at Mr. Easton's store and there you will find them, you will also find a full assortment of "staple" stationery, including blank books, forms, and every kind of office supplies; and you will find pocket books, card cases, bric-a-brac, periodicals, newspapers, in short, all you could expect to find in a first class city stationery and variety store. Mr. Easton receives subscriptions for any publication at publisher's rates, and he does a large business in this department alone, as many prefer to order from him rather than run the risk of sending money by mail. He carries on another large store in Worcester, Mass., and enjoys such relations with the trade as to enable him to easily meet all honorable competition and to quote as low prices as can be named on goods of equal merit. Ample assistance is employed and both large and small buyers are assured prompt, careful and courteous attention.

CENTRAL SQUARE, LYNN.

GEORGE JENKINS, Auctioneer, Real Estate and Insurance, Mortgages Negotiated. 10 Central Square, Room 7, Fuller's Block, Lynn, Mass.—Mr. George Jenkins holds a leading position among the real estate and insurance men of the Shoe City, and it is not in the least surprising that such is the case, for the service afforded by him is not only comprehensive but is very complete in every detail and no one bears a higher reputation for the prompt and satisfactory execution of all commissions placed in his hands. A leading specialty with Mr. Jenkins is the negotiation of mortgages, and if any of our readers contemplate the placing of a mortgage for a large or small amount they would do well to communicate with him as he is in a position to negotiate such loans promptly and on the most favorable terms obtainable. A large insurance business is also done, Mr. Jenkins representing such companies as the Mercantile, of Boston, the Western, of Toronto, and the New England Accident, of Boston, and being prepared to furnish "insurance that insures" at the lowest rates. His office is located in Room 7, Fuller's Block, 10 Central Square, and callers are assured prompt and courteous attention—communications by mail also being promptly responded to.

C. T. CURTIS & SON,
PIANO AND FURNITURE MOVING.
OFFICE, 64 ANDREW STREET.   RESIDENCE, 57 SOUTH STREET.
LYNN, - - - MASS.

Careful people realize the importance of employing the best of service for moving valuable goods, such as pianos and furniture. They cannot afford to take risks, as mended articles can never be made as good as they were before. The firm of Messrs. C. T. Curtis & Son, of Lynn, piano and furniture movers, is one of the oldest and best known of local concerns in this line. For many years they have handled every feature of the business with thorough success and satisfactory results. All kinds of general jobbing and teaming work are promptly attended to. They have a first-class equipment, and can supply suitable teams for every sort of out of town work. The special feature for which they have established the highest reputation is the moving of pianos and fine furniture. This is packed with the most complete and thorough care. Only experienced men are employed, and no pains spared to secure the very best satisfaction to patrons. Promptness and reliability are the two mottoes of this leading establishment. Their rates are equal to the best. They have also unexcelled facilities for storing of furniture on reasonable terms. The office is at 64 Andrew Street. Telephone connection. All orders receive immediate attention.

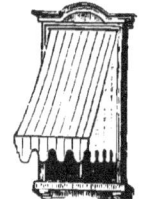

H. H. FULLAM & CO., (Formerly with White & Co.) Makers of Awnings, Tents, Wagon Covers, Bags, Etc. Awnings Taken Down, Stored and Insured. House Awnings a Specialty. 118 Munroe Street, Lynn, Mass.—Awnings are now used very extensively on private houses as well as on public buildings, stores, etc., for it has been found that the saving they make by preventing the fading of carpets, curtains, etc., more than compensate for their cost, to say nothing of the much greater healthfulness and pleasantness of a house equipped with them. Awnings are ornamental as well as useful, that is if they are accurately cut and fitted, for otherwise they look as slovenly as an ill-fitting garment, but there need be no difficulty in getting perfect fitting and thoroughly well made awnings, and one sure way to accomplish this is to place the order with Messrs. H. H. Fullam & Co., located at 118 Munroe Street, for they make a specialty of house awnings and turn out work equal to the best in every respect. Mr. Fullam is a native of Maine and began business for himself here at Lynn in 1887, under the style of H. H. Fullam & Co., having formerly been with White & Co. He manufactures awnings, tents, wagon covers, bags, etc.; does repairing in a neat and durable manner, at moderate rates. Awnings will be taken down, stored, and insured, all postal orders being promptly attended to, and executed at short notice in a most satisfactory manner.

H. H. FULLAM & CO.,
Livery, Boarding and Baiting Stable,
210 UNION STREET,   LYNN, MASS.

W. D. BROWN,

PIANOS, ORGANS,

MUSICAL MERCHANDISE.   TUNING AND REPAIRING.

Haines Bros. Pianos and Other Makes.

84 MARKET STREET,   **LYNN, MASS.**

If the public in general could only understand that no individual, or firm or corporation holds or can hold a monopoly of the making of first-class pianos, there would soon be a change in the business methods of certain manufacturers, who at present are relying largely upon loud boasting and constant belittling of their competitors' work. Of course, many people who know nothing about pianos, feel that they must have a piano of a certain make, or else in all probability get cheated, but if they would only confide in the judgment of a reputable dealer, who is not a manufacturer, they would soon discover the fact that they could get equally as good a piano as though they had paid a much larger price, simply on account of the name. In this connection we call attention to the business conducted by Mr. W. D. Brown, at No. 84 Market street, for this gentleman is considered an expert judge of what constitutes a good piano, and is reliable in his representations to his customers, so that those purchasing an instrument of him are sure of getting just what they pay for. He constantly has some fine pianos and organs besides musical merchandise at his rooms from which customers can select. Those intending to buy or rent a piano or organ would do well to call or communicate with Mr. Brown before engaging elsewhere, as he is prepared to make such terms as will accommodate his patrons. Six reliable assistants are employed, and all orders for tuning and repairing will receive prompt attention and be carefully done.

R. A. SPALDING & CO., Dealers in Foreign and Domestic Dry Goods, 11 and 13 Market Street, Lynn, Mass.—About a third of a century has elapsed since the establishment of the business carried on by Messrs. R. A. Spalding & Co., and as it has always been conducted on legitimate principles and in such a way as to assure satisfactory goods at reasonable prices to patrons, it is not at all surprising that it should rank second to no enterprise in the city in true popularity. The firm is composed of Messrs. R. A. Spalding, F. E. Abbott, and E. A. Merritt, all of whom are natives of the old Bay State. As dealers in foreign and domestic dry and fancy goods they utilize spacious premises at 11 and 13 Market Street, and carry a stock that is large, carefully selected, and complete in every department, for it is constantly being renewed and one can safely depend upon finding the latest novelties in dry and fancy goods at this popular store. Messrs. R. A. Spalding & Co. make no extravagant claims as regards goods and prices—in fact, some think that they go to the other extreme and are unduly conservative in their methods, but however that may be it is an undeniable fact that a more strictly reliable house cannot be found in the county, and that patrons of this store are assured an opportunity to get seasonable, fashionable and generally satisfactory goods at the lowest market rates. Special attention is given to the maintenance of the service at the highest possible standard of efficiency, and employment is given to twenty-five competent assistants, so that callers are waited upon promptly, politely, and intelligently, while the misrepresentation of goods is strictly forbidden, and should mistakes be made they will be promptly and cheerfully corrected.

I. H. ESTES, Wholesale and Retail Dealer in Hay, Grain and Straw, corner of Estes and Broad Sts., Lynn, Mass.—It is fully as important nowadays to see that horses and live stock are provided with wholesome and reliable food as to do this for human beings, partly because they cannot so well judge for themselves, and also because no line of business can be successful without well-kept stocks. It always pays to get the best goods in this line—as to obtain others is practically to throw money away. One of the most popular and successful establishments of Lynn, is that of Mr. I. H. Estes, wholesale and retail dealer in hay, grain and straw at the corner of Estes & Broad Sts. It is also one of the oldest city stores, having been established here by Mr. Estes in 1859. The store building is a substantial structure, two stories in height and 33 x 45 feet in dimensions. Ample storage facilities are enjoyed and the stock is an exceptionally large one, complete in every department. It represents both Eastern and Western centers of supply and can thus afford a very wide range of choice. The prices are uniformly low and reasonable. Three experienced men are employed with good teaming conveniences and all orders delivered without delay. Our readers can count upon the very best goods and service in trading with this old reliable house. Mr. Estes is a native of Lynn and holds a widely recognized place among its most progressive and solid merchants. His experience in his special lines has extended over a third of a century, and the successful trade now conducted represents carefully perfected methods and square liberal dealings from the very first.

HOTEL WAVE.

3 New Ocean St., Swampscott, Mass. - AT KING'S BEACH.

OPEN THROUGHOUT THE YEAR.

MRS. M. A. LITCH, - Swampscott, Mass.

No place on the north shore has a higher reputation for the beauty and eligibility of its situation than Swampscott. Nearness to Boston and intermediate position between Lynn and Salem are also strong points in its favor, apart from its own intrinsic merits. The sea life at Swampscott is equal in attractiveness and wide range to the best sea shore resorts. The scenery of the beaches and harbor is unique for striking and beautiful effects. Among the best hotels of Swampscott, which for years past have afforded homelike and attractive facilities at all seasons of the year, the Hotel Wave, of King's Beach, holds a deservedly high position. It has now been a successful feature of local life since 1886. Its position at this popular beach is all that could be desired. It is within one minute of the electric cars to Boston, and five minutes of the Swampscott station on the B. & M. R. R. The surf-bathing at this point is unexcelled, the beach being of the finest even sand, and the surf itself sufficiently strong to impart a good reaction, yet not too heavy for deep-water swimming when desired. The fishing and sailing between this point and Nahant are too well known to need detailed reference. The Hotel Wave is a fine new structure, three stories high, and with average dimensions of 60x40 feet. It is fitted in the finest modern style, the seventeen guest rooms being large, airy with good view on all sides. Steam heat, running water, and all modern conveniences are on each floor. The hotel is open throughout the year, and is very popular, not only in the summer, but also in the winter, the sheltered position and nearness to the water, giving a milder tone to the atmosphere generally, as is well known. A fine cuisine is maintained at all times, which with uniform moderate terms present advantages not easily equalled. Carriages and good livery service furnished at short notice. Our readers will find a trial of the service at this first class house sure to result in exceptional economy and satisfaction.

CHARLES L. BETTON, Architect, 37 Central Square, Room 1, Lynn.—The steady and rapid growth of Lynn makes it one of the most favorable fields for architects in the State, and the character of the public and private buildings erected in this city of late years shows that the profession is represented here by men who are "up to the times" in every respect, and whose designs embody the latest developments of scientific architecture. Prominent among the most active and successful of our Lynn architects is Mr. Charles L. Betton, whose office is at No. 37 Central Square, Room 1. Having acquired a thorough education in architecture in Boston and vicinity, he is prepared to furnish plans and specifications for private and public buildings at very short notice, and he is very successful in getting the ideas of his clients into practical shape, and in so planning and specifying as to fully protect their interests and ensure the attainment of satisfactory results. Mr. Betton makes a specialty of giving personal attention to the supervision of buildings which are being constructed on plans furnished by him, and he is thoroughly conversant with the details of the building trade, and hence admirably qualified to guard against willful or accidental error in material or construction.

ELBRIDGE S. YOUNG, Wholesale and Retail Dealer in Groceries and Provisions, 113 and 115 Broad Street, Lynn, Mass.—What people want nowadays is solid reliable merit in goods. Showy and much puffed up articles do not have the currency that they once did. A select and first-class trade can only be built up on the basis of goods which stand thorough every day tests and prove by long use to consist of the purest and freshest ingredients. This commercial fact is true of the grocery trade above others, and nowhere in this section more forcibly illustrated than by the valuable trade of Mr. Elbridge S. Young, one of Lynn's most extensive and successful grocers. His trade is both wholesale and retail, including every branch of modern groceries and provisions. A large and finely equipped store is occupied at 113-115 Broad Street, the same being 160 x 45 feet in dimensions, and completely stocked at all times. Staple and fancy groceries are carried in fresh assortments, and sold at lowest market figures, as is also the choicest corn fed beef. Poultry and game in their season a specialty. The finest country vegetables and fruits, in fact all farmers' produce is made a specialty, also canned goods and fresh butter. A number of important lines of flour, directly from leading Western mills, are handled by this house as sole agents. Special attention is called to "Old Gold" brand which excels. The wide busy trade requires the constant employment of thirteen men. The delivery service is first-class in every respect, prompt attention invariably given to orders. Seven first-class teams are constantly in service. For range of selection, moderate prices and uniform excellence of goods, Mr. Young's enterprising store can secure its patrons the very best advantages, which well deserve the careful attention of our readers.

YOULAND & McMANUS, Dealers in Groceries and Provisions, Meats a Specialty, Nos. 169 Market St. and 1 State St., Lynn.—Lynn is a very busy town and there are many well equipped grocers and provision houses located in it, but among them there is not one more deserving of the popularity it has attained than is that conducted by Messrs. Youland & McManus. The business in question was established in 1889 by the present proprietors, who are natives of Maine. The premises occupied are located at No. 169 Market and No. 1 State Streets, comprise one floor 35 x 20 feet in dimensions, and the stock is in harmony with the premises for it is very extensive and is so complete in every department that no trouble is met with in suiting all tastes and all purses. The firm cater especially to family trade, and obtain their supplies from the most reputable sources, thus being in a position to guarantee satisfaction to their customers both as regards the quality and the prices of the goods offered. These include fine groceries and provisions, meats a specialty, choice Vermont butter, cheese and eggs; poultry and game always on hand. Special prices to restaurants and boarding houses. No fancy prices are quoted, but the articles are guaranteed to prove as represented. Three competent and obliging assistants are employed and prompt and courteous attention is assured to every caller.

REPRESENTATIVE BUSINESS MEN OF LYNN. 73

J. WARREN CARSWELL, Dealer in Groceries and Provisions, 43 Broad Street, cor. Green, Lynn, Mass.—The establishment now conducted by Mr. J. Warren Carswell, at 43 Broad Street, corner of Green, may well be called one of the leaders in its special line, for it is one of the oldest of its kind in this city, and what is still more to the point, it constantly contains a very attractive stock. This establishment was originally founded in 1836, and has been conducted by its present proprietor since 1857. Mr. Carswell is a Lynn man by birth and has a large circle of friends and patrons throughout the city, being one of the best known as he is one of the most energetic and popular business men, having served two years in the Common Council, being the only one elected in 1879 on the Citizens' ticket, which indicates his popularity. He served on the finance and Fire Department committees. The premises utilized by Mr. Carswell have a total area of something like 1,360 square feet, but are not a bit too large to accommodate the stock carried, this comprising fine groceries, vegetables, provisions and fruits. Mr. Carswell does an exclusively retail business, carrying a choice assortment of groceries and provisions to select from, and quotes absolutely bottom prices at all times. He employs four competent assistants and is well prepared to assure prompt attention to every caller.

CORNER WASHINGTON STREET AND BROAD STREET.

MISS B. C. STEWART, Millinery Goods, 144 Broad Street, Lynn, Mass.—It would be strange if Lynn which is an acknowledged trade center of this section of the State, should not contain millinery establishments equal to those of any other city, and as a matter of fact the leading Lynn establishments of this kind have no reason to shun comparison in their productions with even those of Boston or New York. Such being the case it is unnecessary to go into details concerning the advantages offered by Miss B. C. Stewart, doing business at No. 144 Broad Street, for the enterprise conducted by her is one of the well-known establishments of its kind in this city having been conducted by Mrs. Radford for very many years and has always held a leading position, Miss Stewart succeeding to the business in 1892, and is making a leading specialty of fine order work, carrying a very choice and carefully selected stock in all lines of millinery goods. Particular attention given to mourning orders. Miss Stewart employs capable and experienced assistants and gives special attention to custom work, and her taste, experience and skill enables her to cater satisfactorily to the most fastidious trade, and to execute commissions at short notice and satisfaction guaranteed.

H. J. SCHMIDT, Dealer in all kinds of Bread, Cake and Pastry, 131 Broad Street, Lynn, Mass.—The establishment now conducted by Mr. H. J. Schmidt is well worthy of prominent and favorable mention, for the entire community are interested in an enterprise which has for its object the furnishing of nutritious and palatable bread, cake and pastry to the public at moderate rates; this is just what Mr. Schmidt is prepared to do, as a visit to the store and a trial of his productions will prove to the satisfaction of the most skeptical. This gentleman occupies premises at 131 Broad Street, where he began business in 1891. His bakery is well equipped with all the necessary facilities to carry on operations to the best advantage. Employment is given to thoroughly competent and careful assistants, and no pains are spared to produce goods that will suit the most fastidious, the material being carefully selected, and the various details being given close personal supervision by the proprietor, who is thus enabled to guarantee that his product shall prove just as represented. Prompt and courteous attention is assured to every caller, and the stock of bread, cake and pastry is so frequently renewed as always to be fresh and tempting, while the prices quoted are as low as can possibly be named on articles of equal excellence.

E. J. KEENLY,

CATERER,

— DEALER IN —

ICE CREAM and CONFECTIONERY

Ice Cream delivered in any part of the City.

HOLIDAY GOODS.

No. 39 Market Square, - West Lynn, Mass.

THE establishment conducted by Mr. E. J. Keenly is well worthy of prominent and favorable mention, for the entire community are interested in an enterprise which has for its object the furnishing of Fine Confections, Ice Cream, etc., to the public at moderate rates, and this is just what this gentleman is prepared to do, as a visit to his establishment and a trial of his productions will prove to the satisfaction of the most skeptical. Mr. Keenly also carries a full line of Holiday Goods which are sold extremely low. He is a native of Lynn, and began operations here in 1892, and has already built up a large manufacturing and retail trade. The premises made use of are located at No. 39 Market Square, West Lynn, comprise one floor 60 x 16 feet in dimensions which is equipped with all necessary facilities to carry on operations to the best advantage, while no pains are spared to produce confections that will suit the most fastidious. Mr. Keenly is a manufacturer of and dealer in Ice Cream and Confectionery, and is prepared to deliver Ice Cream in any quantities and in all parts of the City. He has a large trade at his soda fountain as he makes his own syrups and secures results not excelled elsewhere. With this as with his ice cream the fruit extracts and the various details are given close supervision by the proprietor, who is thus enabled to guarantee that his products will prove just as represented. Mr. Keenly is also a Caterer and is prepared to furnish all articles necessary for Weddings, Parties and Entertainments at the shortest notice, and will cater with or without service. His charges are very reasonable, competent assistance is employed and prompt and courteous attention is assured to every caller. His ice cream parlors will seat about fifty, and are very attractive, a most excellent place to enjoy a rest and first-class ice cream.

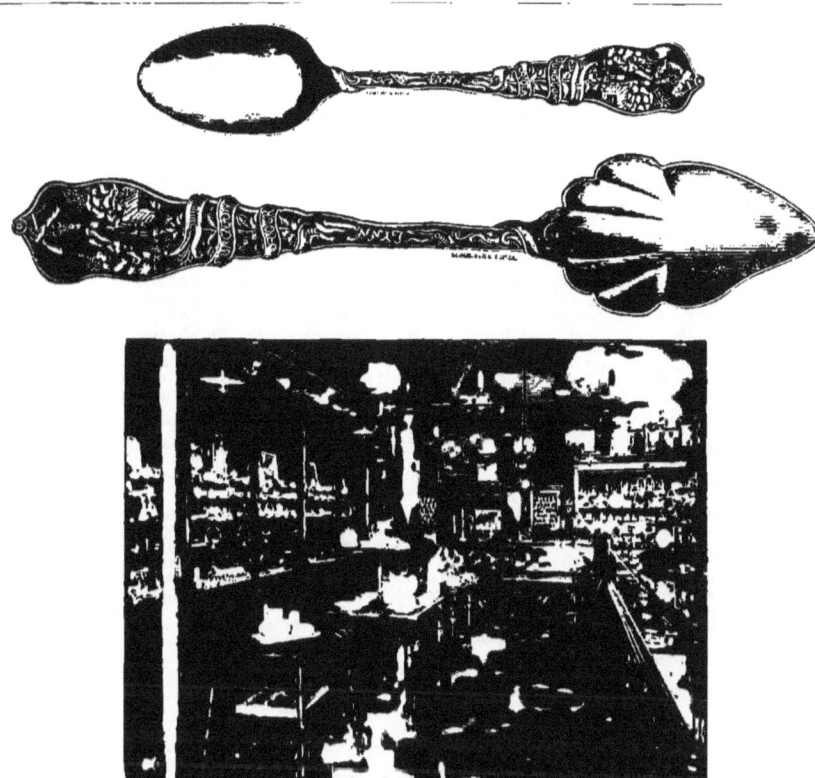

H. M. HILL & CO., Jewelers, 254 and 256 Union Street (Cor. Silsbee), Lynn, Mass.—The spacious, handsome and very finely equipped establishment conducted by Messrs. H. M. Hill & Co., and located at 254 and 256 Union Street, corner of Silsbee, may be briefly described as a metropolitan jewelry store carried on by an enterprising and reliable firm—for the stock will not suffer at all by comparison with that of leading Boston houses, and one who selects from it is given an opportunity to choose from a complete assortment of the latest novelties in the way of jewelry, artistic silverware, optical goods, etc., and is sure not only of getting articles that will prove precisely as represented, but of getting them at positively the lowest market rates. The firm is composed of Messrs. H. M. Hill and C. W. Royce, and they bought out Mr. J. M. Humphrey, who carried on a business established a quarter of a century ago. Mr. Hill was watchmaker for Mr. Humphrey for some three years and is an expert watchmaker and jeweler who has had extended experience in doing the finest work. It is hardly necessary to add that the firm are given a great deal of repairing to do and are capable of successfully doing the most difficult work in that line. Employment is given to two competent assistants, and orders can be filled at short notice. Fine optical work is also done at this establishment, and the charges are as reasonable as the work is excellent. Messrs. H. M. Hill & Co. make a specialty of artistic silverware, and their "Dungeon Rock" spoon has made a most decided "hit;" it being original, artistic and historical. It is made for some twenty different uses; and a special spoon or fork with the Dungeon Rock illustration thereon will be made to order for those desiring an individual pattern that commemorates a historical spot. The stock of watches, jewelry, diamonds and precious stones in general is well worthy of inspection, for it is so complete that all tastes and all purses can be suited from it, and it is so frequently renewed that it is always fresh and attractive and is sure to include the very latest novelties. Messrs. H. M. Hill & Co.'s expenses are of course small in comparison with those of the leading Boston jewelry houses; they do a one-price cash business, and are consequently in a position to quote prices that are literally "as low as the lowest." As an illustration of the scope of their business it may be stated that they carry the largest assortment of hand-painted china to be found in the city of Lynn; and their stock is equally attractive to the admirer of artistic jewelry, rich cut glass and silverware.

L. J. RICHARD & CO.,

◁ MANUFACTURERS OF ▷

Ladies' Fine Boots and Shoes,

REAR 290 BROAD STREET,

LYNN, MASS.

85c. to $1.35.   L. J. RICHARD.   T. A. McKEOWN.

It seems strange sometimes, that certain enterprises fail, while others, started under apparently similar conditions, succeed, but "there is a reason for everything," and investigation will always show that success is by no means the result of "luck." Take for instance the undertaking carried on by Messrs. L. J. Richard & Co. This is a success — there is no room for doubt on that point—and yet that success is not at all due to favorable combination of circumstances, but has been won under decidedly unfavorable conditions. This firm is composed of Messrs. L. J. Richard and T. A. McKeown, both of whom are practical shoe men and both of whom give close personal attention to the work of manufacture. Employment is given to about fifty assistants, and the output of the factory is by no means small, but it is safe to say that no goods leave there without being inspected by a member of the firm, and no trouble is spared to keep them fully up to the standard of the samples in every respect. The result is that the trade are becoming convinced that goods ordered by samples from Messrs. L. J. Richard & Co. can be depended upon, and as the firm manufacture various lines of ladies' fine boots and shoes, and are prepared to quote bottom prices, it naturally follows that their business is steadily increasing. The factory is located rear of 290 Broad street, and is thoroughly equipped, the firm being in a position to fill orders at very short notice.

MISS S. A. WEBSTER, Shorthand and Typewriting, Offices : 333 Union Street, Room 6; Lee Hall, Room 4, Lynn, Mass.—With the telegraph and other applications of electricity, business nowadays moves with a celerity which would be incomprehensible to merchants of a hundred years ago. One very natural feature of this advance has been the development of shorthand and typewriting. Now that it has been carefully perfected, recurrence to the old methods would be an impossibility. The shorthand and typewriting business conducted by Miss S. A. Webster of this city has demonstrated the best standard of ability attained in this line. Two well-equipped offices have been opened at 333 Union Street, Room 6, and at Lee Hall, Room 4. Prompt attention is given to all work in this line, including court reporting, verbatim reports of hearings, lectures, etc., copying of all kinds of manuscript, dictation and general shorthand work. Miss Webster also gives thorough instruction in shorthand and typewriting at moderate figures. Satisfactory results are guaranteed to all who will improve the opportunities here assured. The advantages of first-class work of this kind are too obvious to intelligent people to need extended recommendation. To accomplish the most in the shortest time is one of the chief features of true economy.

J. W. CHASE & CO., Pharmacists, Prescriptions compounded at all hours of day or night, cor. Ireson and Essex Streets, Lynn, Mass.—The standing of a pharmacy can generally be most accurately judged by the magnitude and character of the prescription trade, for although this is dependent to some extent upon the location of the store, it is much more dependent upon the character of the service rendered. Messrs. J. W. Chase & Co. have no reason to shrink from having their pharmacy judged by this standard, for it is not only one of the most popular establishments of the kind in the city, but it is especially popular in its prescription department, as this is very carefully and skillfully managed and the stock of drugs, chemicals, etc., is exceptionally complete and is made up of the best and purest goods the market affords, obtained from the most reliable sources. Prescriptions are compounded at all hours of the day or night, and prompt and accurate service is assured by the employment of an adequate force of thoroughly competent assistants, one of whom is a registered pharmacist, and the use of the most improved apparatus. Moderate charges are made and no trouble is spared to maintain in every way the high reputation of this popular establishment. The proprietors are Messrs. J. W. Chase and C. H. Downing, the former a native of Lynn, and the latter of South Reading (now Wakefield). They have been associated in their present enterprise since 1887, and both are extremely well known in Lynn and vicinity. Mr. Downing has served several years in the Common Council, and has been connected with the Lynn Fire Department for nearly half a century, he first entering it forty-eight years ago, and is now serving his fourth year as chief engineer.

Dr. A. B. MUDGE,

45 MARKET STREET,   -   -   LYNN, MASS.

Preservation of Natural Teeth a Specialty.

....W. W. SMITH.....
Contractor and Builder,
184 OXFORD STREET, - - LYNN, MASS.

Mr. W. W. Smith is a native of the Pine Tree State but has long resided in Lynn, has carried on business here for a score of years and is one of the best known contractors and builders in the city. His shop is located at No. 184 Oxford street, and occupies a building two stories in height and 00 x 25 feet in dimensions. Employment is generally given to about fifteen assistants, although of course, the number varies with the season and the amount of work on hand, and Mr. Smith is prepared to execute even the largest commissions at short notice and to give prompt and careful attention to small orders also. Estimates will be cheerfully furnished on application, and it is hardly necessary to state that one who has had the long and varied experience and controls the extensive facilities of Mr. Smith, is prepared to figure very closely on building work, and to attain results that cannot fail to satisfy even the most critical. Personal attention is given to the supervision of all important work, and such of our readers as have done business with Mr. Smith will agree with us when we say that that is equivalent to a guarantee that all material and workmanship will be strictly in accordance with specifications.

J. G. OLIN, Jeweler and Silversmith, 71 Market Street, Lynn, Mass.—It very seldom pays to buy anything at an establishment that is not thoroughly reliable in every respect, and this is particularly the case where jewelry and silverware are concerned, for the opportunities for fraud in the selling of goods coming under this head are too obvious to need demonstration, and such fraud it is practically impossible to detect at the time or to prove and punish afterwards. The only sensible way to do, then, is to patronize a reputable and firmly established concern, and if you desire to find one that is not only strictly reliable, but is enterprising and liberal in its business methods also, the best advice we can offer is to call on Mr. J. G. Olin, at 71 Market Street, and take advantage of the inducements he is prepared to extend to customers. Mr. Olin is a Massachusetts man by birth, and since beginning operations as a jeweler and silversmith at Lynn in 1867 has gained an enviable reputation. The premises utilized are of the dimensions of 20x50 feet, and a choice assortment of jewelry, silverware, etc., is carried, and every article is fully warranted to prove just as represented in every respect. Three competent and reliable assistants are employed, and the prices quoted on the goods handled are as low as is consistent with the handling of first-class and thoroughly honest goods.

F. F. FRENCH, Wholesale and Retail Dealer in Choice Family Groceries. Butter a Specialty, 32 Market Street, Lynn, Mass.—Among the prominent establishments located in Lynn that conducted by Mr. F. F. French must be given favorable mention for the enterprise carried on by this gentleman has gradually but steadily developed until it now ranks with the important stores of the kind in this locality. An extensive business has been built up, and the establishment has been under the sole management of its present able proprietor since 1868. Mr. French is a native of Pittsfield, N. H., and is thoroughly conversant with all the details of his business. The premises occupied are spacious and well arranged for the business for which they are utilized, comprising a store 2,100 square feet in dimensions in addition to two extensive storehouses. Mr. French's store is located at 32 Market Street, where is carried a large and choice stock of groceries of all kinds especially adapted to family trade and which is offered at the lowest market prices, a specialty being made of choice butter. Employment is given to six competent assistants, so that despite the magnitude of the business, every order is assured immediate and careful attention. In view of the facts already mentioned it becomes almost unnecessary to add that Mr. French is in a position to quote the very lowest prices, and that he does a splendid first class business also that he carries a large assortment of goods which will invariably prove just as represented.

W. E. LEWIS, Successor to Pote & Lewis, Plumbing and Heating, Furnaces and Tinwork. Steam and Gas Piping. 5 Willow Street (Opp. Munroe), Lynn.—The average man doesn't have time to investigate the mysteries of sanitary plumbing and scientific heating, and hence he is generally unable to distinguish good from bad work until he has had opportunity to observe the results attained in the course of practical use; but every ordinarily well-informed man knows that so-called "cheap" plumbing is apt to be unhealthful, and that inferior and badly arranged heating apparatus is sure to be both troublesome and expensive, for it won't do its work satisfactorily and the cost of the fuel consumed is far in excess of that which would be required by first-class heating apparatus doing much better work. Hence the well-informed man makes it a point to place all his orders with a plumbing and heating house that he knows is not only reliable but is fully up to the times, and as that is just the reputation enjoyed by the establishment conducted by Mr. W. E. Lewis, it naturally follows that he does a great deal of the first-class plumbing and heating work done in Lynn and vicinity. Mr. Lewis makes a specialty of the Boynton Furnace a cut of which appears above, and it is a perfect heater. Mr. Lewis has had long and varied experience, and was a member of the firm of Pote & Lewis before he assumed sole control of his present enterprise. His shop is located at 5 Willow Street, opposite Munroe, and is spacious and well-equipped; it having an area of 1,200 square feet, and being supplied with all necessary facilities. The business includes the furnishing, setting up and repairing of furnaces; tin work of all kinds; and steam and gas piping in all their branches. Employment is given to five competent assistants, and all orders are assured prompt and careful attention—all important work being done under the personal supervision of Mr. Lewis.

SEASIDE HAND LAUNDRY,
ESTABLISHED 1885.   JOSEPH A. CALLAHAN.
54 MUNROE STREET, 2d and 3d Stories, - - - - - **LYNN, MASS.**

There are many who object to having washing done at home, and yet do not feel disposed to entrust their linen to public laundries as it is often damaged. But there is no more necessity of having your clothes injured at a laundry than there is of having them done up at home, for the Seaside Hand Laundry under the management of Mr. Joseph A. Callahan, and located at 54 Munroe Street, does careful work and avoids injury to the most delicate fabrics. Mr. Callahan established the Seaside Hand Laundry in 1885, since which date he has built up a thriving business, requiring the services of twenty-six thoroughly experienced assistants. The uniform superiority of the work turned out at this establishment is evident to the most fastidious, and the prices are so low that all can afford to take advantage of the opportunities offered. The premises utilized are spacious and well supplied with every requisite facility, including a 7½ horse-power electric motor. Fancy ironing, fluting, and all kinds of laundry work is done at short notice. Goods will be collected and delivered to any part of the city. First-class work is guaranteed, special attention being given to starch work, and orders by mail will be promptly attended to. Mr. Callahan has seventy-five agencies distributed throughout the city which are in daily communication with the laundry, thus assuring prompt attention to all orders.

F. R. BENNER & CO., Manufacturers of Sails and Awnings, 302 Broad Street, Lynn, Mass.—The people of the North Shore are among the most aquatic of any in the United States. They have furnished many of the finest yachts and sturdiest seamen which this country has produced, and these can be safely compared with any other part of the world. The business of Messrs. F. R. Benner & Co. has long been associated with this line of local interests. They are among the oldest and best-known sail and awning makers anywhere in this section. Their business premises at above address are neatly fitted up and contain every needed appliance for prompt execution of orders. The firm employ only the best of assistance and guarantee thorough satisfaction in all their goods. They can make any class or size of sails promptly to order and at lowest prices; also awnings, tents, canvas work of all kinds, bunting and general decorations. Their political banners and insignia are widely popular for their reliable and first-class workmanship. Nowhere, even in Boston, can better service and prices in these lines be obtained. Many of our readers are probably not aware at what moderate expense, handsome awnings and decorations can be obtained. They will do well to examine the work and figures of this reliable firm and by so doing will without doubt save themselves the expenditure of much time, labor and money.

W. A. STUBBS,
—⋅❖ DEALER IN ALL KINDS OF ❖⋅—
Fresh, Salt, Smoked and Pickle Fish, Clams, Oysters, Lobsters,
➤RAW AND OPENED LOBSTER. FANCY OYSTERS IN THE SHELL.⬅
134 MUNROE STREET, Corner Washington Street, - - **LYNN, MASS.**

It is perfectly safe to say that there are not many persons in Lynn who do not know of the fish market located at 134 Munroe Street, corner of Washington Street, and it is also safe to assert that its popularity is well-nigh universally known throughout this city and vicinity, for this is known as a cash store exclusively. Mr. Stubbs runs no order or delivery wagon, but buys for cash and sells for cash only, giving customers the benefit in lower prices, as there are no poor debts to be provided for by increased profits. There probably is no fish market in the State where you are more sure to find first-class fish, oysters, clams, lobsters, etc., than you are here. Spacious premises are occupied, they being admirably fitted up for the safe and convenient storage of fish, etc., even in the hottest weather. The stock, of course, varies with the season, but it is always "seasonable," that is to say, it is pretty sure to include a full assortment of the goods the market affords. General features may be mentioned, fresh, salt and pickled fish, boiled lobsters, oysters, etc. The proprietor, Mr. W. A. Stubbs, has been identified with his present establishment since 1881, and has developed it extensively by sparing no pains to make the service as satisfactory as possible in every respect. Employment is given to two assistants.

FRANK B. FARMER, Men's Furnishings, Boots and Shoes. Boston Street Laundry Agency, 34 Munroe Street, Tucker Block, Lynn.—It is said that nothing human is perfect, and as the establishment conducted by Mr. Frank B. Farmer is most certainly of human origin, it therefore can't be perfect, but evidently there are many persons who think that it comes nearer to perfection than any similar establishment in Lynn, for they are sure to do their buying here when they want anything in the line of men's furnishings, boots and shoes, etc., and what is more, they try to persuade their friends to go and do likewise, for, as they put it, you can't possibly do better elsewhere and you will very probably do worse. That is the whole story in a nutshell, and nothing would be gained by our going into detail about the goods you will find here, the treatment you will receive here, and the price you will be asked to pay here. But we may say in closing that you are sure of being given an opportunity to choose from the very latest fashionable novelties, and that you can confidently and safely depend upon goods proving precisely as represented to you. Mr. Farmer is agent for the Boston Street Laundry, and occupies premises conveniently located at 34 Munroe Street. Prompt and courteous service is assured to every caller, and whether you wish to buy at once or simply to "look around," you are welcome at this popular store and are assured polite and careful attention.

F. W. KYES, D.D.S.

Room 2, 2d Floor.

OFFICE HOURS: 8 A.M.–6 P.M.

No. 90 MARKET STREET,

LYNN, MASS.

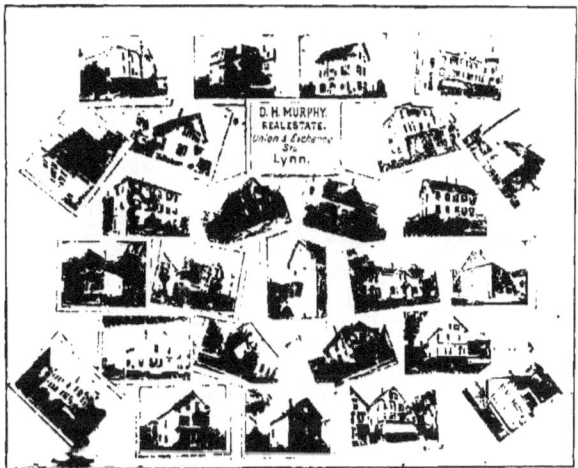

HOUSES TO LET

All parts of City.

D. H. MURPHY,

Cor. UNION & EXCHANGE STS.,

LYNN, MASS.

Fine Confectionery and Bon-Bons

SUSIE M. JENKINS,

281 UNION STREET.   BRANCH, 87 MUNROE ST.,

LYNN, MASS.

The liberal space we have given in this book to notices of the representative retail houses of Lynn and vicinity shows how we appreciate the importance of this branch of trade, and gives sufficient reason why we should make mention of such an establishment as that conducted by Miss Susie M. Jenkins, for this lady ranks with the leading wholesale and retail dealers in fine Confectionery and Ice Cream in this vicinity. Miss Jenkins began operations here some years ago. A rapidly increasing business is transacted and a large stock is carried, as indeed may be judged from the premises occupied, the main store being located at 281 Union Street, 30x35 feet in size, with a branch at 87 Munroe Street, 50x16 feet in size, and both are fitted up with all necessary facilities for the proper handling of the business, which latter fact has much to do with the reputation this house enjoys for filling all orders at short notice and with perfect accuracy. The specialty of this house is the dealing in fine Confectionery, Bon Bons and Ice Cream, of all kinds, which are guaranteed fresh, and made from the purest materials. A competent force of assistants is constantly employed and Miss Jenkins is prepared to supply her goods in quantities to suit at positively bottom prices and to insure prompt delivery.

The fact that the clothing made by Mr. Stanley is cut in the latest styles, is perfect in fit, excellent in workmanship, reveals the secret why the demand for his goods is so large, and rapidly increasing. Mr. Stanley, who is a native of Massachusetts began his present business here at Lynn in 1883, and now occupies premises at 192 Union Street, where he carries an assortment of Domestic and Foreign woolens, including the very latest designs as they appear in the market, and makes a specialty of custom tailoring. Mr. Stanley employs competent assistants, and his facilities are such as to make it easy for him to meet all honorable competition and the residents of Lynn wishing desirable clothing at bottom prices would do well to visit his popular establishment, examine his fine stock and note his prices before placing their orders elsewhere as he personally supervises all work, and strives to render a just equivalent for every dollar charged.

W. F. SMITH, Fine Harness, Blankets, Robes and Whips, Constantly on Hand. No. 173-175 Broad Street (Hotel Seymour), Lynn, Mass.—A good horse and carriage with an inferior equipment are something like a reversal of the old fable, as if the lion were to put on the donkey's skin. Sensible people nowadays uniformly desire and obtain the best quality of goods. Not to speak of the great difference in the satisfaction afforded, they really pay better in the long run. Among the long established and popular stores in this line of trade, that of Mr. W. F. Smith, at 173-175 Broad Street (Hotel Seymour), with its branch store at 94 Central Avenue, has for years been a recognized leader. It was started by Mr. Smith in 1877, and from the first has commanded the finest class of trade. The store premises occupied on Broad Street are handsomely fitted up, (40x30 feet) and contain a valuable stock. This includes fine harness goods of all kinds, blankets, robes, whips, etc., at popular and reasonable prices. The various styles represent the best imported and domestic makes, and quality is uniformly guaranteed A1. Our readers can rely upon obtaining goods exactly as represented at this first class store. Custom work is executed to order, and special designs can be promptly made at any time. Mr. Smith makes a specialty of repairing, and employs four competent and experienced men. He is a native of Massachusetts, and his wide, thorough success fully entitles him to a place among the most progressive business men of Lynn.

W. S. POOLE, Cigars and Tobacco, Fruit and Confectionery, 767 Western Avenue, West Lynn. Agent for Boston Street Laundry. F. C. Cheever, Proprietor, 531 Washington Street, Lynn, Mass.—This enterprise was formerly conducted by Messrs. Poole and Nickerson, but passed into the hands of the present proprietor, Mr. W. S. Poole, in 1892. He has been connected with this undertaking long enough to make many improvements in the business, which is rapidly aiding in its successful development. The premises occupied are located at No. 767 Western Avenue, West Lynn, comprise one floor, 40x25 feet in dimensions, and is in a portion of the city that is rapidly being developed. Newspapers are kept on sale, also magazines and periodicals, which are sold at publishers' rates. Choice confectionery and fruits, cigars and tobacco are a specialty, and largely dealt in, while Mr. Poole has long had the name of selling thoroughly satisfactory cigars at moderate prices, and this name is so well deserved that we feel that we can do our readers no greater service than to call their attention to his fine stock. Mr. Poole is also the agent for the Boston Street Laundry, whose store is located at No. 531 Washington Street, Lynn. All goods left here will be looked after and taken care of. One competent assistant is employed while the proprietor's policy is as simple as it is popular, it being to give full value for amount received, and to endeavor to please every customer.

D. W. CHASE, Piano and Furniture Mover. Light and Heavy Teaming of all Kinds. 18 Andrew Street. Telephone 20. Lynn, Mass.—Among the various little things which are very handy to know is the address of a thoroughly competent, reliable, and well-equipped piano and furniture mover, for it saves money, time and trouble to know just where to place an order so as to have your moving done promptly, carefully, and at reasonable rates. Hence, our readers will do well to note the address of Mr. D. W. Chase, No. 18 Andrew Street, telephone 20, for he has first-class facilities for doing light and heavy teaming of all kinds. He makes a specialty of piano and furniture moving, and he employs experienced and reliable help, and gives personal attention to the filling of all important orders. The business was founded more than a score of years ago, and needs no introduction to the older residents of Lynn, as it has long been known that it is as reliable a local express as can be found in the city. Mr. Chase is uniformly moderate in his charges, and as prompt and careful service, and reasonable prices, make a strong combination, it is but natural that his enterprise is popular, and he does an extensive business.

REPRESENTATIVE BUSINESS MEN OF LYNN.

HOLBROOK'S Central Drug Store, 330 Union Street, Lynn, Mass.— "Holbrook's Central Drug Store" is really one of Lynn's institutions, for it is almost universally as well as very favorably known throughout the city and vicinity, and is spoken of as "the" place, at which to have prescriptions compounded. We don't mean to say that this is the only reliable pharmacy in the city; that, of course would be absurd. But we *do* mean to say that not a few of the residents of Lynn would not think of having their prescriptions compounded elsewhere. They have long had all their prescriptions compounded here; they have learned from experience that the drugs, chemicals, etc., kept in stock are pure, fresh, and in every way the best the market affords; that the compounding is skillfully, carefully, accurately and promptly done, and that the charges are uniformly moderate. Hence it is perfectly natural that they should not only patronize this establishment themselves, but advise their friends to do the same thing. This pharmacy is located at 330 Union Street, and besides a very complete stock of drugs and chemicals, it contains a large and varied assortment of druggists' sundries, toilet articles, and such other articles as one expects to find in one of the best drug stores in Lynn. Employment is given to an ample force of competent assistants, and business can be done here very promptly as well as in a manner that ensures you full value in return for every penny you expend

MUNROE STREET, FROM CENTRAL AVENUE.

R. BACHELLER, Dealer in Groceries and Provisions, Butter, Cheese, Eggs, Flour, Grain, etc., 46 Ocean Street, Lynn, Mass.—It is one of the greatest boasts of our progressive American life that the widest range of daily comforts and even luxuries are now brought within the reach of all. This is well illustrated at the modern and enterprising store of Mr. Rufus Bacheller at No. 46 Ocean Street, Lynn, Mass. No establishment of its kind in the city enjoys a higher reputation for the best class of goods and service than this old established store. A neatly fitted up and attractive store building (25x18 feet) is occupied, and the goods displayed to the very best advantage. Our readers will find a wide range of groceries and provisions at this store, including all staple and fancy lines at lowest market prices. Butter, cheese, eggs, flour and grain are made leading specialties, and the bargains constantly on hand in these and other lines deserve the careful attention of our readers. Two courteous assistants are employed and prompt attention given to all customers. The delivery service has been placed upon the best modern basis. Mr. Bacheller is a native of Massachusetts and one of the most enterprising and reliable of Lynn business men. When you want to get the best return for money expended be sure to visit this wide-awake and modern store.

P. S. DE COSTER, Pharmacist, 91 Washington Street, cor. Lyman, Lynn, Mass.—One of the most difficult things to prove in a court of justice is the "general reputation" of a certain person, for although there are exceptions, of course, it may be stated as a rule, that the moral and social standing of an individual may be generally agreed upon by a community, and yet it may be almost impossible when hampered by the rules which govern the admission of evidence to prove just what that standing is. Within certain bounds the same difficulty is met with in demonstrating the position held by a business enterprise. Old residents of Lynn know perfectly well that the apothecary store carried on by Mr. P. S. De Coster is one of the most reliable and most highly regarded in this city, and indeed they are so thoroughly convinced of the fact as to be willing to swear to it, and yet legal proof of the high standing of this representative establishment might be difficult to obtain. But its prominence is nevertheless unquestionable, and Mr. De Coster may well take pride in it, as the result of faithful service. The store is located at 91 Washington Street, corner of Lyman Street, and contains a complete assortment of pure drugs, medicines, and chemicals, together with toilet and fancy articles. A specialty is made of the compounding of prescriptions, and such orders are filled accurately, promptly, and at uniformly moderate rates.

GEORGE T. SMITH,
HOME BAKERY.

Wholesale Business in Bread. Full line of Home Made Bread, Cake, Pastry, etc., AT RETAIL.
BEANS AND BROWN BREAD, Saturday Nights and Sunday Mornings.   Try our Famous **DOUGHNUTS**.
CIGARS, CONFECTIONERY FANCY GROCERIES, TABLE DELICACIES AND CANNED GOODS, AT BOTTOM PRICES.
COR. FAYETTE AND MASON STREETS.   -   -   LYNN, MASS.

THE BEE HIVE, DRY GOODS STORE. Jona Eldridge Proprietor, 23 Central Square, and 43 Market Square. Residence, 94 Grove Street, Lynn, Mass.—The "Bee Hive" Dry Goods Store was the only dry goods concern which was entirely consumed in the great fire of 1889, but phœnix-like it came up from the ashes and like many other concerns is now located under more favorable circumstances. It is a favorite with the people of Lynn, and it is but natural that such is the case, for the proprietor, Mr. Jona Eldridge, is a thoroughly enterprising merchant who keeps fully "up to the times" in every detail of style, fashion, and price, and hence his store always contains the kind of goods the people want, offered at prices that are sure to be in strict accordance with the lowest market rates. There is no use in trying to decribe in detail such a stock as Mr. Eldridge carries, for it includes dry and fancy goods, gloves, hosiery, corsets, laces, underware, small wares, buttons, fringes, ornaments, men's furnishings, etc., and even a catalogue of it would exhaust our available space many times over. But a description is unnecessary, for all that the people want to know is where they can get staple goods and the latest novelties at bottom prices and that is just what they can do at the "Bee Hive" Dry Goods Store. It is located at 23 Central Square and 43 Market Square, and is very spacious and thoroughly equipped throughout. A large number of experienced assistants are employed and callers can depend upon receiving prompt and courteous attention.

ELECTRIC CONSTRUCTION CO., George C. Millard, Manager, Electrical Contractors, 526 Washington Street, Lynn, Mass.—The importance of electricity is every day making itself felt in the affairs of the business world and general public. It is almost impossible to imagine how present conditions could be maintained without i New ideas and improvements are also being constantly introduced. A house which has taken a leading local position in this line is the Electric Construction Co. under the able management of Mr. George C. Millard, formerly of North Adams, Mass., he having had sixteen years' experience. This company now do a large and thriving business based upon their modern facilities and enterprise. They deal in all kinds of electrical supplies and are prepared at any time to superintend and furnish workmen for the construction of electrical plants. Their regular force includes eight expert electricians. Among their specialties are electric and gas fixtures of every kind and electric wiring, upon which they can offer special figures. Their prices will be found uniformly low and reasonable. The Company is also the local agent of the Boston Art Brass Co., and can furnish a wide variety of goods in this line. They are also Agents for the Eddy motor, the finest motor on the market. Their store premises at 526 Washington Street are handsomely fitted up, being 40x25 feet in dimensions. When in search of the latest and best electrical supplies and A 1 expert service our readers will do well to apply here. The company is the successor of the well-known Perry, Fuller Co., and has maintained the high standing of that house.

E. H. JACOBS, Retailer of Fine Footwear of All Kinds, Bulfinch Block, corner Lewis and Cherry Streets, Lynn, Mass.—No part of the apparel is more distinctive of good taste and refinement than the footwear. It may seem like bringing "coals to New Castle" to enlarge on this topic in connection with Lynn affairs, but those who want the best satisfaction in this line can make no mistake in patronizing the popular and old-established store of Mr. E. H. Jacobs at the corner of Lewis and Cherry Streets (Bulfinch Block.) This store is one of the best retailing establishments in this vicinity for fine footwear of every sort. First-class facilities enable Mr. Jacobs to offer his patrons a wide range of attractive goods and prices unexcelled for liberality, as combining a first-class quality with very reduced figures. We can assure our readers that they can obtain rare bargains here at every season of the year. The stock includes both ladies, men's and children's goods of the most popular make and styles. Rubbers and overshoes of recent and novel patterns are kept always in stock. The manufacture of fine footwear is steadily being improved all the time, and those who would obtain the best satisfaction for their money will do well to examine the advantages of Mr. Jacobs' reliable store.

JOHN SHEEHAN, Contractor for Grading, Blasting by Steam, Licensed Drain Layer, etc., 585 Western Avenue, Lynn, Mass.—Mr. Sheehan has been connected with very many important contract jobs in Lynn and vicinity. He is splendidly equipped, with teams and tools for all kind of heavy jobbing and contract work, either in excavating, steam blasting, drain laying, or cemetery work, he gives all work close personal supervision, is always ready to do work in his line at reasonable prices, and guarantees that all work shall be done thoroughly and up to contract specifications. He will furnish estimates on application and his experience and judgment makes him a wise counselor. His office is located at 585 Western Avenue, and during the many years that he has been engaged in his present line of business he has proved himself capable of filling the most difficult orders with accuracy and celerity. Mr. Sheehan is a practical man and well and favorably known giving employment to a number of men varying with the time of year, and is prepared to make contracts for all kinds of work as above stated and give all work prompt and careful attention, he is also a dealer in Sewer and Drain Pipes carrying an important line. His prices are always moderate and fair and it is not surprising that his business should steadily increase.

FRANK MILLER, JR.,
◁ARCHITECT,▷

Room 32, Woodbury Building, 145 Munroe Street, - LYNN, MASS.

It is the province of the architect to reconcile the ideal and the real, to secure the beautiful without the sacrifice of the useful, and in the majority of cases to so use space and material as to obtain the best possible results at the least possible expense. Where " money is no object " the conditions are greatly simplified, of course, but the true architect, like a true artist, welcomes difficulties, and secures his greatest triumphs where he has the greatest obstacles to overcome. Here in Lynn may be found an architect who faithfully secures the above results. Mr. Frank Miller, Jr., is making a record which not only proves him to possess courage and perseverance, but which demonstrates his natural fitness for his work, his thorough technical education, and his fine discriminating taste. Mr. Miller occupies room 32, Woodbury Building, 145 Munroe Street, where he may be personally consulted, and as he employs an experienced assistant, all commissions can be executed at very short notice despite the magnitude of the business, and all callers are assured most respectful attention.

T. W. PRESTON, Painter and Paper Hanger, 596 Western Avenue, Lynn, Mass.—Experience plainly shows that the best satisfaction in house-painting and decorating can only be obtained by entrusting the work to a leading establishment which can thoroughly supervise and execute every feature of such work from the door-step to the turret roof. This also conduces to economy as the owner thereby secures practically wholesale rates, as well as prompter conclusion of contract and much more durable results. The sad blotches in the way of mixed and inartistic effects disfiguring some of our streets, should be a sufficient warning to sensible people to secure only the best service. Nowhere can this be more thoroughly obtained than at the leading establishment of Mr. T. W. Preston, 596 Western Avenue near Park Street, Lynn, Mass. Mr. Preston has for many years made a careful study of every feature of this business and can guarantee most complete satisfaction. He employs an experienced corps of assistants throughout the year. Beside many large contracts in general house painting, both exterior and interior, he also executes gilding, graining, glazing, white washing and kalsomining work of all kinds. Wall-paper hanging and fresco work carefully attended to. Specialties are also enjoyed for the renovating of oil paintings and regilding frames. At his neatly fitted up and attractive shop, Mr. Preston keeps on hand a large line of all materials needed in his business. His terms will be found moderate and uniform. A good example of the exceptional enterprise and superior service given by his establishment is the new and more thorough process of painting blinds by slipping them into and through the paints prepared by special process used only here. Those who want to save money and obtain better results than in the past, should not fail to try Mr. Preston's special and improved methods of executing this class of work.

SAMUEL S. PERKINS & CO., Dealers in Groceries and Provisions, Flour and Grain, Foreign and Domestic Fruit, Nos. 219 to 223 Lewis Street, Opposite Breed Street, Lynn, Mass.—There was a time when many people were satisfied with an inferior class of groceries simply because it was difficult to obtain the best. That time however has long been passed, as the leading city stores now bring the finest class of goods at moderate prices within the reach of all. The business of Messrs. Samuel S. Perkins & Co. has for the past sixteen years maintained a leading position in its department of local trade, their store having been first opened in 1877. The premises now occupied combine two stores in one, covering a floor space of 60 x 40 feet. A very large and complete stock of fine groceries is kept always on hand. Twelve experienced clerks and assistants are needed to handle their extensive and select retail trade. The stock includes the finest qualities of teas, coffees, sugars, spices, meats and provisions, butter and country produce, flour, grain, hay, etc., also foreign and domestic fruits. The prices of this store are well known for their uniform liberality and fairness. As half or more of the value of groceries depends upon their purity and freedom from adulterations, our readers will consult their own interests very largely by examining and making trial of the high class of goods kept at this store. Mr. Samuel S. Perkins is a native of Lynn and one of the most enterprising and esteemed of its solid business men. The established and leading position which this house has attained is solely the result of sound business principles and liberal dealings.

ISAAC K. HARRIS, Civil Engineer and Surveyor, Room 60, 333 Union Street, Lynn, Mass.—It would seem to be entirely superfluous to point out the importance of having accurate surveys made preparatory to the improving of estates by cutting through streets, laying out house lots, etc., were it not for the fact that the " rule of thumb " method, or rather lack of method is still practiced occasionally even in these enlightened days, and the expensive litigation which almost invariably follows does not seem to deter others from risking the loss of thousands of dollars to save the almost nominal cost of a scientific survey. Surveyors are not infallible, but the results attained by the employment of competent skill in this line are as nearly absolutely certain as anything can be, and it is certainly well worth while to avail one's self of such aid. In this connection we take pleasure in making mention of Mr. Isaac K. Harris, whose office is located in room 60, No. 333 Union Street, for he began operations as a civil engineer and surveyor in 1864, and was city engineer for the city of Lynn from 1869 to 1876, when he established his present office, and has built up an excellent reputation for competency, progressiveness, and close and earnest attention to the interests of his clients. Lack of space forbids our going into details concerning the character and magnitude of the business done by Mr. Harris; suffice it to say it includes civil engineering, surveying, etc., in all their departments. He employs four competent assistants, and is in a position to furnish surveys and plans for the division of estates, plans and profiles for acceptance; to lay out foundations for buildings, etc., and to execute commissions promptly and satisfactorily.

TRASK BROTHERS, Dealers in Shoe Findings and Manufacturers' Supplies of all Kinds. Moulded Shanks and Drill Stays of all Grades a Specialty. Nos. 9 and 11 Willow Street, Mower Bros.' Block, Lynn, Mass.—It has been said that the merits of a firm may be judged by the magnitude of their business, but, like all general statements, this one is not to be interpreted too literally, for "circumstances alter cases," and it is not always the house that does the biggest business that offers the greatest inducements to purchasers. But still, the fact that a business has been established for nearly a quarter of century, has steadily increased until it has become an acknowledged leader in its especial line, and is still steadily increasing, is convincing evidence that the firm who carry it on are in a position to meet all honorable competition in goods and prices ; and such is the record of the business conducted by Messrs. Trask Brothers, dealers in shoe findings and manufacturers' supplies of all kinds. The premises utilized are located in Mower Bros.' Block, Nos. 9 and 11 Willow Street, and have a total area of 7,200 square feet. A large and varied stock is carried, and the manufacturing facilities are extensive, the firm being prepared to fill orders at short notice as well as at the lowest market rates. Among the more important commodities dealt in, may be mentioned leather and straw board, paper, twines, drills, buttons, stays, eyelets, etc., and the firm make a leading specialty of moulded shank and drill stays of all grades. The establishment has telephone connection, and all orders, large and small are assured prompt attention, the business being well systematized, and employment being given to twelve efficient assistants.

J. A. VAUGHAN & CO., Practical Horse Shoers, Carriage Building and Repairing in all its Branches. Strict Attention given to Carriage Painting. 134 Essex Street, Telephone 266-2. Lynn, Mass.—A poor horse well shod can sometimes do more work than a good horse poorly shod, so it is worth the while of every horse owner to see that such work is done as it should be. Messrs. J. A. Vaughan & Co., of 134 Essex Street, have an excellent reputation in connection with this line of work, being practical horse shoers, and as employment in all departments is given to twenty-five experienced and careful assistants all orders can be filled at very short notice. The members of this firm have been identified with their present business for many years. The premises occupied consist of a building two stories in height, 191x40 feet in dimensions. Carriage building and repairing in all its branches is extensively carried on here, strict attention being given to carriage painting, all work being done in the best manner at moderate prices. Messrs. Vaughan & Co. mean to turn out strong as well as neat work and allow no work to leave their shop that will not give satisfaction. They have had an extensive experience in horse shoeing and blacksmithing work of all kinds, and those who have had orders filled at their establishment speak in the highest terms of the work, and the reasonable and low prices charged by them. All orders by mail or telephone 266-2 will be promptly attended to. Mr. Vaughan is an energetic thorough-going and well-informed business man. Prior to coming to Lynn he served as postmaster, justice of the peace, school committee and member of common council five years.

GEORGE E. SMITH, Architect, 19 Central Square or 343 Union Street, Lynn, Mass.—A well known and successful Lynn architect is Mr. George E. Smith, who began the practice of his profession here in 1889, and has already attained a leading position, and gained a high reputation for close devotion to the interests of those making use of his services. Mr. Smith was born in Essex, Mass., and during the four years that he has been located at Lynn has become well known throughout the city. He is a thoroughly practical and expert draughtsman and general architect; having had wide and varied experience, and being a master of the art in all its branches. Contracts, specifications and plans for private or public building, city or country residences, and in fact buildings of all descriptions and classes will be executed in the most skillful and satisfactory manner, and designs and estimates in relation to any proposed work will be furnished at short notice. Mr. Smith has an office located at Room 31, 19 Central Square or 343 Union Street, and employs a competent assistant, all preparations of plans, specifications, etc., being done under his personal supervision. He will give personal attention to the construction of buildings if desired, taking pains to see that the specifications are strictly observed, and guarding the interests of whoever he may represent as carefully as though they were his own.

MASSACHUSETTS TEMPERANCE HOME. President, Frank D. Allen, Boston; Treasurer, Wm. A. Attwill, Lynn; Superintendent of Home, Robert Scott, 27 New Ocean Street, Lynn, Mass.—Great attention has been directed of recent years to highly colored systems of curing the morbid tastes for alcoholic liquors. Bringing matters down to fundamental facts, it will be found that the only sensible and permanent way to overcome these destructive habits is such a complete renovation of the system as a quiet, steady and sound physiological method renders possible. This system, together with the best Christian influences has for years past been that of the Massachusetts Temperance Home, at 27 New Ocean Street, one of Lynn's most noble and important institutions, with an influence which reaches throughout this and other States. This home is entirely non-political, non-sectarian, non-partisan and non-abusive, devoted simply to the reclaiming of those who, with inebriate habits or tendencies, need complete change of atmosphere and influence to get thoroughly on their feet again. During the past year 187 patients have been kindly cared for. The house at the above address is a modern three-story structure with wide verandas and 50 x 60 feet in average dimensions. It has recently been refurnished and painted throughout, making it a most cheery and attractive home. Its work is thoroughly practical and the success obtained in strengthening the physical and moral health of inebriates is too well known to need eulogy. As it depends in large measure on voluntary contributions, we direct the attention of all our readers to its admirable methods and work. The superintendent of the Home is Mr. Robert Scott who has devoted many years to the careful study of this work. The board of officers and directors herewith given indicates the high standing of the Home: Officers, 1893. President, Hon. Frank D. Allen, Room 77, Equitable Building, Boston; Vice-Presidents, Charles O. Beede, Esq., Charles W. Wood, Esq., Worcester; Treasurer, William A. Attwill, City Hall, Lynn; Attending Physician, Frank T. Lougee, M. D.; Superintendent of Home, Robert Scott; Board of Directors, Rev. E. E. Hale, D. D., Rev. J. P. Bodfish, C. O. Beede, Esq., W. A. Attwill, Esq., Mrs. T. A. Scott, Hon. F. D. Allen, C. W. Wood, Esq., Robert Scott. Application for admission to the Home may be made to the superintendent at the Home, 27 New Ocean Street, Lynn, or at the Boston office, 28 School Street, Room 45.

LYNN ICE COMPANY, Wholesale and Retail Dealers in Ice, Office in Currier Block, 333 Union Street, Room 34, Lynn, Mass.—If a city family nowadays should be compelled to go without ice for a single week during the summer they would then realize of what immense importance it is. The amount added to the general health and comfort by this trade is beyond calculation. It seems therefore remarkable that it has been almost entirely developed during the past generation. The Lynn Ice Co.—one of the largest and best known in the State was established in 1879 and has had its hands filled with a prosperous business without interruption since. Its central office is at Room 34, Currier Block, 333 Union Street, this city. The large ice houses of the company situated both at Milton, N. H., and at Lynn, have a total capacity of 42,000 tons. They are therefore prepared to meet the largest demands at any time. They employ fifty regular workmen, drivers, etc., apart from the large corps needed during the ice harvesting season. Their ice is noted in Lynn and adjacent cities for its exceptional purity and reliable character. Their perfected system and facilities enable them to secure very prompt, regular delivery. Both to wholesale and retail trade they can guarantee the lowest market prices, consistent with good service. To convince one's-self that their service and figures are the best it is simply necessary to make a trial of the same. Our readers will consult their own interests in testing this fact.!

JOS. D. VALIQUET, Caterer, 67 Central Avenue, Lynn, Mass.—True success as a caterer can be attained only by one who is really an artist in that line of business, for experience, study and perseverance accomplish but little unless they are backed by that natural ability which is possessed by but few. Hence when we say that Mr. Joseph D. Valiquet occupies a leading position among the caterers of Lynn, it is hardly necessary to add that those who appreciate and desire really artistic catering, cannot possibly do better than to avail themselves of the facilities he offers. The ice cream, sherbets, etc., furnished by Mr. Valiquet are not only made from the best obtainable material, but they are flavored with a delicacy and taste that makes them incomparable; and the same may be said of his frozen puddings, of his fruit ices, of his tutti-frutti, and of his cakes. Mr. Valiquet's establishment is located at 67 Central Avenue, and comprises two floors, measuring 60x40 feet. It is very thoroughly equipped, ample assistance is employed, and orders are assured prompt and accurate delivery at any point in the city. Mr. Valiquet has had extended experience on a large scale, for he has done the catering for the Massachusetts Militia on their annual field days at South Framingham, and also at Fort Warren, and many complimentary reports were made concerning the service he rendered.

J. F. TWOMBLY, House Painting & Decorator, 15 Lewis Street, Lynn, Mass.—This old and reliable business was established by Mr. Twombly in 1863, having held a leading position in the Lynn trade for the past thirty years. Long and thorough experience enables Mr. Twombly to execute a superior class of service in this line and he guarantees uniformly first-class work. His shop at 15 Lewis Street is finely equipped and contains every convenience for house painting and decorating work. Only the best materials are used and great care is taken to secure a fine thorough finish. As is well-known, there are great differences in the way house painting is executed and it often means a matter of many dollars to the house-owner to have this work thoroughly done. The way to be sure is to employ an experienced and thorough master of this branch of trade. Mr. Twombly can execute promptly every kind of paper hanging work. His figures cannot be beaten anywhere in this section. Estimates on large or small contracts will be promptly rendered at any time. Our readers can feel assured of first class satisfactory service in entrusting work of this sort to Mr. Twombly's charge. He is a thorough New England business man in every feature of promptness, energy and strict reliability, as his many patrons in Lynn and vicinity can testify.

PRESTON CAFE, Edward F. Boardman, Proprietor, 78 Exchange Street, Lynn.—A restaurant at which palatable and nutritious meals may be obtained at all hours, at short notice, and at moderate rates is certainly deserving of liberal patronage, and hence no one can justly begrudge Mr. Edward F. Boardman the prompt and decided success his establishment has attained since its opening, for it is a very ably managed restaurant and dining-room and the service is uniformly satisfactory, while the charges are uniformly reasonable. Mr. Boardman gives very close personal attention to every detail of his business and caters successfully to all classes who appreciate good, well-cooked and neatly served food, prompt service and low prices. The premises occupied are located at 78 Exchange Street and are 70x30 feet in dimensions. They are thoroughly fitted up and are kept neat and clean at all times. Seven capable assistants are constantly on hand to serve the numerous patrons who daily patronize this popular cafe, every caller being cordially welcomed and assured prompt as well as courteous attention. One of the specialties of this popular cafe is a regular dinner for the small sum of 25 cents, consisting of soup, fish, roasts, vegetables, pudding and pie. Table board for ladies and gentlemen may be obtained here at low rates.

HOLDER & CO., Apothecaries, 119 Broad Street, Lynn, Mass.—In no branch of modern trade is greater progress constantly being brought about than in that of the apothecary. This is because it represents several distinct lines of scientific advance, all converging here to the alleviation of human suffering and disease. One of the oldest establishments of Lynn in this important department is the well-known apothecary store conducted by Messrs. Holder & Co. at 119 Broad Street. This was established as far back as 1818, and has always maintained a very high position for reliable and accurate service. Under the present management no pains have been spared to keep the store on the best modern basis. It now conducts a trade as select and refined as any in the city. The building occupied is 50x25 feet in dimensions and handsomely fitted up. The stock is complete and constantly renewed with the freshest and purest drugs. Special care is given to preparing physicians' prescriptions, and utmost accuracy guaranteed in this department, the importance of which can not be overestimated. The firm employ four reliable and thoroughly trained assistants. All orders receive prompt attention at any time. A first-class stock of fine toilet and fancy goods also carried in stock at reasonable figures. The firm are natives of Massachusetts and among our best known and solid business men.

W. R. STOVER, Painter and Glazier, Whitewashing and Kalsomining. No. 216 Union Street, Lynn.—The appearance, and to a considerable extent the comfortableness and healthfulness of a house, depends largely upon the manner in which it is painted and papered, and it is well worth while to keep your residence in first-class condition, both as regards exterior painting and interior painting, decorating, and papering. The cost of doing so is by no means large, that is to say, provided you will use reasonable "discrimination" in the placing of the order, and one sure way to get as much first-class work done as possible, at a given price, is to place the order with Mr. W. R. Stover, whose business premises are located at 216 Union Street; for as a house painter, glazier, and paper hanger, he is prepared to do work equal to the best, to quote prices as low as the lowest, and to execute commissions promptly as well as thoroughly. He is a practical painter, glazier and paper-hanger, and also does whitewashing and kalsomining, giving particular attention to all work, and using the best lead, oil, etc. Mr. Stover is a native of Maine, and began business in his present line here at Lynn in 1884, being widely known throughout the city and vicinity. He gives close personal attention to each of the various departments of his business, and employs four competent assistants, being prepared to fill all orders promptly, and at the same time giving each careful and intelligent attention. Mr. Stover is a prominent member of the I. O. O. F., is now Past Grand of Providence Lodge, No. 171, and Past High Priest of Palestine Encampment, No. 37.

W. P. GOURLEY, Teaming, Light and Heavy Expressing, Furniture Moving, Contract Work, Excavating Stone Work, Heavy Trucking a Specialty, Coal by the Ton, cor. Pleasant and Wheeler Street, Lynn, Mass.—The moving of furniture is something which is dreaded by all housekeepers, even when it is done under the most favorable circumstances. We take pleasure therefore in calling particular attention to the business carried on by Mr. W. P. Gourley whose establishment is located on corner of Pleasant and Wheeler Streets, where all orders left for the moving of furniture will receive prompt and careful attention. A specialty is made by him of heavy trucking and any person wishing out of town work done would do well to give him a call. Teaming, light and heavy expressing of all kinds, contract work, excavating stone work, coal by the ton, are all done at short notice, full satisfaction guaranteed, while the terms are extremely reasonable. Six competent assistants are employed and six horses are kept in constant use. Mr. Gourley is successor to Wyman & Son and is becoming very popular among his patrons and others doing business with him, for he is straightforward in his methods and faithfully carries out every agreement. He is a practical business man and gives his personal attention to all orders, and is prepared to do all kinds of jobbing promptly and at short notice.

GEORGE L. WADLIN, Watchmaker, Optician and Jeweler, 75 Munroe Street, Lynn, Mass.—The man who has once carried a really accurate watch will never be satisfied afterwards with a time-keeper that is not to be entirely depended upon. There is a peculiar satisfaction in owning a watch that you can "swear by," known only to those who have experienced it, and if any of our readers should be about to purchase a watch or any article of jewelry, we would advise them to secure full value for their money by buying of a trustworthy dealer and paying a fair price. Those living in Lynn and vicinity cannot do better we believe, than to place their orders with Mr. G. L. Wadlin, located at 75 Munroe Street, for while he does not carry a large stock of goods, he enjoys such relations with the wholesale houses that any orders that may call for any articles not held in stock can be furnished on an hour or two notice and at prices that save to the purchaser the per cent. usually charged to cover interest, insurance, etc., on stock, if carried. Mr. Wadlin is a thoroughly practical watchmaker and jeweler, and has had many years' experience. He makes a specialty of watch repairing, to which he gives his close personal attention and warrants his work equal in excellence to any done in the city, satisfaction being always guaranteed to every patron.

E. W. HALL,
FINE MILLINERY,
17, 43, & 101 Market Street,
LYNN, MASS.

It is often difficult to define the precise status of an establishment located in a city or town where there are many others of the same kind, for "different people have different tastes," and therefore some are apt to favor one establishment and some another, but in spite of this well-known fact the real leaders in any line of trade are quite easily picked out, and hence there is no uncertainty as to the comparative position held by the millinery establishments carried on by Mr. E. W. Hall at 17, 43 and 101 Market Street, Lynn, for these have long been known as representative millinery establishments. The premises at 17 Market Street comprise two floors, being spacious and well arranged. Both a wholesale and retail business is conducted at this store, while in each store the stock is always very attractive, for it comprises the latest novelties in fine millinery goods and is so varied and complete that all tastes can be suited from it. It includes a comprehensive assortment of trimmed and untrimmed hats and bonnets, together with ribbons, velvets, silks, laces, feathers, flowers and mourning goods of all kinds, and the goods are offered at prices that will compare very favorably with those quoted by other dealers. Mr. Hall is a native of Maine, and since beginning operations at Lynn in 1886 has built up an extensive business both wholesale and retail in character. Twelve competent assistants are employed at 17 Market Street alone, and superior custom work is made a leading specialty at each store, and as artistic results are obtained here as at any establishment in the city, while the prices are decidedly lower than those named at many houses devoted to the same line of business.

BON MARCHÉ
Fine Millinery Goods.

Specialty of Fine Order Work. None but First-class Milliners Employed. Lady Attendant who speaks French.

43 MARKET STREET, - - - LYNN, MASS.
Bouquet French and American Millinery,
—FINE STOCK.—
101 MARKET STREET, Odd Fellows' Block, LYNN, MASS.

ALLEN STORY & CO., Boarding, Livery and Sale Stable. Carriages and Harnesses for Sale. Hay and Grain at Wholesale and Retail, 33, 35 and 37 Andrew St.; Telephone 205-2, Lynn, Mass.—A great deal of butter nonsense has been written about the buying, selling and hiring of horses, and if one would believe half the yarns that have been told he would think that there was hardly one chance in ten of one who was not up to all the "tricks of the trade" getting his money's worth. Now, that is not the case. Buy from a reputable house and you may be sure that they will be satisfied with a fair margin of profit, buy from Tom, Dick and Harry, that are here to-day and gone to-morrow, and you will "get it in the neck," for they only want to make a sale and they have no reputation to maintain. The business carried on by Messrs. Allen Story & Co. was founded some ten years ago, and the simple fact that this firm is of unblemished reputation is positive proof that it means to use its customers honorably and can be depended upon to give full value for money received. The firm carry on a boarding, livery and sale stable; and not only sell horses but also carriages and harnesses; and hay and grain—the latter being sold at both wholesale and retail. The premises utilized are located at 33, 35 and 37 Andrew Street,—and it is worth while to note the fact that the harness store is quite distinct from the stable, and contains a fine stock of light, heavy and medium driving and working harnesses. All orders are assured prompt and careful attention and whether you want to buy, sell, or hire a horse, to buy anything in the line of carriages or harnesses, or to buy hay and grain of dependable quality at bottom prices—it will pay you to communicate with this responsible concern.

BOSTON STREET LAUNDRY, Frederic C. Cheever, Proprietor, 531 Washington Street, Lynn, Mass.—The best way to "size up" business enterprises in general and laundries in particular is by the verdict of the people. A laundry may claim to have an elaborate plant of the latest improved machinery; it may claim to do first-class work at bottom prices, and to be prompt and accurate in the filling of orders and the delivery of goods, but unless that claim is supported by the people it is—to say the least—doubtful. Of course, if it is supported by the people the laundry will be a popular one, and as the Boston Street Laundry was never more popular than it is to-day, after ten years' service of the public—it is hardly necessary to add that the work is well done, and the service afforded is very satisfactory. Some idea of the business transacted is shown by the fact that he has over one hundred agents in Lynn and surrounding towns. The proprietor, Fred. C. Cheever, is a native of Saugus, and is very widely known in this section. He spares no trouble to maintain the service at the highest possible standard of efficiency; gives prompt and painstaking attention to every complaint made concerning mistakes or undue delay in the delivery of laundry work, and employs about thirty competent assistants, so that, despite the magnitude of the business, orders are filled promptly and the delivery is regular. The laundry is located at 531 Washington Street, and work is called for and delivered at the residences of customers, if desired.

S. R. ANDREWS, Butter, Cheese, Eggs, Potatoes, Salt, Hay and Grain, 14 Andrew St., Telephone 109-2 Lynn. A review of the prominent business enterprises of Lynn that did not contain mention of that carried on by Mr. S. R. Andrews, would be looked upon as sadly incomplete, and rightly so, for Mr. Andrews has been in the wholesale produce business here for more than a score of years, and is one of the most widely known business men in the city. He utilizes spacious premises located at No. 14 Andrew St., and constantly carries a very large and complete stock; being prepared to fill all wholesale orders—large or small—at very short notice. As a wholesale commission dealer Mr. Andrews has an enviable reputation for promptness in making returns, and it is but natural that he should market the goods of the leading producers who depend chiefly upon the residents of Lynn and vicinity to consume their products. Among the more important commodities handled by Mr. Andrews may be mentioned butter, cheese, eggs, potatoes, apples, hay and grain; also poultry, pure cider vinegar, and salt of all kinds, including crystaline, Liverpool fine, coarse, fine and Turks Island, in 5, 10, and 20 lb. boxes. The business is very thoroughly systematized; is carefully supervised by Mr. Andrews in every department, and it is hardly necessary to add that the service is maintained at a high standard of efficiency. Mr. Andrews is a native of Ipswich, Mass., and has been identified with his present business since 1871.

THE MRS. C. H. KING COMPANY, Manufacturers of Infants', Children's and Misses' Fancy Footwear, Boston Office, No. 139 Summer St.; 7 Willow St., Lynn, Mass.— If proof were needed of the now universally conceded fact that Lynn is the New England headquarters for the manufacture of fine footwear, much would be afforded by a visit to the factory of the Mrs. C. H. King Company, for this company are very extensive manufacturers of infants', children's and misses' fancy footwear that is not only of the finest grade but will compare favorably with the best footwear made in any other part of the country. The factory is located at 7 Willow St., has more than 12,000 square feet of floor space, and is equipped with an elaborate plant of machinery of the most improved type. Employment is given to about 100 hands and the output is so large that orders can generally be filled at comparatively short notice; although it must be confessed that during the busy season the company has to "hustle" in order to avoid falling too far behind in meeting the demand for its goods. And this demand is steadily and rapidly increasing. The goods are sure to be correct in style, excellent in fit and satisfactory in material and workmanship; many new styles are brought out every season; and the prices will always compare favorably with those quoted on any goods of equal merit in the market. A concern offering such inducements is sure to do a good business and the present indications are that the Company will soon have to add to their already extensive facilities.

H. K. WHEELER, Architect, Rooms 59 and 60, Currier Building, 333 Union Street, Telephone 3½2, Lynn, Mass.—A widely observant foreigner visiting this country some ten years ago remarked that all the houses seemed built upon the same plan and with slight application of architectural ability. The past decade, however, has witnessed a great advance in this particular throughout practically the whole country. Like other intellectual and artistic movements it started and centred in Boston and vicinity. Among the most skilled and successful architects of New England, is H. K. Wheeler, of Lynn, who has executed many successful contracts in various sections of Massachusetts as well as other States. The business was first established in 1886. Mr. Wheeler is an experienced and thoroughly trained architect. He has handsomely equipped offices at 59 and 60 Currier Building, 333 Union Street, Lynn, Mass., and employs a large force of competent assistants. He can at any time furnish drawings for buildings of all kinds, complete specifications and contracts—and also superintend work. To ensure thorough results in all the features of a modern dwelling or business house, it is absolutely essential to secure the oversight of such trained and skilled intelligence as is furnished by this office. Apart from the value of artistic excellence and harmony which are now universally regarded as of high importance, a building not accurately constructed as to all the sanitary details unquestionably of vital significance nowadays, will in the end cost much more than one built right at first. The terms and figures of this office will be found in every respect reasonable and moderate. Those who wish to secure the best results of modern scientific and artistic progress will do well to rely upon his complete facilities.

EDWARD S. CLARK & CO., Dry and Fancy Goods, 312 Union Street, Lynn.—The store carried on by Messrs. Edward S. Clark & Co., at No. 312 Union Street, has been described by one Lynn lady who has had a good deal of experience in shopping, as "A place big enough to accommodate as large and complete a stock as one expects to find in a first-class dry and fancy goods store, and small enough to avoid the bothers and delays of a big department store, and to enable one to have mistakes promptly and satisfactorily corrected." There you have the whole story in a nutshell, and it is hardly necessary to add that this is a very popular establishment— especially as the prices quoted on all the goods handled are as low as the lowest, and the service is such that prompt and courteous attention is assured to every caller. The premises occupied are 125x25 feet in dimensions, and contain as "clean" a stock of dry and fancy goods as can be found in the city. This technical term "clean" means free from unseasonable, unsalable goods, and at this establishment there is no room for goods of that kind, for every inch of available space is required to accommodate the extensive and complete assortment of foreign and domestic dry and fancy goods that is constantly carried. The stock is being renewed; one is sure to find here the latest novelties, and if one is looking for "back numbers" he must search elsewhere, for this carefully and skillfully chosen stock is always fully up to date in every department.

WM. TABOUR, Established 1861, Manufacturer of Fine Cigars, 180 Union Street, Lynn, Mass. —There is but one sure way of distinguishing a good cigar and that is to smoke it, for in spite of the claims of self-styled "experts" we question if there is a man living who can infallibly judge by any other means. Examination will tell whether a cigar is well or ill made, and whether it is well seasoned or not, but beyond this it avails but little and therefore the smoker has only one security that he will not be imposed upon, and that is the reputation of the dealer from whom he buys. Mr. Wm. Tabour has the name of selling thoroughly satisfactory cigars at moderate prices, and this name is so well established and deserved that we feel that we can do our readers no greater service than to call their attention to this gentleman's establishment, located at 180 Union Street, for here may be found a remarkably complete assortment of cigars, tobacco, etc., of all kinds, and the prices are as satisfactory as the goods themselves. The premises occupied comprise one floor measuring 1,000 square feet, giving ample room for the manufacture of fine cigars, as well as for the transaction of an extensive wholesale and retail trade in all the finest grades of cigars, tobacco, pipes, etc. Mr. Tabour is a pioneer in the cigar trade, having started the first cigar store in the city of Boston in 1847 where the Lowell depot now stands; this was burned out. He was for some time located at the junction of Lancaster and Merrimac Streets, Boston. In 1860 he went to Salem, Mass., where he conducted business for a short time. Then removed to Lynn in 1861. For three years was on the corner of Munroe and Market Streets, but for the past twelve years has been at his present stand, No. 180 Union Street. Mr. Tabour is a native of Massachusetts. He is an energetic and reliable business man, employs seven well informed assistants and is thus in a position to assure every patron prompt as well as polite attention.

LUTHER S. JOHNSON & CO., Slipper Manufacturers, Lynn, Mass. Salesroom 83 Bedford Street, Boston.—Just about a score of years have passed since the establishment of the business conducted by Messrs. Luther S. Johnson & Co., it having been founded in 1873. Mr Johnson was sole proprietor until 1886, when Mr. James W. Hitchings was admitted to partnership, and the present firm name was adopted. As slipper manufacturers this concern rank with the largest in the country, and their goods are shipped to every section of the United States, being placed with the largest and best jobbing houses in the trade. Their factory facilities are immense, the factory having an area of over 52,000 square feet, and employment being given to from 300 to 400 operatives, but even these resources are sometimes insufficient, as the demand for this firm's productions is enormous, and seems destined to continue to increase every year. This demand may be said to be due to a combination of style, neatness, comfort, beauty and cheapness, for it is conceded by the trade that the goods manufactured by this representative house are unsurpassed in these important respects. The salesroom is at 83 Bedford Street, Boston, and orders are assured prompt and careful attention.

CHAS. C. BLANCHARD (Successor to J. W. Cushing), Carpenter, Builder, and Jobber. Telephone, 146-2. 819 to 823 Washington Street, Lynn, Mass.—Architecture is the outgrowth of centuries of genius, and finds its first impetus in the buildings of the Greeks. In this day it is required of the builder that his abilities shall combine the talents of the architect, if he would defeat, or even meet the competition of his fellow builders. The imposing edifices of Lynn, Mass., afford a living example of this statement, and in many is seen the excellent handiwork of Chas. C. Blanchard, who conducts a very extensive business as carpenter, builder and jobber, at 819 to 823 Washington Street. Mr. Blanchard, who is a native of Maine, entered upon his calling in 1884, after having gone through a very long apprenticeship, and carefully prepared himself for the prosecution of his duties. He is a thoroughly trained architect and builder, and, in addition to his abilities as a carpenter he has the ability to handle and command his men, his force comprising fifty of the most skillful carpenters in this city. He has convenient and eligible premises, 40x60 feet in area, and has provided his shop with all of the most modern appliances used in the work of constructing high class dwellings, stores, offices, etc. Mr Blanchard succeeded Mr. J. W. Cushing in business, and, while he found a good basis to work upon, his own energies were quickly brought into requisition, with the result that he has gone on increasing his patronage, until his half a hundred clever mechanics constantly have their hands full in meeting the requirements of customers. Mr. Blanchard's work from an artistic standpoint can perhaps be judged to no greater advantage than by a view of his own fine residence at No. 11 Bloomfield Street, East Lynn. Here he has a beautiful home, and enjoys the confidence and respect of his townsmen. He is content to let political and social ambitions alone, and continue in a hard drive at his business, which is daily increasing. His work stands as a living monument of its excellence, and in this the builder is far in vantage of the manufacturer of stuffs, because the builder's work does not perish. Likewise does the reputation of an honorable man withstand all the storms of criticism, and in his daily application to every sort of fine cabinet and carpenter work Mr. Blanchard's name stands out boldly for integrity and fair dealing.

WOODWARD HOUSE, S. T. Woodward, Proprietor, 10 Pearl Street, Lynn.—People who care more for style than they do for comfort, and who judge of the desirability of the service offered at a public house entirely by the charges made in connection with the same, will not be especially interested in the Woodward House, and will hardly find it worth their while to read this brief notice of the same; but the majority of our readers are not included in this class, and therefore, we need no apology for devoting space to a consideration of the hotel in question. The proprietor, Mr. S. T. Woodward, seems to have but one object in view, and that is to make his guests feel entirely comfortable and at home. Of course he is not in the business for the fun of the thing, and he proposes to make a fair profit on his investment, but he evidently believes that a liberal policy pays the best in the long run. This house was opened in 1885 by the present proprietor, who is a native of Poland, Maine, and well-known in this vicinity. The Woodward House is very pleasantly and conveniently situated at No. 10 Pearl Street, consisting of a good sized building which contains sixty-three well furnished rooms for the accommodation of guests, which are nicely kept. A specialty is made of renting rooms to transient or permanent guests, and all are treated in a civil and polite manner. The table is supplied at all seasons with an abundance, the bill of fare showing a good variety; the cooking and service is first class, and the prices reasonable.

OSGOOD & FISH, Dealers in Choice Family Groceries and Provisions, Teas, Coffees and Spices a Specialty, 8 Union Street, Lynn, Mass.—One of the most reliable grocery and provision houses doing business in this city is that carried on by Messrs. Osgood & Fish, located at 8 Union Street, but if any of our readers should make the common mistake of assuming that age and reliability must necessarily mean more or less "old fogyism" and lack of enterprise they would be most decidedly wrong so far as this firm is concerned at all events, for a more trusty progressive firm cannot be found in Lynn, and Lynn contains many enterprising business men. They have had an experience in this line of trade for about twenty years, having opened their present establishment to the public in 1871. Spacious premises occupied, and the stock handled is proportionately large, it comprising choice family groceries and provisions of all kinds it being very complete in each of its departments. A specialty is made of teas, coffees and spices and orders for anything usually found in a first-class city grocery and provision store may be placed here in the full assurance that they will be filled at short notice and at the lowest market rates, and it is superfluous to add that all goods will prove just as represented in every respect. The individual members of this firm are Mr. J. S. Osgood and Mr. Geo. A. Fish, both of whom give close personal attention to the details of the business and they have won the respect and high esteem of all who patronize their store, by their liberal business methods.

JAMES B. SMALL, PH. G., Apothecary, 606 Essex Street and 169 Central Avenue, Lynn, Mass.—As health is the most valuable possession that any person can have, it follows that every reasonable person should take pains to preserve his health, and to regain it as soon as possible if by any cause it is taken away. Therefore, everyone should know the address of a skillful and trustworthy physician, and also that of an equally competent apothecary, for the most eminent physician can do but little unless his prescriptions are filled from a fresh and complete stock of drugs, etc., and compounded with that skill which is the outcome of education and practical experience. In this connection, we may be excused for calling attention to the establishment conducted by Mr. James B. Small. The premises utilized are located at 606 Essex Street and 169 Central Avenue, they being centrally located at the junction of the above named streets. A full line of goods desirable in an apothecary store, will be found here, and every effort made to retain the reputation which this house has gained from having been so long established, and as we live in the age of progress, when new methods are used and improvements are desirable in all kinds of business, Mr. Small will be found equal to the occasion, and all customers will be served in a courteous and satisfactory manner. Mr. Small, who is a native of Maine, has been for twenty-four years actively engaged in the pursuit of his calling. Graduating from M. C. P. in class 1874, twenty-one years of the time being spent in Lynn, and since 1881 he has conducted a successful and honorable business for himself.

Professor JAMES H. READY,
DANCING * ACADEMY,
FULLER BUILDING, ROOM 16,
10 CENTRAL SQUARE, - - LYNN.

Many parents appreciate the advantages of dancing, and would see that their children were instructed in the art, were it not for their fear of entrusting them to an incompetent instructor, for they know that inferior teaching is really worse than none at all. But it is not difficult to find a thoroughly skillful and reliable dancing master if the search be intelligently carried on, and we take pleasure in calling attention to the dancing academy of Professor James H. Ready, for we are convinced that this gentleman is not only a most skillful and graceful dancer, but has that faculty for teaching which is indispensable to the attainment of the best possible results. Instruction is given in all the latest ball room dances; and such care is taken in even the minutest details of tuition that one who graduates from Professor Ready's Academy is assured of proficiency and has not the least reason to fear appearance in the very highest society. Lessons are given every day and evening, both public and private, at the academy in the Fuller Building, 10 Central Square, Room 16, and pupils will be attended at their residence if desired. Communications to above address are assured prompt attention.

L. C. HOLDSWORTH, Carpenter and Builder. Shop, 821 Washington Street, Residence, 27 New Chatham Street, Lynn, Mass.—Of course in order to attain the best possible results in building operations, it is necessary to secure the services of an experienced and skillful architect and a reliable, responsible and experienced builder, but if circumstances are such as to force one to choose between a first-class architect and a first-class builder, it is doubtless better to choose the latter: for a thoroughly competent builder will so carry out his contract as to correct many minor errors and omissions on the part of the architect while an unreliable or unskillful builder will do unsatisfactory work in spite of the most skillfully and thoroughly prepared plans and specifications. Happily such a choice has very seldom to be made in this vicinity; good architects and very good builders are many and one of the most prominent and successful of the latter is Mr. L. C. Holdsworth, who has carried on operations in Lynn for the past nine years having established this business in 1884. The premises utilized for business purposes are located at 821 Washington Street, or he may be seen at his residence, 27 New Chatham Street. The shop consists of two floors 40x30 and 20x20 feet in dimensions. Mr. Holdsworth has executed many important commissions. He employs fifteen experienced men, and large orders can be filled at very short notice in cases where haste is essential. Mr. Holdsworth is in a position to figure very closely on building work; and those placing contracts with him have the decided advantage of knowing that the work will be executed strictly in accordance with the agreement. Jobbing is done at short notice and at reasonable rates, and estimates will cheerfully be furnished on application.

J. L. WHITTREDGE, Mason and Builder, Jobbing in all its Branches. Lime, Sand and Cement of all Kinds. Plaster, Kaolin, Common, Face, and Fire Brick in Stock. No. 843 Washington Street, Lee's Wharf, Lynn, Mass.—There is no more important profession or trade among the various enterprises that go to make up the business interests of a community, than that of the mason and builder. With him rests, largely, the making of the city beautiful, for, according to his skill and practical knowledge, the architectural appearance of the city is improved, or kept at or below mediocrity. Among the prominent builders and masons of Lynn, none has a higher or better deserved reputation as a thorough master of his business than Mr. J. L. Whittredge. His is one of the largest and most important enterprises of its kind in New England, giving steady employment to eighteen hands. The establishment is located at 843 Washington Street, Lee's Wharf, and dates from 1883, when Mr. Whittredge began business in Lynn. In addition to his large business as a mason and builder, Mr. Whittredge does an extensive wholesale and retail trade in lime, sand, masons' supplies and drain pipe; loading and unloading from vessels at the wharf, which gives him an advantage in the handling of these bulky materials over other dealers not so advantageously located, and enabling him to make lower prices than are possible where the stock has to be carted from the wharves. His lime, sand, and cement are kept under cover in a building especially provided for their protection. In fact, Mr. Whittredge's every facility is of the best, and through them he is able to fill orders at the shortest possible notice, and with a promptness that is much appreciated by buyers of this class of goods. Besides the articles already mentioned, he carries a full stock of plaster, kaolin, common, face and fire brick. He is agent for the celebrated Original Akron Company's drain pipe, which he furnishes and lays at the lowest price. Mr. Whittredge is also agent in Lynn, for the Hematite Mortar Red, which he is prepared to sell at a reduced price, making it one of the cheapest and most desirable articles of its kind in the market.

LYNN DYE HOUSE, George H. Johnson & Co., Proprietors, Dyeing, Cleansing and Finishing of every description, 306 Broad Street, Lynn, Mass. Office at 56 Market Street. New Bedford Office, 6 Pleasant Street. Newburyport Office, 25 Pleasant Street.—The people of New England are noted for their economical and careful habits. This is one of the main reasons why they are so well off and able to furnish money to the rest of the country. One striking example of this fact locally is the great success which has been achieved by the Lynn Dye House during the past twenty years. The business was established by Mr. George H. Johnson in 1873, and is now organized as Geo. H. Johnson & Co., Mr. Thos. J. Houlding being also a member of the firm. Both of these gentlemen are natives of Massachusetts and widely experienced business men. Their establishment is one of the largest and best of its kind in the State and does a very extensive business. The building occupied at 306 Broad Street is three stories high and 60x25 feet in dimensions. There is also a branch office at 56 Market Street. Twelve experienced hands are employed in the various branches of the work here. In addition to the Lynn offices there are also branch offices at New Bedford and Newburyport. Every sort of dyeing, cleansing and finishing work is handled with the utmost care and dispatch. The large facilities of this establishment enable them to secure the highest degree of satisfaction. All work attended to and delivered promptly, while the charges will be found equal to the best. The high reputation of the Lynn Dye House is based upon the most careful and accurate service. A specialty is made of handling delicate and valuable fabrics, utmost care being guaranteed. Our readers in all parts of the State will find it to their advantage to entrust work of this kind to the old established Lynn Dye House and by so doing secure most gratifying results.

J. RUTH & SON, Dealers in Groceries and Provisions, Butter, Cheese and Eggs, 319 Essex Street, Lynn, Mass.—The management of a retail store, and especially of a retail market, is what makes the difference between success and failure, and plain as this would seem to be it is very often lost sight of, and the result is that some dealers who handle satisfactory goods and quote moderate prices, utterly fail in establishing or in holding a business. What we mean by good management may be seen by a visit to the establishment of Messrs. J. Ruth & Son, at 319 Essex Street. Here you will find an attractive store and an attractive stock. This business was established by J. Ruth in 1868, his son being admitted to partnership in 1892. Mr. Ruth, Sr., has had a long and varied experience in this business, therefore he knows what his customer's want, and what's more, he proposes to see that they get it, provided, of course, it is anything in reason, and we need hardly add that Lynn people are not at all apt to be unreasonable in their demands. Orders are filled intelligently; their delivery is looked after sharply, and somebody is held responsible for the prompt and faithful performance of each of the various duties incidental to the business; hence the service is uniformly accurate and satisfactory. As the stock includes full lines of choice groceries and provisions, butter, cheese and eggs, orders can be filled at short notice. Both members of the firm are natives of Massachusetts, and are widely and favorably known throughout Lynn and vicinity. Employment is given to four polite and experienced assistants, and the premises occupied are 30x22 feet in dimensions.

GEORGE H. ROBIE, Dealer in Ladies', Misses', Childrens' and Infants' Cloaks, Suits, Millinery, and Furs, 315 Union Street, Lynn, Mass.—There is probably no house in Lynn deserving of a more extended notice in a work of this kind than the one which heads this article. Experience in any pursuit in life is justly regarded wherein the ability exists to profit by it, as equal to the capital, and when this is found in connection with sound business principles, the possessors are entitled to recognition. Mr. George H. Robie, evidently merits to be ranked with this class, having in the judgment of his fellow citizens been found worthy their entire confidence and esteem. The premises utilized by him are located at 315 Union Street, comprising one floor some 1,600 square feet in dimensions, and are well stocked with a large variety of Ladies', Misses', Children's, and Infants' Cloaks, Suits, Millinery and Furs. The extensive retail trade already acquired gives employment to a number of capable and efficient assistants, and we can assure our interested readers that all transactions entered into cannot but result in connections both pleasant and profitable. Mr. Robie deals in only fashionable Cloaks, Suits and Millinery, Furs, etc., offering the same at very moderate prices. He is well-known throughout Lynn and vicinity as a man of artistic tastes, and rare business ability who is prepared to execute any order that his numerous patrons may entrust to either department of his establishment in a most satisfactory manner.

THE CONTINENTAL, Dam & Warner, Dealers in Clothing, Men's Furnishings, Hats, Caps, Trunks, etc., 323 & 325 Union Street, Lynn, Mass.—For many years Lynn has had an enviable reputation as a trade centre, or more properly as a purchasing centre; for the enterprise, the business sagacity and the integrity of her merchants have so favorably impressed the residents of this section that Lynn has been and is the centre of supply for a large radius of country, and there is every reason to believe that the condition of affairs will be not only continued, but intensified in the future, for the present merchants are even more enterprising than their predecessors. Among the most progressive merchants in this vicinity mention should be made of the proprietors of The Continental who furnish thoroughly desirable and dependable goods at bottom prices. The individual members of the firm are Mr. S. N. Dam and George Warner, both of whom have made many friends throughout this city by their straightforward and liberal business methods. The premises utilized are located at 323 to 325 Union Street, Lynn, comprising one floor 100 x 28 feet in dimensions and a basement 75 x 75 feet in size, containing a choice and varied assortment of clothing, men's furnishings, hats, caps, trunks, etc. This stock is carefully selected, complete in every department, and made up of goods that are guaranteed to prove as represented. Messrs. Dam and Warner do an extensive retail trade, requiring the services of competent assistants; they quote positively bottom prices, and are prepared to suit all tastes and all purses, and to assure prompt and courteous attention to every caller.

GEORGE A. HAZLETT, Horse Shoeing, Carriage Smith, Wheelwright, and Carriage Painting, Light and Heavy Jobbing of Every Description, 212-214 Chestnut Street, Telephone 158-4, Lynn, Mass.—If every one who pretends to be a competent horse shoer were really what he claims to be, it would be an excellent thing for horses, to say nothing of their owners, for it is a notorious fact that many a valuable animal has been crippled and in some instances ruined by improper shoeing. Too much care can not be taken to entrust such work to thoroughly skillful and reliable hands, and as first-class horse shoers are by no means common, we take special pleasure in calling attention to the shop carried on by Mr. George A. Hazlett, and located at 212-214 Chestnut Street, for Mr. Hazlett is a professional horse shoer in the full sense of the term, for he suits his work to the requirements of the animal and spares no pains to attain the best results possible. Mr. Hazlett's energies are not all expended on horse shoeing however, as he also attends to carriage painting, carriage building and trimming as well as light and heavy jobbing of every description. He founded his present business in 1890. Mr. Hazlett's shop consists of two floors 120x43 feet in dimensions, and is very completely fitted up, and as employment is given to from eight to fifteen experienced assistants all orders are assured prompt and careful attention. Telephone 158-4.

W. F. GOLDSMITH & CO., Dealers in Carpetings, Draperies, Upholstery Goods, Window Shades, etc., 273 Union Street and 16 Buffum Street, Lynn, Mass.—From the earliest times no form of household decoration has been held in such high esteem as carpetings or rugs and draperies. In our day great artistic ability has been devoted to the perfection of new and elegant designs in this department of industrial art. The well-known house of Messrs. W. F. Goldsmith & Co. has long been recognized as representing the very finest and best developments in this line. At its large and handsome salesrooms, 273 Union Street and 16 Buffum Street, the stock of fine carpetings, draperies, upholstery goods, window shades, etc., kept constantly on hand, is unrivalled for combined variety, elegance and liberal price, by any similar assortment in this immediate section. All the grades of best carpetings, Axminsters, Wiltons, Moquettes, body Brussels, tapestries and ingrains, as well as straw mattings, oilcloths, linoleums, rugs, etc., are carried. Fresh and original designs are offered each season. Nowhere can more attractive and economical goods be obtained than at this leading store. A complete assortment of draperies and upholstery goods is also handled, including lambrequins, porticres, window shades, curtains, etc. These goods are guaranteed A1, and are sold at special figures. The best service is also afforded in making and laying carpets, also in all kinds of upholstering work. Nine experienced employes are kept constantly busied by the extensive and growing trade of this house. In prompt and courteous attention no less than in the high quality of bargains offered its facilities are unsurpassed. Mr. Goldsmith is prominent in local affairs and is serving his second term in the Common Council.

E. A. TIBBETTS & CO., Employment Bureau, Auctioneers and Dealers in Personal Property and Real Estate. Mortgages Negotiated, Estates Cared for, Tenements to Let, Bills Collected, Etc., 319 Union Street, Rooms 4 and 5, Lynn, Mass.—One of the most active and enterprising concerns in one of the most progressive cities in Massachusetts is that of E. A. Tibbetts & Co., who have offices in Rooms 4 and 5, 319 Union Street, and as enterprise and reliability are highly appreciated in the lively "shoe city" it is hardly necessary to add that the facilities offered by this firm are very generally availed of and that their business is steadily increasing. As dealers in real estate, and furnishing first-class service in their Employment Bureau department, and as auctioneers they are prepared to render service that is as efficient as it is comprehensive, and some idea of its comprehensiveness may be gained from the fact that it includes the care of estates, the negotiation of mortgages, the collection of rents and bills, the letting of tenements, and in fact all the many duties incidental to the carrying on of an extensive and complete business which includes the handling of personal property and real estate of all kinds. A specialty, is made of auctioneer service—the selling of real estate and personal property of every description. The firm is composed of Messrs. E. A. Tibbetts and C. F. Hathorne both of whom are widely known in business and social circles throughout the city. Both have served in minor offices in the city government. Mr. Tibbetts was in the legislature two years and has been Milk Inspector for this city. Personal attention is given to the carrying out of all the business entrusted to the firm, and the results attained are such as to fully explain the popularity of the enterprise. The public will find the service afforded by their employment bureau very efficient to those desiring reliable information in that line.

WALDO THOMPSON & SON, Established 1849. Real Estate and Insurance Agents, Mortgages Negotiated, Summer Cottages to Let. Notary Public; Justice of the Peace. 10 Central Square, Lynn, Mass., also Swampscott, Mass.—The history of the business carried on by Messrs. Waldo Thompson & Son, may truly be said to form a part of the history of the city, for this enterprise was inaugurated nearly half a century ago, and has been very closely connected with the many and radical changes in real estate matters which have taken place since that time. A real estate business which was established away back in 1849, and has been successfully conducted ever since, certainly needs no further proof of its stability, and it goes without saying that a firm carrying on such a business should be in a position to offer unsurpassed advantages to those wishing to buy, sell, exchange, rent or lease realty of any kind. Two specialties with this firm are the negotiation of mortgages and the purchase, sale and letting of summer cottages, and the magnitude of the business done in these departments alone, affords convincing evidence that the service rendered is thoroughly satisfactory. Mr. Fred O. Thompson is a native of Swampscott, and resides on Elmwood Road in that town, and is now alone in the business, his father having died in September, 1892. The business is carried on without change of firm. He is so generally known throughout this section as to need no extended personal mention. The office of the firm is located at 10 Central Square, and they also have an office in Swampscott, as many of the summer cottages controlled by them are situated in that town. A large insurance business is done, as the concern is prepared to place insurance in large or small amounts at short notice and at bottom rates, while the perfectly reliable character of the insurance furnished needs no further proof than that afforded by the standing of the companies represented, the list being as follows: German American, Liverpool, London and Globe; Mutual Citizens of Boston, Cambridge of Cambridgeport, Dedham & Norfolk of Dedham, Holyoke of Salem, Dorchester of Dorchester, Traders & Mechanics, Worcester, Mutual of Lowell.

BOSTON DRY GOODS STORE.

Hosiery, Underwear,
Gloves, Small Wares,
Laces, Corsets,
Ribbons, Domestics,
Cotton Underwear,
Men's Furnishings, &c.

PATON & TRUEMAN,

No. 38 MARKET STREET, LYNN, MASS.

It must be confessed that the "Boston Dry Goods Store" is a somewhat pretentious name for a dry goods establishment, as Boston is the headquarters for dry goods, small wares, etc., and so one naturally expects that a store bearing that name should offer a large assortment of goods that are fully "up to date" at positively the lowest market rates. But in the case of the "Boston Dry Goods Store" carried on by Messrs. Paton & Trueman, at No. 38 Market Street, the name is not pretentious, for the expectation it excites is fulfilled by examination of the stock and prices, and if you are an experienced "shopper" you will fully endorse our statement that many a dry goods store in Boston itself makes a less favorable showing. Spacious premises are occupied, and the stock is very complete in every department, it including foreign and domestic Dress Goods, Hosiery, Underwear, Gloves, Small Wares, Laces, Corsets, Ribbons Cotton Underwear, Men's Furnishings and other goods, literally "too numerous to mention." You are sure to find the latest novelties here; you are sure to be given opportunity to choose from the productions of the leading manufacturers, and you are sure to get full value in return for every dollar expended, as the prices are always in strict accordance with the lowest market rates, and every article is sold strictly on its merits. The relations of this firm in the past and present to the Scotch syndicate have been and are of such a character, that they are enabled to secure the benefit of first cost prices. Employment is given to 18 efficient assistants, and the service is prompt, accommodating and accurate, and so well systematized, that, should any mistake be made, it can be promptly and satisfactorily corrected. Aside from the satisfaction and pardonable pride felt by the managers of a successful business, when contemplating the profits of their establishment, there is an added degree of pleasure if they can reflect that their prosperity is due, in a great measure, to the confidence reposed in them by their customers—the confidence born of practical tests and actual results. Judging of the future by the past, the present store will soon be inadequate to the needs of this thriving business, and we shall expect to hear of extensive additions to the space now occupied. The proprietors are young men, of large experience, alive to every detail and need of the business, devoting to it all their time and energy, and their success is well deserved.

Lynn is a pretty big city, but it is not the kind of a city that attracts what is known as "transient trade," and hence a merchant who builds up a big business here, does it by satisfying "regular" customers. Hence the simple fact that Mr. James H. Conner does a very extensive business in Diamonds, Watches, Clocks, Jewelry, Silverware, Opera Glasses, Spectacles, etc., may be accepted as positive proof that he sells goods that prove just as represented and quotes bottom prices, for a heavy permanent patronage can be built up in no other way. The business was founded by Mr. Geo. Howe, in 1849, and in 1870 Mr. Conner was admitted to partnership, after having worked for Mr. Howe for four years. After the death of Mr. Howe, in 1886, Mr. Conner purchased the entire business, and has not only fully maintained the honorable reputation of the establishment, but has materially increased its patronage. He is an acknowledged connoisseur of precious stones, and his diamond trade is one of the most important features of the business; his customers being by no means confined to residents of Lynn. His spacious store is located at No. 81 Pearl Street, and one is always sure to find here a heavy, varied and most skillfully chosen stock, which includes the very latest novelties, as well as staple goods (like certain makes of watches, etc.,) which are always in demand. Particular attention is given to fine watch repairing and engraving, and some idea of the magnitude of the business in this department alone may be gained from the fact that employment is given to two skilled watchmakers, while two clerks are also employed. Of course one is assured prompt and courteous attention at this establishment, and equally of course he is sure of getting excellent value in return for every dollar expended. In May, 1893, a special department for optical work was established and is under the direct care of Mr. S. E. West, who is a professional optician of long experience, having been in business in Boston prior to forming this connection. Everything pertaining to his profession is skillfully attended to; a full line of everything pertaining to the eye is carried in stock, so that patrons are promptly served at Mr. Conner's store, and prices in this department defy competition for equally skillful service.

SWEENEY & DELANEY, Dealers in Fine Groceries and Provisions, Fancy Cereals a Specialty, No. 297 Essex Street, Lynn, Mass.—So much trouble and time can be saved by dealing at a store where a complete and carefully selected stock is carried, where effort is made to ascertain the preferences of each customer and to furnish him with goods that will suit his tastes, that it is no wonder that the establishment carried on by Messrs. Sweeney & Delaney should be largely patronized, for this is just such a store as we have described, and its merits have become very generally known since its inception in 1891. Messrs. Sweeney & Delaney are dealers in fine groceries and provisions, making a specialty of fancy cereals. They make a specialty of catering to family trade in both departments of their business, and handle goods that they are prepared to guarantee will prove just as represented in every respect. The premises utilized are located at No. 297 Essex Street, and are 40 x 18 feet in size. The members of the firm are Messrs. E. S. Sweeney and J. F. Delaney, both well and favorably known. Bottom prices are quoted on all the articles dealt in, and as two assistants are employed goods can be delivered at very short notice.

SANBORN, HURD & CO., Wholesale Dealers in Pork, Lard, Hams, Sausage, Pigs' Feet, Tripe, etc., No. 32 Andrew Street (Telephone 203-4), Lynn, Mass.—At No. 32 Andrew Street is one of the handsomest and best-equipped stores in the city, with great plate-glass windows, extensive refrigerating apparatus and every convenience for the prompt handling and neat and wholesome storage of pork by wholesale. The proprietors, Messrs. Sanborn, Hurd & Co., sell at wholesale only, so their establishment is not visited by the general public, but so many "fairy stories" have been circulated about the improper handling of meats in general and pork in particular by the wholesale dealers that it would pay the average citizen to inspect this store and become convinced that no trouble or expense is spared to deliver pork to the trade and to all wholesale buyers in the best possible condition. This firm deal in pork, lard, hams, sausage, pigs' feet, tripe, etc., and number among their customers the leading marketmen doing business in Lynn and vicinity, for it is known that their goods are equal to the best and their prices are as low as the lowest, quality considered. Employment is given to ten assistants and all orders are assured immediate attention.

H. W. HEATH,

STEAM AND WATER HEATING, GAS FITTING AND PLUMBING.

DEALER IN

BOILERS, ENGINES, ETC.

75 CENTRAL AVENUE, LYNN, MASS.

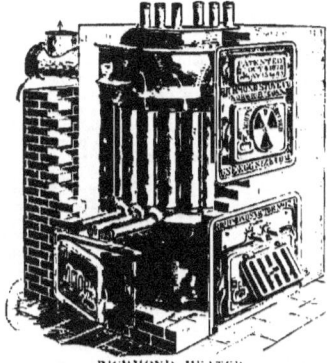

RICHMOND HEATER.

Mr. H. W. Heath is a native of Salisbury, N. H., but has long resided in Lynn, has carried on business here since 1880, and is extremely well-known in both business and social circles. He is a practical mechanic as well as an active and energetic business man, and makes a specialty of Steam and Water Heating, he being engaged in introducing the famous Richmond Heaters, and carrying on one of the largest enterprises of the kind in this section of the State; but still he finds time to devote to public affairs, and has been a member of the City Council. His shop is located at No. 75 Central Ave., and if you wish to place orders for steam or water heating apparatus; for gas fitting or plumbing; or for boilers, engines, etc., you would do well to communicate with Mr. Heath, for he is prepared to render strictly first-class service and to quote prices as low as can be named in connection with apparatus, material and workmanship of equal excellence. As his leading specialty is heating, he has made a special study of how best to solve the problem of satisfactorily and economically heating houses, stores, factories, and public and private buildings in general; and his record is such as to afford the best possible evidence that he is fitted to successfully meet special conditions and to furnish and set up heating plants that are not only satisfactory when run by experts, but also when subjected to the tests of common everyday use and managed by those who make no pretensions to be mechanics. In fact, Mr. Heath's heating plants are "built for business," and the better they become known the more heartily are they commended.

E. L. PACK, Steel Letter Cutter, Shoe Stamps, Gilding Stamps, Steel Letters and Figures, Burning Brands, Seal Presses and Stencils, 593 New Washington Street, Lynn, Mass.—The superiority of steel for all cutting purposes has long been recognized. Its application to stamps and dies is of somewhat more recent origin, and is now widely and justly celebrated. The leading establishment in this department of Lynn business is undoubtedly that conducted by Mr. E. L. Pack at 593 Washington Street. It was started by Mr. Pack in 1892 and has rapidly come to the front as the representative of modern and improved facilities in this important line. Mr. Pack has a neatly fitted up office and manufacturing premises at above address. He employs first-class and competent assistance. His specialty is the steel letter cutting, and he is prepared to show its superior qualities to all having use for this kind of stamp. His stock includes all kinds of shoe stamps, gilding stamps, steel letters and figures, also burning brands, seal presses and stencils. He can manufacture these goods at any time promptly to order and guarantees A1 satisfaction. His prices will be found exceptionally reasonable and low. Mr. Pack is a native of the State of New Hampshire, and has won a firm place among the reliable and energetic business men of this great shoe center. Those who desire to obtain the very latest and best results in the lines mentioned, will do well to call upon him. We commend his first-class facilities to the attention of all our readers.

RICHARD McBRIEN, Manufacturer of Ladies', Misses' and Children's Fine Medium Grade Spring Heel Shoes, 495 Union Street, Lynn, Mass.—Somebody has said : "A business man's customers are his best advertisements," and there is certainly a good deal of truth in that so far as Mr. Richard McBrien is concerned for we have yet to hear from a customer of his who did not speak in the highest praise of his goods, his methods and his reliability. This favorable showing is doubtless largely due to Mr. McBrien's giving close personal attention to the supervision of the many details of his business, for he leaves nothing to chance, and therefore is in a position to be reasonably sure that all his goods will prove just what they are claimed to be. His factory is located at 495 Union Street, and is admirably equipped for the manufacture of ladies', misses' and children's fine spring heel shoes. Mr. McBrien makes a specialty of spring heel shoes, and is very successful in producing goods that give entire satisfaction to both consumers and the trade, both as regards quality and price. Employment is given to sixty capable assistants, and all orders are assured prompt and careful attention.

A. H. SPRAGUE, Manufacturer of Rubber Stamps, 302 Broad Street, Lynn, Mass.—The principle of the use of the die is one of the most ancient and renowned of all devices, being seen in seals and stamps of many kinds. It was only, however, when it was first reproduced in rubber goods that it obtained its most popular and practical use. The business of Mr. A. H. Sprague, Manufacturer of Rubber Stamps is one of the oldest and best known in this vicinity. He has made a thorough mastery of every feature of the business and represents the latest improvements and patented ideas. A number of his specialties can be obtained nowhere else—outside of the largest cities. Mr. Sprague can promptly manufacture to order any kind of rubber stamps, for business or general purposes. His figures will be found very reasonable and attractive. Special designs and figures reproduced if desired and satisfaction guaranteed. Work for societies, corporations, banks and so forth is given careful and thorough attention. Our readers desiring the very best kind of service in this line will do well to call upon Mr. Sprague and examine his complete facilities.

WM. P. CONNERY, Dealer in Coal and Wood, Connery's Corner, Cor. Pleasant and Wheeler Streets, Opp. State Street. Telephone No. 4 2, Lynn, Mass.—There are few households in which the question of fuel is not an important one. To purchase this necessity to the best advantage, it is first of all necessary to find a house in which confidence may be placed. It is extravagance instead of economy to deal at a so called cheap house, for the goods there sold are bound to be inferior. There is, of course, in a place of the size of Lynn, more than one reliable coal merchant, but we feel entitled to say that those parties who place their confidence and their orders with Mr. Wm. P. Connery will not have cause to regret the step. This enterprise was established in 1879 by the present proprietor. He is a native of Lynn and too widely known in business circles to require extended personal mention. The premises occupied are located on "Connery's Corner," corner of Pleasant and Wheeler Streets, opposite State. Mr. Connery is a retail coal and wood merchant, and his yard which covers a large area of ground is stocked with the finest grades of coal and wood, which he is prepared to furnish at the lowest market prices as he buys in large quantities and maintains the most favorable relations with producers. Employment is given to five assistants while all orders whether sent by mail or telephone (Call No. 4 2) are promptly and carefully attended to, the system of delivery being uniformly reliable and the coal and wood furnished being strictly the best in the market. A branch is also conducted on Market Square, West Lynn, in charge of Andrew Welsh.

H. J. POTE, Practical Plumber and Tinsmith, Steam, Gas and Water Piping, Jobbing Promptly Attended to. 89 Central Avenue, Valpey and Anthony Block, Lynn.—The average man has enough to do in keeping up to the times in his own business without bothering with the business of others, and so all of us cannot be acquainted with the latest advances in sanitary plumbing, drain laying, etc., and must depend upon the ability and integrity of those with whom we place our orders for the attainment of satisfactory results. Hence we can't afford to do business with inexperienced or irresponsible parties, for bad plumbing and bad health are so closely connected that the former is very frequently the cause of the latter. There are many excellent plumbers in this city, but there is not one more able, experienced and reliable than is Mr. Henry J. Pote, and as he has carried on operations here for years, is well known to the people and is moderate in his charges, it naturally follows that he does an extensive business and is entrusted with many important contracts besides doing an immense amount of general jobbing and repairing. His shop is located at 89 Central Avenue, in the Valpey and Anthony Block, and the premises are very extensive, they having an area of 1,500 square feet. Employment is given to six efficient assistants, and the facilities are such as to enable even the largest orders for plumbing, tinsmithing, steam, gas and water piping, drain laying, tin roofing, etc., to be executed at short notice; while all orders, however small, are assured prompt and careful attention. Estimates will be cheerfully furnished on application, and Mr. Pote is prepared to figure closely on any work in his line.

REDDING & TEDFORD, House Painting and Paper Hanging, Whitewashing and Kalsomining. Shop, 245 Broad Street, Lynn.—The service of taste and refinement in all features of house painting and decoration has been very noticeable in recent years. Among the most modern and progressive firms in the department of Lynn's business affairs is that of Redding & Tedford, whose office and shop is at 245 Broad Street. This house has demonstrated its ability to handle every kind of painting and paper hanging work in the most able and thorough manner. Both members of the firm are experienced business men and by many years of careful attention are well acquainted with all the requirements in this line. Their figures for house-painting, wall paper hanging, whitewashing, kalsomining, etc., will be found equal to the best, and work is guaranteed satisfactory. They employ competent assistance and all orders receive prompt attention. In both exterior and interior decoration work they can furnish original and handsome designs. A specialty is made of hard-wood finish and oil stains. All work undertaken receives the constant oversight of the firm. They furnish estimates on request and our readers will consult their own interests in examining the figures and facilities of this enterprising firm before letting out contracts for work of this sort.

WASHINGTON SQUARE FISH MARKET. H. M. Jacobs, Proprietor, Dealer in all kinds of Fish, Clams, Oysters and Lobsters; also Smoked, Pickled and Dry Fish. Sea Clams and Fresh Halibut a Specialty. 110 Broad Street, Lynn, Mass.—The old belief that there was a large amount of brain food in the various kinds of fish so popular in this section of the country is not without foundation. That the same is conducive to health is shown by the strong constitution and longevity of our native population. One of the oldest and best known establishments in this line of Lynn and vicinity is that conducted by Mr. H. M. Jacobs at 110 Broad Street, well known as the Washington Square Fish Market. The business was formerly conducted by Mr. Jacobs who, after selling it, again re-purchased it in 1889 and has since that time maintained it upon the highest standard of good service and reliability. Long experience enables Mr. Jacobs to select and carry only the finest class of fish, clams, oysters and lobsters, which constitute the leading staples of his trade. He can furnish patrons with halibut and other fish directly upon the arrival of the same. He makes a specialty of sea clams, fresh halibut and cod; having also a full line of smoked, pickled and dry fish. Our readers will find that Mr. Jacobs can secure for them the very best quality and lowest prices. A trial of his facilities will be sure to prove satisfactory.

W. F. NEWHALL, Watches, Clocks, Diamonds, Silverware and Jewelry. Optical Goods. Fine Watch Repairing. Established 1872. 52 Market Street, Lynn, Mass.—It very seldom pays to buy anything at an establishment that is not thoroughly reliable in every respect, and this is particularly the case where jewelry is concerned, for the opportunities for fraud in the selling of goods coming under this head are too obvious to need demonstration, and such fraud it is practically impossible to detect at the time, or to prove and punish afterwards. The only sensible way to do, then, is to patronize a reputable and firmly established concern, and if you desire to find one that is not only strictly reliable, but is enterprising and liberal in its business methods also, the best advice we can offer is to call on Mr. W. F. Newhall, at No. 52 Market Street, and take advantage of the inducements he is prepared to extend to customers. Mr. Newhall is a native of this city and began operations here in his present line of business in 1872. The premises utilized comprise one floor 70x25 feet in dimensions, and a choice assortment of gold and silver watches, French and American clocks, diamonds, silverware, and jewelry, with a choice line of music boxes, are carried in stock, while a specialty is made of optical goods, and the testing of the eyes, and the proper adjustment of spectacles and eyeglasses to individual needs. The store is elegantly furnished in black walnut. The high wall cases on either side of the store, with the counter cases all extending from front to rear, and filled with a large and imposing stock of high grade goods, with an elegant and expensive burglar proof safe placed at the rear and center of store, all combine to make this one of the most attractive stores in the city. The genial proprietor, with his four courteous assistants, spare no pains to make a visit to the store both pleasant and profitable, for Mr. Newhall invites a careful inspection of his stock and prices, for he guarantees his goods to prove as represented, and the prices as low as can be named on goods of equal merit. Fine watch, clock and jewelry repairing is made a specialty, one of the two rooms at the rear of the store being devoted to this work, while the other is for the optical department.

M. B. McLAUGHLIN, Plumbing, Steam and Hot Water Heating, Gas Fitting and Water Piping, Corner of Broad and Washington Streets, Lynn, Mass.—Mr. M. B. McLaughlin does a very extensive business and it is not at all surprising that he does, for the people of Lynn know that the best is most emphatically the cheapest when placing orders for plumbing, steam and hot water heating, etc., and they know that work done by Mr. McLaughlin is sure to be done not only thoroughly and skillfully, but in accordance with the latest approved scientific methods. Another thing that makes this shop popular is the fact that all orders, whether large or small, are assured prompt attention. Mr. McLaughlin is called upon to execute many very extensive commissions including factory work, etc., and also to do a great deal of "family work," such as the setting up and repairing of plumbing apparatus, heating apparatus, gas piping, etc., but he does not allow either department of his business to interfere with the other, and the result is that when you place an order at his shop you can depend upon it being properly attended to. Very spacious and well-equipped premises located at the corner of Broad and Washington Streets, are occupied, and employment is given to ten competent assistants. A specialty is made of cutting and threading pipe from ⅛ to 6 inch inclusive, and all sizes of pipe fittings and valves are constantly on hand, so that even the most extensive and difficult orders for steam and gas fitting or water piping can be filled at very short notice. Only thoroughly competent and reliable help is employed, and all work is fully guaranteed to prove just as represented in every detail of workmanship and material.

M. S. CAMPBELL, D. D. S., Office hours 8 to 1 A. M., 2 to 6, 7 to 8 P. M., 145 Munroe Street, Lynn, Mass.—Many of our readers will not need to be reminded that Dr. M. S. Campbell has excellent facilities for the practice of dentistry in all its branches, as he is well and favorably known in this city, but as this book will pass into the hands of many who are strangers or comparative strangers in this vicinity and as some of these may have occasion for the service of an experienced and competent dentist we take pleasure in calling attention to the advantages Dr. Campbell is so well prepared to offer. The premises occupied are at 145 Munroe Street and comprise two nicely appointed rooms, they being very completely fitted up, and the latest improved apparatus utilized and every operation is carried on in accordance with the most approved methods. In addition to the regular practice of dentistry, he makes a specialty of painless extraction of teeth with a local anæsthetic which he himself first introduced in practice and which is giving universal satisfaction. There is no need of going further into detail concerning the kind and variety of dental work done; suffice it to say it includes all branches of dentistry, and therefore satisfactory treatment is assured to every patron. Dr. Campbell is a graduate of Howard University, Washington, D. C.

W. O. HOSMER, Dealer in Pianos and Organs, Musical Instruments of all kinds, Sheet Music, etc. Pianos to Rent, Family Sewing Machines, 27 Central Square, Boyce Building, Room 4, Lynn, Mass.—Mr. W. O. Hosmer began operations in this city in 1887, and has built up a very large trade in musical instruments in general and pianos and organs in particular, for the people have learned from experience that he is a "hustler," making a success by handling first-class pianos, is square in his methods, and low in his prices. Although a young man he has had extended experience in the piano trade, hence it is but natural that those who have done business with him should recommend his store to their friends and assure them that they could safely depend upon getting full value for every dollar expended. Mr. Hosmer makes a specialty of the celebrated McPhail pianos, but he handles all the standard makes and is prepared to suit all tastes and purses, as he deals in both new and second-hand instruments and sells both for cash and on instalments. Pianos and organs are rented by him at very reasonable rates, and, if desired, arrangements can be made by which the amount of the rental will be deducted from the price of the instrument. Thoroughly competent assistance is employed, and pianos will be tuned, polished and repaired at short notice, in first-class style, and at the lowest rates consistent with the attainment of thoroughly satisfactory results. The premises utilized are located in the Boyce Building, 27 Central Square, Room 4, and contain a fine stock of musical merchandise in general including a full assortment of sheet music. Standard instruction books, including the books of the Normal and Cecilian Series in Sight Singing by John W. Tufts can be procured at the warerooms. First-class family sewing machines are also largely dealt in, and there is no surer way of getting a satisfactory machine at a bottom price than to place the order with Mr. Hosmer. He very closely supervises the many details of his business, and callers are assured prompt and courteous attention. In the piano department Mrs. Hosmer receives pupils. Her card is appended.

Mrs. LIZZIE TREEN HOSMER,
Teacher of VOICE CULTURE, SIGHT SINGING and PIANO.
Director of Music in Public Schools. -- Normal Music Course.
STUDIED WITH THE FOLLOWING INSTRUCTORS:
Mrs. J. H. Long, Madam Edna Hall, Mr. J. W. Tufts, Mr. Carl Zarahn.
OVER 20 YEARS EXPERIENCE.
RESIDENCE, 51 TUDOR STREET, - - - LYNN.

B. F. HASKELL, Dealer in Choice Family Groceries and Provisions, Fine Teas, Coffee, Sugar, Flour, Grain, Butter, Cheese, &c., 176 Chestnut Street, Lynn, Mass.—Should a person thoroughly acquainted with the comparative standing of the various business houses in this town be asked to name half a dozen of the leading grocery firms of Lynn he would unquestionably include Mr. B. F. Haskell in the list, for he has long held his present high position, and is generally conceded to have few if any rivals in his particular line. The reasons for this favorable judgment are not difficult to learn, for no one can visit his establishment without being impressed by the magnitude and variety of the stock, the dependable character of the goods and the low prices quoted on the same, while the prompt and courteous attention extended to every caller is of itself enough to entitle this representative house to particularly favorable mention. The premises made use of comprise the ground floor 60x25 feet in dimensions, and located at 176 Chestnut Street. Choice standard family groceries and provisions of every description are dealt in, and as employment is given to five competent assistants all orders can be accurately filled at short notice. Fine teas, coffees, sugar, flour, grain, butter and cheese will be found here all at reasonable prices. Mr. Haskell caters so intelligently to family trade that the inducements cannot easily be found elsewhere.

F. LOVERING, Machine and Job Forging, Machinists' Tools Made to Order and Warranted. Machine Knives for Wood or Leather, Plumbers' Tools of all Kinds. Rear 141 Oxford Street, Lynn, Mass.—In almost all lines of manufacturing interests new machinery can be obtained already made, but there are exceptions to this rule, especially in machinists' tools. Machine knives of certain designs and some lines require special work in job forging. To meet these special demands, Mr. F. Lovering is specially prepared. He is a thorough mechanic and at his place of business, rear of No. 141 Oxford Street, he is prepared to do all kinds of machine and job forging. All kinds of special tools for machinists' use are made to order and warranted, also machine knives for wood or leather, and plumbers' tools of all kinds. Mr. Lovering gives his work his personal attention which is a sufficient guarantee that all work entrusted to him will be thoroughly done. He has carried on his present enterprise for many years. The premises occupied comprise one floor 40x30 feet in size, and every facility is at hand for the doing of first-class work. Orders can be filled at very short notice.

D. W. CLARK, House Painter, Graining, Whitewashing, and Kalsomining, 213 Lewis Street, Lynn, Mass.—The beauty and tastefulness of our New England homes is a point which impresses every beholder and nowhere is this truer than in Lynn. The great explanation of this fact is the thoroughness and artistic ability of local house painters who are to the houses what the tailors are to the persons of the best apparelled people, determining the general appearance of the same. The business of Mr. D. W. Clark, the well-known house-painter of Lynn, is at 213 Lewis Street. He has an experience in this line of thirty years, and has maintained a position of unexcelled excellence in its line. Mr. Clark has carefully perfected his facilities for handling this work and makes a specialty of house-painting, including graining, whitewashing and kalsomining. He employs only competent assistance and guarantees the very best results—as well as figures equal to the lowest anywhere. Orders by mail receive prompt attention and no pains spared to thoroughly meet every requirement of the best trade. We can assure our readers that Mr. Clark's facilities are unusually complete, and an examination of his estimates will also convince them that they will consult economy by entrusting work of this kind to his reliable care.

JOHN H. MADDEN, Real Estate and Insurance, Fire, Plate Glass and Liability. Justice of the Peace, 408 Union and 9 Exchange Street, Earl's Building, Lynn, Mass. — When the gentleman whose cut and card we print above, opened his office in Lynn to engage in the real estate and insurance business, many considered it almost a presumption and hazardous experiment, for Lynn had many firms engaged in this line of business, some of whom had spent years of active effort to establish the same, and hence some people felt that the field was already abundantly preoccupied, but Mr. Madden thought otherwise; his push, enterprise and honorable business methods and conscientious devotion to the interests of his clients had not been put to the test and his capabilities measured. He opened his office, laid his plans, advertised for certain lines of business, and awaited results—he had not long to wait, for people came to him, he served them promptly, faithfully and satisfactorily, his success has been phenomenal. He stands to-day one of Lynn's most prominent young business men. His specialty is buying and selling real estate and negotiating loans and mortgages. If one wishes to buy, sell, exchange or mortgage real estate, it is certainly wise to utilize the facilities offered by Mr. Madden, for he is in a position to render valuable assistance and to cause the early consummation of plans that might otherwise be long delayed. He is also prepared to render efficient aid in the placing of fire, plate glass and liability insurance in large or small amounts, for he represents some of the largest American and Foreign Insurance Companies, both Stock and Mutual, and can issue policies at short notice and at the lowest possible rates. The negotiation of mortgages is a prominent feature of his business and in aid of which he has recourse to Trust Funds for conservative and first-class investments, no one is better qualified to place mortgages on favorable terms. Mr. Madden was appointed a Justice of the Peace and Notary Public by Gov. Russell, and will discharge all the duties incidental to those offices promptly. His rooms are No. 13 and 14, located in Earl's Building, at 408 Union and 9 Exchange Street, overlooking Central Square and are spacious and well-equipped. Competent assistance is employed, so that orders are assured prompt and careful attention.

TAYLOR & GOODING, Builders of Fine Machinery, Gears and Cams Cut. Experimental Work and Developing Novel Machinery a Specialty, 747 Washington Street, Lynn, Mass.—A live progressive concern, is that of Messrs. Taylor & Gooding of 747 Washington Street, Lynn, Mass. It was organized in 1885, and in the intervening years it has met with continuous and well-earned success. There are no more competent builders of fine machinery in the country, and the great reputation the members of the firm have gained, is due to their intimate knowledge of their business, their practical ability and their invariable promptness and close attention to details. The senior partner, Mr. Eugene H. Taylor, is a mechanical engineer and draughtsman of high ability, and is particularly skillful in the designing and perfecting of machinery, even to the most intricate pieces of mechanism. The junior member of the firm, Mr. George F. Gooding, beside being a finished workman, is a business man through and through, so that with a combination of professional and mercantile ability the firm is far better equipped than many of its competitors, and it is, therefore, not a matter for wonder that it should have forged rapidly to the front. Messrs. Taylor & Gooding make a specialty of experimental work, and the development of novel machinery, in addition to their general business of building machines of all kinds and the cutting of gears and cams. In the lines first mentioned they have no superiors and few equals, their success in this department being marked. Their establishment covers an entire floor, having an area of six thousand square feet, and here, at all times, activity prevails, as Messrs. Taylor & Gooding have no dull season. Their orders come from all parts of New England, and they have many customers in the various manufacturing centers of the country among those who know by experience the reliability, and high class work of this firm. Employment is given, on the average, to from fifteen to twenty mechanics, and they are all skilled workmen, as no others are employed in this house.

T. F. GAFNEY, Carpenter and Builder, Shop and Yard, 117 to 127 Central Avenue. Residence, 5 Albany Street, Lynn, Mass.—One of the best-known carpenters and builders in Lynn, is Mr. T. F. Gafney, who carries on a business founded about thirty years ago, and is prepared to execute commissions promptly, skillfully, and at prices which are literally " as low as the lowest," quality, of course, being duly considered. His shop and yard are located at Nos. 117 to 127 Central Avenue, and his residence is at No. 5 Albany Street, communications to either address being assured immediate and careful attention. Mr. Gafney's business includes building and jobbing of all kinds; also theatrical construction work, scenery, etc. Men furnished who are experienced in this line. He makes a specialty of the furnishing and erection of iron fire escapes and iron window shutters, and is prepared to figure very closely on work of that kind. He is also prepared to furnish window and door screens in any desired quantities, at very short notice, and is agent for the famous Norton door checks and springs. Special attention is given to pattern making. Employment is given to nine experienced and reliable assistants, and jobbing is promptly attended to, all important work being done under Mr. Gafney's personal supervision. Particular attention is paid to contract work, and those who contemplate building operations would best serve their own interests by giving Mr. Gafney an opportunity to bid, as this is a live house, and he is in a position to figure very closely, and can be depended upon to faithfully carry out every agreement.

ORIENTAL COFFEE HOUSE, J. A. Littlefield, Proprietor, 65, 71 and 73 Blake Street, corner Almont, Lynn, Mass. In most of our large cities are to be found lunch rooms, or in other words "quick lunch rooms" which are largely patronized by business men, who do not feel that they can spend fifteen minutes or so in waiting for their order for lunch to be filled, but prefer to patronize a "quick lunch room" where they can be served at once with good food at reasonable prices. Such an establishment is "The Oriental Coffee House," of which Mr. J. A. Littlefield is the proprietor. These rooms are located on Blake Street at Nos. 65, 71 and 73, corner of Almont, with an entrance also on Almont, and employment is given to 19 competent assistants, and all needs of customers in this line are waited on promptly and with care. Thoroughly competent skill is employed in the preparation of all foods, and individual tastes are carefully observed. We can recommend this establishment to our readers. The establishment is run on the Boston or European plan, low prices—pay for only what you order. A specialty is made of furnishing the best cup of coffee to be found in the city. Seating capacity 125, and feeding from 500 to 800 persons per day.

F. H HOUGHTON, Dealer in Flexible Innersoles, and Shoe Manufacturers' Supplies, 462 Union Street, Lynn, Mass.—Very few people, excepting those identified with the business, have any idea of the complexity of the process of shoe manufacturing, and the many materials which are required by the modern shoe manufacturer. Some idea of the latter, however, may be gained by reading the following list of the more important articles handled by Mr. F. H. Houghton, who makes a specialty of the manufacture and sale of flexible innersoles, but deals in shoe manufacturers' supplies in general; cut soles, flexible innersoles, canvas inner soling, leather board, straw board, shanking, veneering, filling, paper soles, tacks, nails, shanks, stiffenings, sock linings, welting, McKay thread, McKay wax, sandpaper, twines, cut laces, paste, packing paper, drafting paper, toilet paper, colored tissues, paper bags. The premises occupied by Mr. Houghton are located at No. 462 Union Street, and have an area of 2,800 square feet, giving ample opportunity for the carrying of a large and varied stock. Employment is given to seven competent assistants, and orders are assured prompt and careful attention, and can be filled at very short notice and at bottom prices.

A. B. FLANDERS, Real Estate, 10 Central Square, Room 4, Lynn, Mass.—Such of our readers as wish to buy, sell, exchange, rent or lease real estate, would do well to communicate with Mr. A. B. Flanders, of 10 Central Square, Room 4, for he is thoroughly well posted on real estate affairs, and is in a position to save time and trouble for intending investors or sellers. He will assume the entire care of estates, including the securing of tenants, the collection of rents, keeping in repair, etc., and non-resident owners will find it well worth their while to take advantage of the service he offers. Another specialty with Mr. Flanders is the negotiation of mortgages, and his success in placing mortgages for large and small amounts on favorable terms, and his care in protecting the best interests of all parties concerned, commends him to both investors and borrowers. Mr. Flanders gives personal attention to every detail of his business, so the trustworthiness and completeness of the service can be implicitly depended upon.

FRED. I. HOPKINS, Apothecary, Corner Essex and Chestnut Streets, Lynn, Mass.—When purchasing goods of any kind it is, of course, well to use some discrimination in the placing of the order, but when buying drugs, either singly or in form of a prescription, careful discrimination becomes an absolute duty, for it is of the first importance that the articles obtained shall be pure and reasonably fresh, and it is a notorious fact that by no means all the drugs in the market are of this character. Doubtless many of our readers (and certainly many of those residing in Lynn and vicinity), have satisfactorily solved the problem of where to get dependable drugs at fair prices, by placing their orders with Mr. Fred. I. Hopkins, doing business at the corner of Essex and Chestnut Streets, for not only is he prepared to furnish such commodities of standard quality at reasonable rates, but he shows enterprise in acquainting the public with the fact, and hence his facilities are as well known as they are reliable. Mr. Hopkins was born in Maine, and succeeded to his present business in 1882; it having been established in 1871. The premises occupied are 18x18 feet in dimensions, and contain a carefully chosen stock comprising drugs, medicines and chemicals, together with toilet and fancy articles, and such other goods as are usually found in a well-appointed pharmacy. The compounding of prescriptions is of course given special attention, and no trouble is spared to insure absolute accuracy in every part of the work, while the charges made are uniformly moderate, and as employment is given to a thoroughly competent assistant, all orders are assured immediate and intelligent attention.

BOYD BROTHERS,
(Successors to G. F. Sleeper),
MANUFACTURERS OF THE
◁CELEBRATED▷
REVERE ♦ BEACH CHIPS.

The Oldest Established Potato Chip Business in the Country.

116 and 118 Central Ave.,
LYNN, MASS.

"Imitation is the sincerest flattery" and the many attempts that have been made to imitate the celebrated Revere Beach Chips made by Messrs. Boyd Brothers, proprietors of the oldest established potato chip business in the county, afford the best possible proof that these chips suit the people and the trade to perfection. But have any of these attempts been successful? No, they have not. Read what one of the largest grocery houses in New England has to say on the subject: "Boston, April 27, 1893. We have sold Boyd Bros.' Potato Chips, ever since they first commenced to put them upon the market. They have proved very satisfactory. In fact, we have never seen any better, none that we should care to change for Boyd Bros. Cobb, Bates & Yerxa. Wright." We might present many more equally favorable testimonials from prominent houses, hotels, etc., throughout this section of the State, but "a word to the wise is sufficient," and no further proof is needed that the way to get the best potato chips the market affords is to use those made by Messrs. Boyd Brothers. The business was established in 1876 by Mr. G. F. Sleeper, and came under the control of the present proprietors in September, 1889. The premises then occupied consisted of one room, 30 feet square. Before the first season was over the business increased so that it was removed to a two-story building, 28 x 40 feet in dimensions; but even that decided increase of facilities was not long sufficient, and at the end of more seasons the firm removed to their present commodious quarters at Nos. 116 and 118 Central Avenue. This is the largest establishment of the kind in the country, and some idea of its capacity may be gained from the fact that it contains four large kettles, each of which can fry 30 barrels of potatoes per day. All work is done by hand here, and the firm generally employ about 25 assistants, but can accommodate double that number if occasion requires. They buy potatoes by the carload, receiving them direct from the producers, and thus saving "middlemen's" profits and getting fresh and first-class material. Hence they are in a position to quote bottom prices on first-class chips and they are also in a position to fill the largest orders at short notice. Patrons are supplied with their glass showcases, which have proved a great convenience to the trade. The business extends all over the New England States, and the magnitude of the local trade alone is indicated by the fact that five large covered teams are engaged in the reception and delivery of orders.

TORRENCE, VARY & CO., Wholesale and Retail Dealers in Flour, Grain and Hay, 147 Oxford St. Lynn, and Summer Street, Nahant.—As bread is the staff of life, it is of first importance that the flour, from which it is made, should be the best that the market affords. There are many good brands of flour, but there is none better than that which Messrs. Torrence, Vary & Co. sell, as wholesale and retail dealers, at Lynn. This old established house has a high reputation as handlers of flour, grain and hay, and the extensive business they do here, as well as at their branch house in Nahant, is the best evidence of their desire and ability to serve the trade in the most acceptable manner. The business was begun in Lynn, in 1873, under the firm name of A. Ballard & Co., but in 1887 the style was changed to Torrence, Vary & Co., and has so continued to the present time, although death has claimed the senior member, Mr. Torrence. The present head of the firm, Mr. Charles D. Vary, is a native of New York, and a man of large experience and great executive ability, while his associate, Mr. F. C. Spearin, who claims Maine as his birthplace, is a man of keen business ability and untiring energy. A firm so constituted cannot but be successful, and the degree of success that has attended all the enterprises of Messrs. Torrence & Co., has been well deserved. The business of the firm is conducted in a fine two-story building, having a breadth of 25 feet and a depth of 60. Here are located the wholesale and retail departments, while at the Pleasant Street Court, a warehouse, 90x40 feet in dimension, and two stories high, is used for storage and shipping purposes. The Nahant store, which is situated on Summer Street, in that place, is a two story building, 20 feet wide by 30 feet in depth. The facilities enjoyed by this firm, for the prompt dispatch of business, are unequalled, and those who have occasion to buy flour, grain or hay from them will have no cause to complain of delay in the shipment of goods.

REPRESENTATIVE BUSINESS MEN OF LYNN.

OSBORNE & CO., Dealers in Groceries and Provisions, 17 and 21 Market Square, West Lynn, Mass.—No observant stranger can have strolled about much in West Lynn in the morning without having noticed many square yellow cards in the windows of residences, upon which is printed a big capital O. If he is at all inquisitive he will ask somebody what that means, and when he is told that it is a signal for one of Osborne & Co.'s teams to call and take an order for groceries and provisions, he will naturally conclude that that firm must do a big business. And so indeed they do. The business carried on by them was founded by Mr. E. W. Osborne in 1861. In 1870 the firm name was changed to E. W. Osborne & Son, and in 1877 the present style was adopted. It goes without saying that a business that has been successfully carried on for so many years must have a firm hold upon the public, and the more thoroughly you inquire into the enterprise the more thoroughly will you be convinced that it stands so high in public favor that it can safely challenge competition in its chosen fields. Above is a cut of the building erected by Wallace Osborne in 1891, the lower floor and basement are fitted up first-class and devoted entirely to their business. Visit the store, which is located at Nos. 17 and 21 Market Square, and note the goods, the prices and the service. Then you will need no further explanation why this is a very popular establishment, or why its patronage is steadily increasing. The stock includes fresh, salted, smoked and corned meats of all kinds; all sorts of seasonable vegetables and fruits; a full line of bottled goods, comprising every variety of sauces, catsups, flavoring extracts, etc.; canned goods of all kinds, put up by the most reputable packers; a complete assortment of staple and fancy groceries, and choice butter and lard. Particular attention is paid to the selection of teas and coffees. A year's stock is secured when the market is at its best in regard to quality and prices, enabling them to give to their customers the same uniform goods throughout the year. Their coffees are always fresh roasted, and ground by the Cyclone Motor Mill as sold. The prices are always in strict accordance with the lowest market rates, and all goods are guaranteed to prove just as represented. Employment is given to 13 competent assistants, and orders are assured prompt and careful attention; every department of the business being thoroughly systematized.

THE BOSTON BRANCH GROCERY, A. M. Babb, Proprietor, cor. Market and Andrew Streets, Lynn.—In compiling such a book as this, one is often reminded of Daniel Webster's famous saying, "There is always room at the the top," for numerous instances are met with where superior merit has won a high degree of success in what was apparently a crowded field of effort. There for example is the business carried on by Mr. A. M. Babb, proprietor of the "Boston Branch Grocery," located on corner of Market and Andrew Streets. This enterprise was founded in 1878 by the present proprietor. He is a native of Maine and a dealer in groceries and provisions, and we need hardly say that when this undertaking was started there were many of a similar character in successful operation here, but still "there was room at the top," and by hard and intelligent work this business has been placed at the top and is expanding rapidly and steadily. The premises utilized comprise one floor 100x25 feet in size and are conveniently and attractively fitted up, this being one of the first-class stores of the kind in Lynn. A large and complete stock of the choicest groceries, superior teas, coffees and spices, canned goods and provisions are always carried, while employment is given to eight competent and obliging assistants, so that all callers may depend upon receiving immediate and polite attention.

H. A. MACMANNON, Dealer in Watches and Jewelry, Diamonds, Silver and Plated Ware, Fine Watch Repairing a Specialty, 22 Market Street, Lynn, Mass.—That Mr. H. A. MacMannon understands his business thoroughly will be readily granted when we state the fact that he served seven years to learn the trade in England, and in this country has had twenty-three years experience on the road as a traveling salesman in this line. Some time since he founded his present business and is prepared to give the public first-class service in his special line. The premises occupied are located at 22 Market Street, comprise one floor 40x20 feet in dimensions, and contain a very complete stock of watches and jewelry, silver and plated ware, etc., etc., comprising the productions of the most reputable manufacturers, and including the very latest fashionable novelties. Only competent assistants are employed, and moderate prices are quoted on all goods handled which are guaranteed to prove just as represented, so it is natural that this store should be one of the most popular in the city. Those of our readers who have valuable watches needing repair should entrust them to Mr. MacMannon, as he makes a specialty of fine watch repairing in all its branches and his charges are always reasonable.

RAYMOND & PARKER, Dealers in Coal and Wood, 211 Chestnut Street, Lynn, Mass.—The trade in coal and wood is not excelled in importance by that of any other line, and as the colder season approaches every household realizes how impossible it would be to do without it. It is then that one realizes the importance of dealing with a house that fills orders promptly when promised. There is no commodity in which increased demand so quickly raises the price, and only regular patrons of prompt establishments can rely upon the most satisfactory service. Such an establishment is the one conducted by Messrs. Raymond & Parker of this place. The business has been established several years, the present firm assuming control in 1893; the business is steadily increasing. They make a speciality of domestic trade and are able to supply the best quality of the different kinds of coal and wood at very attractive rates and in any desired quantity either large or small orders. The firm occupy for business purposes premises located at 211 Chestnut Street. They are prepared to fill all orders in a prompt and careful manner, and our readers are assured in trading with this house of obtaining most prompt and satisfactory service.

CHARLES F. BULFINCH,

PHARMACIST,

COR. LEWIS AND CHERRY STREETS.

Among the most enterprising and successful drug stores of Lynn, that conducted by Mr. Chas. F. Bulfinch, at the corner of Lewis and Cherry Sts., has long held a recognized place. We need not remind our readers of the importance of obtaining the very best service in this line. The danger not only to health but even to life of inferior and careless service has frequently been shown, and no sensible person will take any chances in this matter. Mr. Bulfinch's establishment stands among the very first in the city for the complete care and reliability of its service. It occupies spacious and handsomely equipped store premises, with elegantly carved fixtures with bronze settings, being well stocked with fresh, reliable drugs and medical preparations of all kinds. A specialty is made of filling physician's prescriptions and no efforts are spared to prepare the same in the most careful and accurate manner. Mr. Bulfinch employs three experienced assistants, two of them being registered pharmacists. He can thus guarantee the most accurate service in this line at any hour of the day or night. We can assure our readers that for modern facilities this store is equal to any Boston establishment and its prices not surpassed anywhere. In addition to the regular stock, there is also a large line of fancy and toilet articles. These are of the finest designs and especially appropriate for gifts. Another point worthy of mention, is the elegant marble soda-fountain, one of the most elaborate in this section. Popular beverages, with a distinctive flavor which is superior to that of most places, are dispensed here at all seasons, and only the purest ingredients are used. The absolute purity and freshness of goods purchased here can always be relied upon. No establishment of its kind in this part of the State has more thorough endorsement by the faculty, the long experience and standing of Mr. Bulfinch forming a solid basis for the large and successful trade which has been built up.

OLIVER R. HOWE, (Howe's Rubber Store,) Rubber Clothing, Footwear, Rubber Goods of all Descriptions. A specialty of Ladies' and Gents' Fine Mackintosh Garments, 50 Central Square, Lynn, Mass.—When one stops to think of the many uses to which rubber is put, he wonders how in the world the people managed to get along without it until comparatively few years ago, but when one visits such an establishment as Howe's Rubber Store, he is apt to wonder how a market can be found for such an almost endless variety of rubber goods. The stock is simply immense; it is almost as immense in variety as it is in quantity, and even the merest catalogue of it would occupy pages of our space. But there is no need of our printing such a catalogue, for the residents of Lynn and vicinity know from experience that the management of this representative establishment can with truth say "If its rubber, we have it." And their stock is not confined to rubber goods either, for it includes belting and engine supplies of all kinds, as will be seen by an examination of the following list:

Belting, Leather,
" Rubber,
Belt Awls,
Belt Dressing,
Belt Hooks,
Belt Punches,
Blake's Belt Studs,
Cement, Leather,
" Rubber,
Cotton Waste,
Gaskets,
Hose, Cotton,
" Rubber,
" Steam,
Lacing, Cut,
" in Sides,
" Indian Tan'd,

Lacing Raw Hide,
" Tipped,
Oil, Castor,
" Cylinder,
" Dynamo,
" Engine,
" Lard,
" Neat's Foot,
" Paraffine.
" Sperm,
" Whale,
Oilers, Brass,
" Steel,
Packing, American,
" Asbestos,
" Clinton,
" Eureka,

Packing Flax,
" Garlock's,
" Hemp,
" Jenkin's,
" Phœnix (red)
" Plumbago,
" Sheet Rubber,
" Square Flax,
" Tuck's
" Usudurian,
Round Belt Couplings,
Round Leather Belting,
Tubing, Rubber,
Water Glasses,
Water Glass Rings,
Wicking, Asbestos,
" Cotton.

A specialty is made of rubber goods, however, and a leading specialty of ladies' and gents' fine mackintosh garments, made by the leading manufacturers and guaranteed in every respect. In fact, one reason why Mr. Oliver R. Howe has built up so great a business is because he has made it a rule to handle the productions of reputable houses and to furnish goods that are as positively reliable as such goods can be. Everybody knows that there is much difference in rubber goods, that some are dear at any price, and that others are well worth double their cost, but everybody does not know how to distinguish good from bad, and so the only safe course to pursue is to patronize a thoroughly reliable dealer. Mr. Howe's business is by no means confined to Lynn, for customers at a distance are able to buy by mail as cheaply as those who come to his store, and they can buy as intelligently too, for Mr. Howe has just issued a large illustrated catalogue and price list, which will be sent free on application. Ample assistance is employed and all orders are assured prompt and careful attention.

SPINNEY & RICHARDSON, Dealers in Dry and Fancy Goods, No. 226 Summer Street, Lynn, Mass.—The popularity of some stores, like that of some men, is very difficult to account for—it is evident that it exists, but when we try to trace out the cause of it we are unable to find any good reason why the establishment should attract special favor. Not so with the store of which Messrs. Spinney & Richardson are proprietors, for any competent observer can see abundant cause for the high esteem in which this is held by the purchasing public. To begin with, the stock is always varied, seasonable and complete, then the prices are low, the service prompt and polite and the representations made are strictly in accordance with the facts, surely an exceptional combination of advantages. The latest novelties in dry and fancy goods are always to be found here, together with all kinds of notions which are always in demand. The premises occupied are located at 226 Summer Street, comprise one floor 25x25 feet in size, and are conveniently fitted up, while every caller is assured prompt and careful attention. This enterprise was founded about a quarter of a century ago, by the present firm, which is composed of F. A. Spinney and E. M. Richardson both natives of this city. They give the business close personal supervision and spare no pains to fully maintain the high reputation so long associated with this establishment. This firm are the agents for the Troy Laundry, and all orders left at their store will be promptly and satisfactorily attended to. In connection with the business F. A. Spinney conducts a circulating library containing about 1,600 volumes.

THE LYNN BUSINESS EXCHANGE, Jas. F. Haley & Co., Proprietors, Furnish First-class Male and Female Help Free of Cost. Domestic Servants' Headquarters, 28 Market Street, Lynn, Mass.—Messrs. Jas. F. Haley & Co., proprietors of the "Lynn Business Exchange" at 28 Market Street in this town, enjoy the distinction of having built up the largest and most successful business of this character in town. They successfully introduced that which had heretofore not existed in Lynn, viz., the supplying of both male and female help for any capacity, and that too, in the face of seemingly insurmountable obstacles. This exchange will furnish employers with any class of help, male or female, except domestics, free of cost, recommending none whose ability they have reason to doubt, while at the ladies' exchange, conducted by the same proprietors, they will furnish employers with any lady mercantile help free of cost, and families are supplied with domestic help by paying an office fee, this is domestic servants' headquarters, and this department of the business has been found to be a great convenience to the people of this vicinity. This house also makes a specialty of negotiating sales on business places and also have houses to sell, receiving $5 down and $1 weekly thereafter. They are also agents for Clyde line of steamers to Florida. Their office is on the second floor of 28 Market Street. Two reliable clerks are employed and all callers are treated with promptness and courtesy.

JOHN C. GARROOD, Manufacturer and Dealer in Bicycles and Tricycles, Skates, Guns, Typewriters, etc., No. 126 Munroe Street, Cor. Washington Street, Lynn, Mass.—"Experience is the best teacher," and a man who has ridden, manufactured, repaired and sold bicycles for more than a quarter of a century certainly ought to know about all there is worth knowing about those popular vehicles, especially when he is a practical mechanic, a progressive man and has introduced improvements which have been adopted by all the leading cycle manufacturers. Such is the record of Mr. John C. Garrood, who had thirteen years' experience in England, six years in Boston, and seven years in Lynn. He was the originator of the hollow fork of weldless steel tubing and has made many more patented improvements to the cycle, so it goes without saying that he is not only fully up to the times but is somewhat ahead of the trade in most things having to do with cycles and cycle building and repairing. Mr. Garrood makes a leading specialty of light cycles and cripples' machines, and is prepared to furnish wheels admirably adapted to individual needs, and to fill orders at short notice, as his facilities are ample and employment is given to thoroughly competent assistants. He handles such standard cycles as the Rover, Black Hawk, Crescent, Brookes, Columbus, Relay, Waverly Belle, Rob Roy and Juno, and carries in stock a great variety of new, shop-worn and second-hand machines, which he is prepared to sell for cash or on credit at bottom rates. A large assortment of sundries and parts is also carried in stock, and repairing is done with a neatness, strength and despatch that is as gratifying as it is rare. But the cycle business has its "dull season," and so Mr. Garrood (who is one of those business men who are always "on deck" and don't depend on big profits at one season to carry them through the year) deals in skates, shot guns, rifles, air guns and pistols, revolvers and ammunition, and also in typewriters. He makes a specialty of die making and light machine work to order. His store is at 126 Munroe Street, corner of Washington Street, and as enterprise and square dealing are sure to be appreciated by the public, we need hardly say that it is a very popular establishment.

BIRD'S EYE VIEW OF LYNN.

WOODWARD & COCHEY, Leather and Findings, 667 Washington Street, Lynn, Mass.—The business carried on by Messrs. Woodward & Cochey was established in 1891 by Mr. H. W. Woodward, in Stoneham, Mass. It then came under the control of Messrs. Woodward & Boynton, then to the present firm. In 1893, under the name of the Acme Trimming Co., it was removed from Stoneham to Lynn, and the subsequent changes of firm mentioned occurring in Lynn. It is now doing business under the style firm of Woodward & Cochey. The company utilize spacious premises equipped with an elaborate plant of the most improved machinery for the manufacture of tips, trimmings, etc., and give employment to about thirty-five assistants. Their trade is by no means confined to Lynn, and is so extensive and so constant that this is doubtless one of the busiest concerns of the kind in the State. Leather is largely dealt in, and the company are prepared to fill orders at very short notice, and to quote prices in strict accordance with the lowest market rates, their specialty being high grade tips and trimmings.

SARGENT, MERRILL & PORTER, makers of Ladies', Misses' and Children's Fine and Medium Grades Footwear, Machine and Hand Sewed, 505 Washington St., Lynn, Mass.—Lynn offers a very striking example of the commercial fact that the more of a good thing there is the better. The increase of competition in the shoe-trade has not only served to perfect methods of manufacture and the finished product, but also has greatly extended the business. The well-known firm of Sargent, Merrill & Porter is one of the oldest, solid houses in the manufacture of Ladies', Misses' and Children's Footwear. Their business has now been in successful operation since 1881. They occupy new and thoroughly equipped business premises, at above address, representing the latest ideas in machinery and management. The employee-force averages about 100, and is kept constantly busied. They make every kind of medium and fine-grade footwear for the trade at liberal prices. Their goods command everywhere a ready sale and both in quality and in style are among the most popular sent out from Lynn to all parts of the country. Both machine and hand-sewed shoes are turned out here, and a number of styles made which have proven popular leaders. In solid wearing features as well as beauty, their goods will stand the most thorough tests, and should receive the careful attention of all our readers. Those who want A1 boots and shoes at a moderate price can rely with confidence upon the superior qualities of these goods. The individual members of this firm are Messrs. J. M. Sargent, Henry Merrill and George S. Porter. All are Massachusetts men and thoroughly acquainted with the demands of the modern shoe trade. The steady development of their business in season and out has been the result of careful enterprise based upon untiring energy and uniform fair dealings.

EMERY & RYAN, Decorators, Frescoers, Gold Gilders, and Picture Framers, Dealers in Etchings, engravings, etc., Fine Portrait-copying a specialty, 136 and 138 Central Avenue, near City Hall, Lynn, Mass.—In the early ages, the skill and art of the decorator and gilder was only employed by royalty and the favored and aristocratic few, but as the masses have gradually become elevated, educated and refined and acquired wealth, the demand for genius and skill in this field has become very great, until now in this present age in almost every community, are those whose wealth and cultured taste have demanded the service of the artist in this as also in other lines, to a greater or less extent, so that in the prosperous city of Lynn it is only what would be expected, to find a firm meeting such demands from the public in a most able and skillful manner. Such is the firm of Emery & Ryan, whose card we print above, they are located at 136 and 138 Central Ave. near City Hall. They are interior and outside decorators, doing all kind of work in this line; frescoing, gold gilding and regilding, decorating in paper maché and carton piére. They make a specialty of churches, fine residences and nice furniture and utilize a new style of ornamentation. They are also manufacturers and dealers in picture frames, etc. The effect of a painting, engraving, etching, photograph or any other kind of a picture is so largely dependent upon the manner in which it is framed that there is as much opportunity for the display of taste in the choice of a frame as in that of the picture itself, and it is to be regretted that the high prices quoted on handsome and artistic frames by many dealers prevent their being utilized so generally as they otherwise would be. Of course such frames are expensive to manufacture, and cannot be furnished at prices as low as are quoted on cheap and showy frames so common in the market, but on the other hand this is no good reason why fancy prices should be demanded for them, and hence Messrs. Emery & Ryan are prepared to furnish all styles, sizes and kinds of picture frame at a small margin of profit. They carry a large and well selected line of mouldings, and money can be saved and prompt and otherwise satisfactory service assured by making use of the facilities offered by them. These gentlemen deal also in Etchings, Engravings, Water Colors and Oleographs, also Easels, Picture Cords, Mouldings, Hooks, Mats, Panels, Etc. Messrs. Emery & Ryan, make a specialty of fine Portrait Copying, and having in their employ an artist of rare ability in Portrait Copying, in Crayon, India Ink, Oil, Pastel or Water Colors, they can safely guarantee satisfaction, and hope to merit a continuance of your generous patronage. Being Picture Frame Manufacturers, and having had long experience in Portrait Work, they defy competition in quality and price.

J. B. SWEETLAND & CO., Manufacturers and Designers of all Kinds of Boot and Shoe Patterns, 64 Oxford Street, Lynn, Mass.—The business carried by Messrs. J. B. Sweetland & Co. was founded a score of years ago, and the firm have met with such success in the manufacturing and designing of boot and shoe patterns that no other Lynn concern is more widely and favorably known among the shoe trade. This house is fully "up to the times" in every respect, and shoe manufacturers know from experience that one of the surest ways to obtain plain and ornamental shoe patterns in the latest styles at the shortest possible notice is to place the order with Messrs. J. B. Sweetland & Co., who have had twenty years' experience. They are agents for lasts of every description, and are prepared to supply them in quantities to suit, at bottom prices, and to promptly execute every commission. It is safe to say that no business card is more highly valued and more carefully preserved by the shoe trade than is that of this enterprising concern, for it is printed upon a most ingeniously arranged "sliding card," which gives the standard measurements of lasts as adopted by the retail boot and shoe dealers at the National Association. It accurately indicates the dimensions of the ball, waist, instep, ankle and bottom of a last of any width and size, and truly "must be seen to be appreciated," for it is so simple, efficient and convenient that no description can do it justice. This card was copyrighted in 1887, but it is freely distributed by Messrs. J. B. Sweetland & Co., and is one of those unpretentious but highly valuable appliances which no member of the shoe trade can afford to do without.

I. H. STEARNS, M. D., Physician and Surgeon, and recognized Pension Claim Agent. Room 4a, 113 Munroe Street, Lynn, Mass.—In these days when the operation of the United States pension law is being more rigidly enforced than at any previous time, it behooves those who have just claims, to place them in the hands of the most responsible and experienced agents. Many claims have been lost, or their recognition delayed, through want of proper handling, or because the claimant has entrusted them to pension sharps, who were more interested in getting for themselves all there was in it, than in seeking to serve the old soldier for a reasonable recompense. Dr. I. H. Stearns, who served as surgeon of the 22d regiment, Massachusetts infantry, and who besides serving in the same capacity at the National Soldiers' Home in Maine and Wisconsin, was, until recently, United States Examining surgeon for Pensions, is, consequently, better equipped than the majority of so-called pension claim agents. His vast and particular experience in the public service enables him to give the best judgment on claims for pensions, and to push these claims with every prospect of success where others have failed. As proof of his ability in this direction, Dr. Stearns points to hundreds of pensioners in Lynn, and elsewhere, for whom he has secured pensions, and whose claims had, in a number of instances, been previously rejected. He particularly requests those who have a case which is "exasperating" from any cause, as so many are, to give him points about it or come and see him, and he will freely advise them what to do, and perhaps put them on the road to success. Any letter, with a stamp, will be promptly answered.

I. FRAZIER & SON, House, Sign and Fresco Painting, Plain and Decorative Paper Hanging. Also Dealers in Paints, Oils, Glass, Paper Hanging, Etc. 27 Andrew St., Lynn, Mass.—The enterprise conducted by Messrs. I. Frazier and Son is of special interest, not only on account of the magnitude and character of the business, but also because the senior partner has been longer engaged in the painting business than any other man in this section, and probably in all New England. Mr. I. Frazier is a native of the Pine Tree State, and served as captain in the Sixth Maine Regiment for two years. He is now eighty-seven years of age; has been in the painting business for seventy-two years, and founded the business with which he is now identified nearly sixty years ago, or in 1835. His son, M. Frazier, has been associated with him for twenty years, and was also in the late war, serving as Lieut. in the same Company under command of his father. The firm have long held a leading position among the house, sign and fresco painters of Essex county. They deal largely in Paints, Varnishes, Stains, Oils, Glass, Paper Hangings, etc., handling the productions of the most reputable manufacturers, and always quoting the lowest market prices on goods that can be depended upon to prove just as represented in every respect. Special attention is given to the sale of artistic Wall Papers, and to plain and decorative Paper Hanging; and those who wish to secure the latest accepted novelties in Wall Paper effects and to have paper hanging done by skilled workmen cannot possibly do better than to place their orders with this responsible concern. They also make a specialty of enameling drawing rooms, halls, etc., the work warranted to retain its brilliancy, and the results being permanently satisfactory. Messrs. I. Frazier & Son have extensive facilities, and all orders are assured prompt attention and can be filled at short notice.

G. WILLIS HANSON, Cut Sole Leather, 777 Washington Street, Lynn, Mass.—No small part of the labor involved in the making of foot gear, is the cutting of the soles, and this part of the business necessitates the use of so much space, for the storage of hides, that the majority of manufacturers prefer to buy their leather conveniently cut into pieces, suitable to be turned into soles when needed. There has consequently grown up, within a comparatively few years, a special industry for the supplying of cut sole leather, and those who are engaged in it, find it a very lucrative business. It gives employment at good wages to many men, and is steadily increasing in importance. Of the people who are engaged in this line of business in the city of Lynn, Mass., probably one of the best known, as well as one of the largest cutters of sole leather, is Mr. G. Willis Hanson, a native of the Old Bay State, and a man universally liked and esteemed for his many sterling attributes. Mr. Hanson began business here in 1885, and succeeded beyond what most men could accomplish in the interim. He occupies the whole of a large floor at 777 Washington Street, giving him a front of 20 feet and a depth of 90 feet. This space is all required for the conduct of his flourishing business, which, on the average gives employment to four skilled workmen. Mr. Hanson has facilities and carries sufficient stock, at all times for the prompt execution of orders, and is prepared to furnish unlimited quantities of cut soles at prices which competitors find it hard to meet. Manufacturers who are not already doing business with him, will consult their own interests by obtaining quotations from Mr. Hanson, before placing their orders elsewhere.

ELIHU B. HAYES, Wholesale News Agency, rear 332 Union Street, Lynn, Mass.—This important agency for the distribution of newspapers in Lynn and vicinity, was established in 1892 by the present proprietor who has developed it into very important proportions, until now it is the distributing center for the great mass of publications that find their way daily to the numerous news stands throughout this vicinity. The proprietor, Hon. Elihu B. Hayes, is a native of West Lebanon, Me., and came to Lynn in 1865. Since that time he has been so identified with city and State interests that in this review of Lynn's representative business men, we give space to briefly mention some of his personal history which is so inseparably connected with some of the most important legislation of this generation. He was formerly an editorial writer for the Lynn *Daily Bee* and Lynn *Reporter*, of which papers he was a part owner. While engaged in this work he began his public career as a member of the Board of Aldermen of 1883. In 1885 he became the publisher of the Boston *Daily Advertiser* and the *Evening Record*, continuing as such until illness compelled his retirement. With returning health he gave his attention once more to local matters. He was thrice elected Representative to the Legislature from the 18th Essex District, serving in the years 1887, '88 and '89. He was largely instrumental in achieving most important measures in the House, one of which was the Australian ballot law, which he introduced and which was adopted by the Massachusetts Legislature in 1888 and went into effect in 1889, and which has since been adopted in various forms in thirty-five States. He was also the author of the amendment to the constitution adopted in 1890 to prevent the disfranchisement of voters because of change of residence within the State limits and was the father of the bill regarding fire escapes attached to window frames in hotels and boarding houses. The question of public libraries also received his attention and mainly through his efforts was carried through the bill granting $100 worth of books to any town not provided with a public library, which has been the means of establishing more public libraries in Massachusetts, than are possessed by all other States in the Union. Mr Hayes was elected Mayor of Lynn in 1891 and re-elected in 1892. He will be a candidate for the Republican nomination for Congress from the Seventh District in 1894. Having demonstrated his superior fitness to serve the best interests of the people, they will undoubtedly elect him to represent them in that capacity.

MRS. H. A. RUBLEE, Lynn's Complexion Specialist, Superfluous Hair Permanently Removed, 36 Market Street, 2d story, Lynn, Mass.—No observing person can have failed to notice that there has been a decided increase in what may be called the average of personal beauty of late years, for there are now more "pretty girls," more "beautiful women," and more "good-looking men" than ever before, and the proportion is steadily increasing every year. Well, why is this thus? Why is it that we Americans are, as a people, steadily gaining in attractiveness? The answer is simple. It is because we are beginning to appreciate the fact that health is the foundation of beauty, and that careful living, outdoor exercise, and care for the body are the foundations of health. The time was when it was necessary for a lady to be pale and fragile in appearance in order to be "interesting," and when she should carefully avoid long walks or other exercise, for fear she would become masculine in appearance. But we know better now, and the ladies we admire are those who have rose-tinted cheeks, clear eyes, glossy hair, smooth and "satiny" skin—all of which are but evidences of good health and intelligent physical culture. Read an account of a gathering of "society people" and you will notice many references to the "well-groomed" appearance of the ladies and gentlemen. There you have the main secret of success in presenting an attractive appearance. Society ladies profit by the advice, the treatment, and the preparations of specialists in the art of gaining and maintaining beauty—hence, they are handsome, healthful and charming. But this service is by no means monopolized by the few—at all events it is not here in Lynn, for Mrs. H. A. Rublee, Lynn's complexion specialist, is prepared to serve the many, and her service is unsurpassed by that of any specialist in any of the great cities. We would like to go into detail concerning her many special toilet preparations, and her method of treatment for the prompt and permanent removal of each of the defects in complexion which so seriously mar the appearance of many an otherwise beautiful woman, but lack of space forbids, and we will simply say that Mrs. Rublee has made a special study of the subject of beauty for years, and is thoroughly conversant with it in every detail. She utilizes a thoroughly equipped suite of rooms at 36 Market Street, where may be found an improved Turkish bath, plunge and sulphur baths, and other accessories to the gaining of health and beauty; and where attention is given to massage and to steaming the face to remove blackheads, and in fact to all treatment incidental to the beautifying of the complexion. Ladies' hair dressing is skillfully attended to, and manicuring in all its details is carefully carried out, as is also the treatment of corns, bunions, and ingrowing nails without pain. Mrs. Rublee is moderate in her charges and gives personal attention to all patrons. She began operations in Lynn in 1891, and has already established an extensive business which is still steadily increasing.

HIGHLAND HOUSE, C. M. Rhodes, Proprietor, 472 Essex, cor. High Street, Lynn, Mass.—This house was opened to the public by the present proprietor, Mr. C. M. Rhodes during the present year, and has already become one of the favorite stopping places in Lynn. Rooms can be obtained here by the week, there being twenty-five finely furnished apartments for the accommodation of guests. The Highland House is centrally located at 472 Essex, corner of High Street, and there is a first class dining-room under the house on the High Street side where meals can be obtained, the prices per week being $3.25 for gentlemen and $2.75 for ladies, this making it fully as convenient as though board could be obtained of Mr. Rhodes. There are six polite assistants employed, and the rooms are kept in first-class condition. Mr. Rhodes is a native of Massachusetts and is a considerate, accommodating host, ever vigilant to anticipate and supply the wants of his guests. This house is run in a neat and attractive manner, and the dining-rooms on High Street are all that could be wished for. Those who are obliged to board will find a pleasant home at the Highland House, and we feel that we can conscientiously recommend it to all.

PLACIDE HEBERT, Shoe Manufacturer, No. 587 Washington Street, Lynn, Mass. — Experienced retailers say that a shoe that fits perfectly sells itself, so it is easy to account for the popularity of the ladies' and misses' shoes manufactured by Mr. Placide Hebert, for he has an enviable reputation for making perfect-fitting shoes, and he makes shoes that not only fit perfectly but feel easy and comfortable also. But, of course, that is not the only reason why the demand for his goods often exceeds the supply, for shoes must combine both style and durability with perfection of fit and comfort in order to be permanently popular, and this combination is to be found in the footwear made by this representative manufacturer, so it is able to "hold its end up" in any company, and when once fairly introduced in a given section the demand for it is steady and pronounced. Mr. Hebert's factory is located at 587 Washington Street and is fitted up with machinery of the most improved type. Employment is given to 150 assistants, and the capacity of the establishment is great enough to admit of even the largest orders being filled at comparatively short notice. The business is thoroughly systematized, and there is but little chance of errors in the filling of orders or of imperfect goods being allowed to leave the factory.

DEARBORN BROS. & CO., Masons, Contractors and Builders. Office, 34 Central Square, Lynn, Mass. Box 116, Mechanics' Exchange, 35 Hawley Street, Boston. — One of the oldest established businesses of its kind in Lynn is that carried on by Messrs. Dearborn Brothers & Co., for it was founded nearly forty years ago, operations having been begun in 1855. Their business has extended over New England and Canada they having built five business blocks in Canada, several large blocks in Boston, Mass., on Summer and High Sts., nine business blocks in the city of Portland, Maine ; County Buildings for York Co., Maine ; Female College Building, Kent's Hill, Maine ; fourteen large public buildings and several large woolen and cotton mills; sixteen blocks for the Waumsetta Mfg. Co., New Bedford, Mass., twenty business blocks and factories in Lynn, some of the finest depots and other buildings for the Boston & Maine R. R., and at present are building the large State Armory, situated on South Common St., Lynn, Mass. As masons, contractors and builders, they are in a position to give prompt and careful attention to all orders, large and small, but their leading specialty is the erection of public buildings, and they are prepared to figure very closely on plans and specifications, and to execute even the most extensive commissions at the shortest possible notice. The office is at No. 34 Central Square, and communications to that address are assured prompt and careful attention. The firm is composed of Messrs. J. W. Dearborn, A. J. Dearborn, and C. W. Dearborn, all of whom are so well known in this section as to render further personal mention entirely unnecessary.

WALTER I. WILEY, Sanitary Plumbing in all its Branches. Drain Laying a Specialty. Jobbing Promptly Attended to. 51 Market Square, Lynn, Mass. — If those who are about to "begin housekeeping" would only bear in mind the fact that "whatever is worth doing, is worth doing well," and look sharply after the drainage and sanitary condition of a house before they consent to occupy it, there would be less sickness, less loss of time, and less doctors' bills to be paid, and we might truthfully add, less undertakers' bills also. Mr. Walter I. Wiley, whose card we print above, has had over ten years experience in his line of business, and is prepared to do sanitary plumbing in all its branches. Special attention is given to drain laying, both in new and jobbing work, he being a "licensed drain layer ;" all work in steam and gas fitting or pump work promptly attended to, and all work guaranteed to be first-class and at reasonable prices. He also carries a line of stoves and ranges. Mr. Wiley is a native of Lynn, and takes a just pride in his native city. He is an Odd Fellow, and member of the Encampment, also of the Lincoln Club, and Order of Red Men. His place of business is at 51 Market Square, where he is prepared to do all kind of work pertaining to his line of business, in the most satisfactory manner, employing from six to ten skilled workmen so that all orders can be filled with the utmost dispatch.

HASKELL, RICH & CO., Manufacturers of Ladies' Fine Boots, 465 Union Street, Lynn, Mass. — Messrs. Haskell, Rich & Co. began operations in 1890, and the steady growth of their business affords the best possible proof that both their goods and their prices suit the trade. The uniformly satisfactory quality of the ladies' fine boots made by this firm is very easy to explain, for Messrs. F. S. Haskell, J. F. Rich, and F. O. Marston — who constitute the concern — are practical shoe men, every detail of the work of manufacture from the selection of the stock to the shipping of the finished product — is carefully supervised, nothing is left to chance, and care is taken to employ operatives who are reliable as well as experienced. The result is that the firm produce goods that are equal in every respect to the samples from which orders are taken, so that they soon gain the full confidence of those with whom they do business, and the fact that footwear was made by Haskell, Rich & Co. is accepted as good evidence that it is fully up to the times and will prove as represented in every detail. The goods are sold direct to the retail trade, and are extensively as well as favorably known; orders being received from all parts of New England, New York and Pennsylvania. The factory is located at 465 Union Street, and is equipped with machinery of the most improved type. Adequate assistance is employed, and both large and small orders are assured prompt attention and can be filled at short notice.

MRS. H. GRANT, Dress and Cloak-making, 191 Chestnut Street, Lynn, Mass. — As a large portion of our readers consists of ladies, we are confident this article will prove of interest to many, as of course ladies like to learn of an establishment where they can depend upon the taste and skill therein displayed in the line of dressmaking. Just such an establishment is that conducted by Mrs. H. Grant at 191 Chestnut Street, and she is not only prepared to make dresses in an entirely satisfactory manner, but will also teach, to those wishing to learn either for their own private use or to fit themselves as dressmakers, the system of dress cutting she uses in her business. This is an entirely scientific system, being new, novel and complete, it is not a chart but a rule. A cordial invitation is extended to all ladies interested in the art of dressmaking to visit Mrs. Grant's rooms. Her business has been established since 1865 and has steadily increased, for she has had an unusual degree of success in fitting and one of the chief factors of her popularity is to be found in this important particular, as also in the economical utilization of the material furnished to her. She gives employment to sufficient help to enable her to fill her orders promptly and endeavors to meet all sensible expectations, and to make her work first-class in every respect, and her charges as low as are consistent with the doing of thoroughly good work. Mrs. Grant is a native of Maine and is well and favorably known. The premises used for her business are centrally located and are 30x20 feet in dimensions.

INDEX.

Architects.

Betton, Charles L. 72
Miller, Frank, Jr. 83
Smith, George E. 84
Wheeler, H. K. 88

Bakers.

Arroll, G. W. 44
Ross, C. I. 53
Schmidt, H. J. 73
Smith, George T. 82

Blacksmithing.

Duffy & Oulton 45
Hazlett, George A. 94
Langham, J. A. & Co. 84
Wood, John A. 40

Boot and Shoe Patterns.

Bailey, J. C. 36
Sweetland, J. B. & Co. 108

Boots and Shoes.

Farmer & Lemmon 50
Jacobs, E. H. 82
Lee, Agnes 52
Manufacturers' Shoe Store 39

Boot and Shoe Manufacturers.

Barnard, Geo. E. Co. 40
Brown & Balcom 60
Harris & Story 41
Haskell, Rich & Co. 111
Hebert, Placide, Shoes 111
King, The Mrs. C. H., Co. 88
Sargeant, Merrill & Porter 108
McBrien, Richard 97
Richard, L. J. & Co. 76
Spinney, F. L. & Co. 51

Carpets, Etc.

Gifford, W. B. 61
Goldsmith, W. F. & Co. 94

Caterers.

Keenly, E. J. 74
Valiquet, Jos. D. 85

Cigars, Tobacco, Etc.

Boynton, Mrs. G. A. 60
Breed, Henry G. 44
Hovey, A. S. 61
Katzes, Harry 38
Poole, W. S. 80
Tabour, Wm. 89
Tucker, G. M. & Co. 32
Tupper & Grant 54
Welsh, Andrew 68

Coal and Wood.

Connery, Wm. P. 98
Raymond & Parker 104
Sexton, T. J. 54

Confectionery, Etc.

Jenkins, Susie M. 79
Jepson, Oliver F. 58
Lorendo, F. G. 59
Skinner, F. W. 34

Contractors and Builders.

Blanchard, Charles C. 90
Crosscup, J. A. 61
Gafney, T. F. 101
Hatch & Fernald 57
Holdsworth, L. C. 92
Smith, W. W. 77

Dentists.

Campbell, M. S. 99
Griffin, Daniel 67
Kennedy, J. 39
Kyes, F. W. 79
Lindstrom, C. R. 46
Mudge, A. B. 76
Runals, R. F. 68

Dress and Cloak Makers.

Burnsville, F. A. 34
Grant, Mrs. H. 111

Druggists.

Bulfinch, Chas. F. 105
Chase, J. W. & Co. 76
DeCoster, P. S. 81
Faulkner & Hoyle 60
Fenning, H. C. 47
Flint, Frank E. 56
Harriman, J. M. & Co. 49
Hodges, C. A. 52
Holbrook's "Central Drug Store" 81
Holder & Co. 86
Hopkins, Fred. I. 102
Small, James B. 99
Stinson, Arthur A. 58

Dry and Fancy Goods.

Bee Hive, The 82
Boston Dry Goods Store 95
Cate, Josie E. 56
Clark, Edward S. & Co. 88
Spalding, R. A. & Co. 71
Spinney & Richardson 106
Watson, E. J. 52

Engineers and Surveyors.

Harris, Isaac K. 83
Smith, Edward H. 46
Winkley, E. E. & Co. 43

Fancy Goods.

Boston Novelty Store 57
Gerry, Miss G. L. & Co. 57

Fish Dealers.

Cape Cod Fish Market 57
Stubbs, W. A. 78
Washington Square Fish Market 98
Williams Bros. 43

Furniture.

Bean, C. A. & J. H. & Co. 60
Merrill & Durgin 58
Ready, T. J. 51

Gent's Furnishings.

Butman, M. & Co. 59
Continental, The 93
Dermody, J. F. & Co. 32
Dow, Fred F. & Co. 35
Farmer, Frank B. 78
Gunn, S. G. 68

Groceries and Provisions

Bacheller, R. 81
Blood, Josiah B. & Co. 53
Boston Branch Grocery Store 104
Carswell, J. Warren 73
Colby, L. I. 65
French, F. F. 77
Haskell, B. F. 100
Kellam, Theo. H. 64
Osborne & Co. 104
Osgood & Fish 90
Perkins, Samuel S. & Co. 83
Ruth, J. & Son 91
Ryan, S. 56
Shannon, C. T. 59
Sweeny & Delaney 96
Young, Elbridge S. 72
Youland & McManus 72

Harness Makers.

Burton, W. J. 44
McElhinney, E. S. & E. M. 46
Smith, W. F. 80

Hotels.

Anderson Hotel 36
Columbus House 65
Highland House 110
Hoffman House 53
Hotel Wave 72
Tucker House 56
Woodward House 90

Jewelry, Etc.

Barnard, F. L. 61
Conner, Jas. H. 96
Hill, H. M. & Co. 75
Machmannon, H. A. 104
Newhall, W. F. 99
Olin, J. G. 77
Wadlin, George I. 86

Laundries.

Boston Street Laundry 87
Seaside Hand Laundry 78
Troy Laundry 46

Leather.

Hamden & Blanchard 60
Hanson, G. Willis 109
Woodward & Cochey 107

Livery Stables.

Fullam, H. H. & Co. 70
Kearney, Stephen R. 49
Murphy, Thomas F. 48
Story, Allen & Co. 87

Machinists.

Embree, Wm. F. 55
Lovering, F. 100
Taylor & Gooding 101

Manufacturers.

Benner, F. R. & Co., Awnings 78
Bubier Laboratory Co., Pharmacists 63
Flexity Stain Co., Bottom Stains 51
Fullam, H. H. & Co., Awnings 70
Garwood, John C., Bicycles 107
Kelley & Green, Dongola 48
Kent & Smith, Enamel Stains 40
Lynn Gas & Electric Co. 30
Murphy, P. R., Cutting Dies 48
National Popcorn Works 67
Nickerson, J., Inner Soles, etc. 46
Russell & Co., Moulded Counters 68
Sprague, A. H., Rubber Stamps 97
Young, W. L., Moulded Counters and Counter Machinery 36

Masons.

Dearborn Bros. & Co. 111
Whittredge, J. L. 92

Meats, Provisions, Etc.

Chicago Beef Market 48
Doyle, John A. 62
Hardy, H. 45
Sanborn, Hurd & Co. 90

Millinery.

Bon Marché 87
Farley, Miss Alicia M. 62
Hall, E. W. 87
Stewart, Miss B. C. 73

Miscellaneous.

American Dye House 50
Andrews, S. R. (butter, eggs, etc.) 88
Boynton, Elmer S. (clothing cleaned.) 34
Blanchard & Curry, (clothing cleaned.) 56
Boyd Bros. (potato chips) 103
Curtis, James H. (kalsomining) 47
Emery & Ryan (art decorators) 108
Estes, I. H. (hay, grain and straw) 71
Electric Construction Co. 82
Hayes, Elihu B. (news agent) 110
Hosmer, Mrs. Lizzie Treen (music teacher) 100
Howe, Oliver R. (rubber clothing) 106
Johnson, N. D. (general repairs) 67
Lewis, Joseph C. (sign writer) 64
Lynn Ice Co. 85
Lynn Dye House 92
Lynn Business Exchange 106
Lamphier, Wilbur C. (photographic supplies) 54
Lynn Mutual Fire Ins. Co. 68
Millett, D. K. (ice cream, etc.) 64
Moloney, John J. (fruits, etc.) 51
Massachusetts Temperance Home 84
Novelty Popcorn Works 33
Pinkham, Lydia E. Co. (medicines) 43
Pack, E. L. (letter cutter, etc.) 97
Pine Grove Marble and Granite Works 34
Ready, James H. (dancing academy) 91
Ranger, J. M. (paper hangings) 59
Robie, George H. (cloaks, suits, etc.) 93
Rublee, Mrs. H. A. (complexion specialist) 110
Sisson, A. H. (gunsmith) 51
Sheehan, John (grading, blasting, etc.) 82
Stearns, I. H. (pension agent) 109
Tyler, T. W. (belts, engine supplies, etc.) 55
Tufts, A. M. (taxidermist) 64
Torrence, Vary & Co. (flour, feed, etc.) 103
Webster, Miss A. (shorthand and typewriting) 76
Weinberg, S. J. (tailors' trimmings) 35

Painters.

Adams, A. K. & Co. 32
Clark, D. W. 100
Frazier, I. & Son 109
Pollard, C. F., Jr. 70
Preston, T. W. 83
Redding & Tedford 95
Stover, W. R. 86
Twombly, J. F. 85

Photographers.

Bowers, W. T. 47
Shorey, C. E. 50

Pianos, Organs, Etc.

Brown, W. D. 71
Hosmer, W. O. 100

Plumbers.

Curry, James H. 33
Dame, Melvin A. 62
Harnwer & Quinby 45
Hannaford & Perkins 54
Heath, H. W. 97
Lewis, W. E. 77
May, The L. A., Co. 39
McLaughlin, M. B. 99
Pote, H. J. 98
Reardon, T. B. 42
Stevens, F. B. 37
Wiley, Walter I. 111

Real Estate.

Atkins, Frank W. 38
Cook, H. W. 49
Flanders, A. B. 102
Frizzell, F. H. 48
Higgins, George C. 47
Jenkins, George 69
Lake Shore Improvement Co. 31
Madden, John H. 101
Murphy, D. N. 79
Newhall, George H. 58
Newhall, Israel Augustus 36
Pitman, Benj. 38
Snow, Willis I. 34
Suburban Land Improvement Co. 66
Thompson, Waldo & Son 94
Tibbetts, E. A. & Co. 94

Restaurants.

Gurney, Kingman 32
Oriental Coffee House 102
Oxford Ladies' & Gents' Dining Rooms 33
Preston Cafe 86
Windsor Cafe 65

Shoe Parts.

Atkins, Hoyt & Co. 61
Houghton, F. H. 102
Sutherland, J. T. & Co. 44
Trask Bros. 84

Slipper Manufacturers.

Cook, J. A., Slippers 52
Hoyt & Rowe, Slippers 63
Johnson, Luther S. & Co., Slippers 89
Kollock & Easp, Slippers 58

Stationery.

Easton, F. A. 69
Graves, Mrs. H. D. 62
Herbert, Geo. C. & Co. 50
Wheeler, C. A. 54

Tailors.

Berkley, Ludlow 65
Dearborn & Blanchard 52
Dowling & Co. 38
Stanley, F. D. 80
Williams, John C. 50

Truckmen, Etc.

Chase, D. W. 80
Curtis, C. T. & Son 70
Gourley, W. P. 86

www.ingramcontent.com/pod-product-compliance
Lightning Source LLC
Chambersburg PA
CBHW020142170426
43199CB00010B/848